T0212103

Data Structures and Algorithms: *A First Course*

Springer

London
Berlin
Heidelberg
New York
Barcelona
Budapest
Hong Kong
Milan
Paris
Santa Clara
Singapore
Tokyo

Iain T. Adamson

Data Structures and Algorithms: *A First Course*

 Springer

Iain T. Adamson, BSc, MSc, AM, PhD
Department of Mathematics
University of Dundee
23 Perth Road, Dundee DD1 4IIN, UK

ISBN-13:978-3-540-76047-4

British Library Cataloguing in Publication Data
Adamson, Iain T.
   Data structures and algorithms : a first course
   1.Data structures (Computer science)   2.Algorithms
   I.Title
   005.7'3
ISBN-13:978-3-540-76047-4

Library of Congress Cataloging-in-Publication Data
Adamson,   Iain T.
      Data structures and algorithms : a first course / Iain T. Adamson.
         p.   cm.
      Includes index.
      ISBN-13:978-3-540-76047-4   e-ISBN-13:978-1-4471-1023-1
      DOI:10.1007/978-1-4471-1023-1

      1. Data structures (Computer science)   2. Computer algorithms.
      I. Title.
      QA76.9.D33A33   1996   96-9537
      005.13'3 - - dc20   CIP

Apart from any fair dealing for the purposes of research or private study, or criticism or review, as permitted under the Copyright, Designs and Patents Act 1988, this publication may only be reproduced, stored or transmitted, in any form or by any means, with the prior permission in writing of the publishers, or in the case of reprographic reproduction in accordance with the terms of licences issued by the Copyright Licensing Agency. Enquiries concerning reproduction outside those terms should be sent to the publishers.

© Springer-Verlag London Limited 1996

The use of registered names, trademarks etc. in this publication does not imply, even in the absence of a specific statement, that such names are exempt from the relevant laws and regulations and therefore free for general use.

The publisher makes no representation, express or implied, with regard to the accuracy of the information contained in this book and cannot accept any legal responsibility or liability for any errors or omissions that may be made.

Typesetting: camera ready by author

34/3830-543210 Printed on acid-free paper

PREFACE

In 1976 Niklaus Wirth, the inventor of Pascal, published a book entitled *Algorithms + Data Structures = Programs*. If the assertion of Wirth's title is correct—and it would be hard to dispute it—all young computer scientists who aspire to write programs must learn something about algorithms and data structures. This book is intended to help them do that.

It is based on lecture courses developed over the past few years and I hope that at least some of the informality of the classroom and the spoken word has been transferred to the printed page. The lectures were given to first and second year students in The University of Dundee who had been well-grounded in Pascal and who had therefore already met some elementary data structures and sorting and searching algorithms; but only the syntax of Pascal was taken for granted, as it is in the book. My students had rather varied mathematical backgrounds and some were not very well-disposed to old-fashioned algebraic manipulation. A little of this (and a brief mention of limits) does appear in the book; but readers of a book are more fortunate than students in a classroom—they can skip all the details and concentrate on the final results.

The book is divided into four parts. Part I on Data Structures introduces a variety of structures and the fundamental operations associated with them, together with descriptions of how they are implemented in Pascal. Chapter 1, on arrays, records and linked lists, and Chapter 3, on binary trees, are largely (but not entirely) recapitulation of ideas from any introductory programming course. Chapter 2, on stacks and queues, introduces these structures and describes various ways of implementing them; it also discusses some of the many applications of stacks in computer science. Heaps (priority queues) are introduced in Chapter

v

4 as a way of modelling constantly changing collections in which the only item of interest at any moment is the one with highest priority. In Chapter 5 we introduce graphs, which are much less regular structures than any of the earlier ones, and we describe how, in spite of their irregularity, they can be handled in the computer science environment.

Part II on Algorithms begins with the short Chapter 6 in which the concept of algorithm is discussed informally and the notion of the complexity of an algorithm is introduced. Although some of the mathematical details can be skipped over, it is important even at the beginning of one's education in computer science to have at least an inkling of the ideas introduced here.

In Chapter 7 we cover a variety of sorting algorithms, both internal and external, paying particular attention to their complexity (though of course the mathematical details can be skipped). It may be that a smaller proportion of the world's computer resources are used for sorting nowadays than the 25 to 50 per cent mentioned by Knuth in his 1973 volume *Sorting and Searching*; but sorting is still an everyday problem and it is right for students to acquire an armoury of sorting methods.

Chapter 8 is devoted to two types of graph algorithms, dealing with shortest path and spanning tree problems. In both sections of this chapter there are several pages which readers may find difficult; they may, I suppose, be described as 'mathematical', but only in the sense that they involve close logical reasoning and proof by contradiction. I would like to encourage readers to persevere with these hard proofs, which provide justification that the algorithms described do in fact solve the problems to which they apply.

The shorter Chapter 9, as its title indicates, includes an assortment of algorithms which were included in my lectures 'as time allowed'. Most students enjoyed particularly the stable marriage algorithm which is described in Section 9.3.

Part II refers in passing to various approaches to algorithm development—the divide-and-conquer method, greedy methods and dynamic programming.

Part III is concerned with the description of successively more elaborate structures for the storage of records and algorithms for retrieving a record from such a structure by means of its key (this is what is meant by the 'searching' of the title). The collections of records we are concerned with are supposed to be constantly changing; so we must examine how to deal not only with searching but also with insertion and deletion of records.

Part IV consists of very full solutions to nearly all the exercises in the book. It would have been more conventional (and easier for the author) to give more abbreviated solutions, perhaps only final results, to only a selection of the exercises; but my students have always said how helpful they have found my solutions to tutorial problems and claim to have learned from them. Of course readers ought to try the exercises for themselves before consulting the solutions.

Acknowledgements

My first word of thanks must go to the several generations of Dundee students whose favourable comments on my lectures encouraged me to turn them into a book. Next I have to thank Keith Edwards, who read and commented on some of my manuscript and gave me much helpful advice about mathematical typesetting. My chief thanks, as always, go to my wife for her constant love and support.

Iain T. Adamson

Dundee,
April 1996.

CONTENTS

Part I
DATA STRUCTURES

Data was originally a Latin word, meaning simply *given things*, but as computer scientists use it in English its meaning has been extended—for us it covers not only the objects which we are given to work with at the start of our problems, but also all the objects which we use in the course of solving them. (We remark that although *data* is a Latin plural it is nowadays considered excessively pedantic—however correct—to insist on treating it as a plural in English.) The objects we work with in our problems are of many different kinds: we call these different kinds of objects **data types**. Not only are the objects we use of different kinds—we can also organise or arrange them in different ways: we say that we have various possible **data structures**.

In a real-world situation, when we are working with an actual problem on a real live computer, we are restricted in a number of ways. We are restricted by the capabilities of the machine we are using, especially by the word size and by the capacity of its memory—for example in a machine with n-bit words the range of integers readily available is limited to $[-2^{n-1}, 2^{n-1} - 1]$ if the usual twos complement representation is used. We are restricted also by the programming language we use: no doubt we can exercise our ingenuity and *make* our chosen language do everything we need, but, for example, the older versions of Fortran do not readily handle Pascal-type records, nor does Pascal have a built-in basic type **complex** as Fortran does. Different languages, we say, support different data types and different data structures.

These practical considerations are clearly important when we are dealing with a particular practical problem, and we must not allow ourselves to forget about them completely; in this book, though, our concerns are more theoretical than practical, and in our discussions of data structures we shall be looking at them primarily from an abstract viewpoint untrammelled by machine or language considerations.

This abstract approach has the great advantage that it enables us to concentrate our attention on the essential features of the data structures we are concerned with. Nevertheless we have to remember that these data structures are thought up as contributions towards solving practical problems by means of computer programs. With this in mind we shall offer for each data structure which we introduce some suggestions about how it may be implemented in Pascal.

When we talk of *implementing* a data structure we have in mind not only how it can be defined using the facilities available in Pascal but also how we we can work with it—for each data structure has associated with it a number of fundamental operations and we must show how these operations can be carried out on the Pascal model of our data structure.

Chapter 1

ARRAYS, RECORDS AND LINKED LISTS

1.1 Arrays

Practically every high-level programming language supports a data structure called an *array*. Different languages have different rules for working with arrays, but the basic idea is common to them all—namely, to describe an array we have to specify an index set I, an element set E and for each index i in I a unique corresponding element of E. The collection of all such arrays is called **array**(I, E).

In working with **array**(I, E) we shall require a number of basic operations: we shall need to have a method for defining or creating an array; we shall also want to have a method for extracting the unique element of the set E which is associated with a given index i in a given array a; finally, we shall require a method for updating an array entry, that is changing the element of E associated with a given index i.

In our description of **array**(I, E) in the first paragraph above the index set I and the element set E were completely arbitrary; but when we come to implement **array**(I, E) concretely the programming language we use may impose restrictions on I or E or both. We consider first one-dimensional arrays. In Pascal the index set I is restricted to be an ordinal type—**boolean**, **integer**, **char**, any enumeration type, any subrange type—but the element set E is completely unrestricted:

5

it may be any type supported by the language, including user-defined types, **array**, **record**, **set** and **file** types. In Fortran77, however, the index set I is restricted to be a finite subrange of the integers and the element set E must be one of the basic types of the language. When we come to consider n-dimensional arrays with n greater than 1 we see that they can be thought of as forming a collection **array**(I, E) where the index set I has the form $I = I_1 \times I_2 \times \ldots \times I_n$, with elements $(i_1, i_2, \ldots, i_n)$ where each i_k belongs to the corresponding set I_k $(k = 1, \ldots, n)$. In both Pascal and Fortran77 the component sets I_k are restricted to be sets which would be admissible as index sets of one-dimensional arrays; in Fortran77 the dimension n is restricted to be no greater than 7, and later versions of Fortran have not removed this restriction.

To implement **array**(I, E) in Pascal we must first of all declare the types *Index_type* of the index set I (which must be an ordinal type) and the type *Element_type* of the element set E, unless these are pre-declared types. If we are dealing with multidimensional arrays, where the index set I is a product $I_1 \times I_2 \ldots \times I_k$, the types of each of the factors $I_1, \ldots, I_k$ must be declared, unless they are pre-declared.

We may then make a type declaration

> **Type** $T =$ **array** [*Index_type*] **of** *Element_type*;

(for a one-dimensional array) or

> **Type** $T =$ **array** [*Index_type_1*, ... , *Index_type_k*] **of** *Element_type*;

(for a k-dimensional array). T is then the Pascal implementation of **array**(I, E).

To create a single array a in this collection we make the usual declaration

> **Var** $a : T$;

and to initialise it we must make assignments

> $a[i] :=$ some object of *Element_type;*

for each element i of *Index_type*.

To extract the i-th component of the array a, where i is a member of *Index_type* we introduce a variable of type *Element_type*, say x, and make the assignment

$$x := a\,[\,i\,];$$

To change (update) the i-th component of the array we make the assignment

$$a\,[\,i\,] := b;$$

where b is a variable of *Element_type*.

1.2   Storage of arrays

Underlying our informal, intuitive notion of arrays is the fundamental idea that, when we have a given array before us, then, as soon as we are given one of the indices of the array, we can find at once the corresponding component of the array. In order to achieve in practice our idea of getting direct access to an array component as soon as its index is known, we need a mechanism which, given any index, will find the address of the storage location in the computer's memory which holds the array component corresponding to the given index. The calculation of a machine address from an array index is carried out by means of an **array mapping function**. The operation of this function is hidden from naïve users of the programming language, who simply reap its benefits without soiling their fingers with such sordid matters as machine addresses. None the less it is interesting to see how the array mapping function is organised to produce the required machine addresses with the same amount of effort for all indices.

We look first at one-dimensional arrays. In Fortran the index type of such an array is a finite subrange of the integers; in Pascal more general index sets are allowed, but they are all ordinal types and so they can be put in one-to-one correspondence with finite subranges of the integers. (This is true even if the index set is the Pascal type **integer**, since in any implementation of Pascal this is restricted to a finite subrange of the infinite set of all integers.) So there is no loss of generality if we deal with arrays indexed by such a subrange, say $l \mathbin{..} u$; we call l the **lower bound** and u the **upper bound** of the range. Notice that the number of entries in an array indexed by $l \mathbin{..} u$ is $u - l + 1$. (If you believe it to be $u - l$ just consider an array indexed by $1 \mathbin{..} 2$!) Suppose that to store an object of the element type of our array requires L bytes: we call L the **component length** of the array.

Let us assume that the memory of our computer is one-dimensional and that we are to store the entries of our array in adjacent memory locations, each capable of holding one byte. Suppose that the first byte of the first component of the array (i.e. the component indexed by l) has address b: we call b the **base address**. Then the first component is stored in the L bytes with addresses

$$b, b + 1, b + 2, \ldots, b + L - 1.$$

So the address of the first byte of the second component, indexed by $l + 1$, is $b + L = b + ((l + 1) - l) L$. In general, when we come to store the component indexed by i ($l \le i \le u$) we will have used up $(i - l) L$ bytes starting with b to store the $i - l$ preceding components. So the address of the first byte of the i-th component is

$$b + (i - l) L$$

which we can rewrite as

$$(b - lL) + iL = c_0 + c_1 i$$

where

$$\begin{aligned} c_1 &= L, \\ c_0 &= b - lL = b - c_1 l. \end{aligned}$$

Thus, once the constants c_0 and c_1 are calculated for a given array, the calculation of the address of the first byte of any component requires one multiplication ($c_1 i$) and one addition ($c_0 + c_1 i$) whatever the index of the component. If a is an array indexed by $l \mathbin{..} u$ its **array mapping function** $addr$ is given by

$addr(i) = $ address of first byte of i-th component of $a = c_0 + c_1 i$.

Consider now a two-dimensional array, indexed by $I = I_1 \times I_2$ with elements (i_1, i_2) where $i_1 \in I_1$ and $i_2 \in I_2$, I_1 and I_2 being sets which are admissible as index sets for one-dimensional arrays. Without loss of generality we may assume that I_1 and I_2 are subranges $l_1 .. u_1$ and $l_2 .. u_2$ of the integers.

As in the one-dimensional case we shall assume that the array components are stored in adjacent memory locations. We notice at once that there are two natural ways of doing this:

(1) **Row major order**. This method consists in storing the array components row by row; that is, we store first the components of the first row in increasing order of column index, then the components of the second row in increasing order of column index, followed by the components of the third row and so on. This method of arrangement is also known as **lexical** or **lexicographic** or **dictionary order**: we notice that $a(i_1, i_2)$ precedes $a(j_1, j_2)$ in this arrangement if and only if either $(i_1 < j_1)$ or $(i_1 = j_1$ and $i_2 < j_2)$, that is if and only if the "word" $i_1 i_2$ comes earlier in the dictionary than $j_1 j_2$.

Suppose the component length is L and the base address (the address of the first byte of the (l_1, l_2)-th component) is b. The number of components in each row is $u_2 - l_2 + 1$; so, when we come to store the (i_1, i_2)-th component we shall already have stored $i_1 - l_1$ complete rows, requiring $(i_1 - l_1)(u_2 - l_2 + 1)L$ bytes, together with the preceding $i_2 - l_2$ components in the i_1-th row, requiring $(i_2 - l_2)L$ bytes. So the address of the first byte of the (i_1, i_2)-th component is

$$b + (i_1 - l_1)(u_2 - l_2 + 1) L + (i_2 - l_2) L$$

which we can rewrite as

$$c_0 + c_1 i_1 + c_2 i_2$$

where

$$
\begin{aligned}
c_2 &= L, \\
c_1 &= (u_2 - l_2 + 1) L = (u_2 - l_2 + 1) c_2, \\
c_0 &= b - (u_2 - l_2 + 1) l_1 L - l_2 L = b - c_1 l_1 - c_2 l_2.
\end{aligned}
$$

So once the constants c_0, c_1, c_2 are calculated for a given array, the calculation of the address of the first byte of any component requires two multiplications and two additions.

(2) **Column major order.** Here we store the components of the array column by column instead of row by row. Fortran actually requires that two-dimensional arrays be stored in column major order. An easy modification of the discussion of row major order produces the result that when column major order is used the address of the first byte of the (i_1, i_2)-th component is

$$b + (i_2 - l_2)(u_1 - l_1 + 1) L + (i_1 - l_1) L.$$

We mention briefly higher-dimensional arrays indexed, say, by the product set $I = I_1 \times I_2 \times \ldots \times I_k$, where we may assume that $I_1, \ldots, I_k$ are the ranges of integers $l_1 \ldots u_1, \ldots, l_k \ldots u_k$. If we store the components in the k-dimensional analogue of dictionary order we conclude after some modest algebraic manipulation that the address of the first byte of the $(i_1, i_2, \ldots, i_k)$-th component is

$$c_0 + c_1 i_1 + c_2 i_2 + \ldots + c_k i_k$$

where

$$c_k = L,$$
$$c_{j-1} = (u_j - l_j + 1) c_j \text{ for } j = 2, \ldots, k,$$
$$c_0 = b - c_1 l_1 - c_2 l_2 - \ldots - c_k l_k.$$

As in the one- and two-dimensional cases we see that as soon as the constants c_0, c_1, $\ldots$, c_k have been calculated we can find the address of any component of the array by carrying out k multiplications and k additions.

Clearly in the running of a program it is important for every array to have associated with it an **array descriptor**—an identity card, so to speak—which gathers together its important characteristics. These would include (1) the name of the array, (2) some indication of its element type, (3) the component length of its elements, (4) the base address, (5) the lower and upper bounds in each dimension and (6) the constants of the array mapping function. The naïve user will never have to be concerned explicitly with array descriptors, but they are implicit in the running of programs which involve arrays.

1.3 Records

An array with index set I and element set E is a composite object made up of a number of components, one for each index i in I. These components are all of the same type E: we say that arrays are *homogeneous* structures. Frequently, however, we want to gather together into a single package a collection of pieces of information which are not all of the same type—such a structure would be called *heterogeneous*. For example a university record department would want to hold together for each student an identification number (presumably of type **integer** or perhaps some subrange), a name (no doubt thought of as a **packed array of char**), an indication of gender (M or F), and various other pieces of personal and academic information (nationality, marital status, whether undergraduate or postgraduate, courses being studied and so on). Now of course it would be possible without too much trouble to represent all these disparate pieces of information by integers, for example, and so represent each student by an array of integers, with one component corresponding to each piece of information. But this is clearly unnatural and it would be preferable to introduce a new type of data structure which gathers together into a single whole a collection of items of different types.

We call this new kind of structure a **record**, and each of the items is called a **field** of the record. Each of the fields of a record has a name and a set. Suppose we have n fields, with names $id_1, \ldots, id_n$, and corresponding sets $E_1, \ldots, E_n$. Then a record with these fields is an ordered n-tuple $(x_1, \ldots, x_n)$ where each component x_k belongs to the corresponding set E_k ($k = 1, \ldots, n$); such an n-tuple is an element of the cartesian product set $E_1 \times \ldots \times E_n$. So for each collection of ordered pairs (id_k, E_k) ($k = 1, \ldots, n$) we define a collection which we denote by **record**$((id_1, E_1), \ldots, (id_n, E_n))$.

In dealing with this collection we need to have some basic operations analogous to those for arrays. We shall require a method for creating a record and we shall want to have ways of extracting and updating a given field of a record.

To implement **record**$((id_1, E_1), \ldots, (id_n, E_n))$ in Pascal we must first declare the types $T_1, \ldots, T_n$ of the element sets $E_1, \ldots, E_n$ (unless they are pre-declared types). We then make the declaration

Type T = Record
$$id_1 : T_1;$$
$$id_2 : T_2;$$
$$\ldots$$
$$id_n : T_n$$
        end;

whereupon T is the Pascal representation of our collection of records. To create a single record of this type we make the declaration

Var $r : T$;

and to initialise it we make assignments

$$r.id_k := \text{ some object of type } T_k;$$

for each $k = 1, \ldots, n$.

To extract the k-th field of the record r we introduce a variable x_k of type T_k and make the assignment

$$x_k := r.id_k;$$

while to update the k-th field of r we make the assignment

$$r.id_k := b_k;$$

where b_k is a variable of type T_k.

Records, like arrays, should have descriptors associated with them, in which their "vital statistics" are collected together. These would include (1) the name of the record, (2) the base address, which for a record would be the address of the first byte of the first field of the record and (3) for each field, its name, some indication of its type and its offset, which is the total number of bytes required to store all the preceding fields.

1.4 Linked lists

In everyday life when we make a list of jobs to be done we usually have it in mind to start at the top (or head) of the list and work through the list in order until we reach the end. So we might think of defining a list as a (finite) sequence

$$x_1, x_2, \ldots, x_n$$

of items, all of the same type. At first sight this may not seem very different from an array of items indexed by 1 .. n; but there are some important differences between arrays and lists. First of all, arrays are usually thought of as random access structures (and we have seen that we can organise the storage of an array in such a way that the same amount of work is required to access each array entry) while the entries in a list are usually dealt with in order, starting at the head. Next, once an array is set up its size remains constant, although individual entries may be changed; lists, on the other hand, are subject to alteration—for example, our list of tasks to be performed is constantly changing as some tasks are completed and the corresponding items are removed from the list while new tasks present themselves, causing items to be added to the list, perhaps at the end or at some intermediate point or even at the head. We notice, too, that with luck, if we are assiduous in carrying out all the tasks on our list, then we shall no longer have any tasks left on the list—the list is empty. If we are to carry out our intention of working through our list of jobs in order then it is clear that as we deal with each item we must know where to go next (unless we have reached the end of the list).

This informal discussion leads us to the following definition. For each set E the collection **list**(E) consists of the empty list together with all objects made up of an element of E (called the **head** of the list) followed by an object in **list**(E) (called the **tail** of the list). This is, of course, a recursive definition, but it is well-founded since we have been careful to give one member of the collection **list**(E) explicitly, namely the empty list.

Associated with the collection **list**(E) we have a number of fundamental operations. At the very least we shall require an operation to create a list; we shall want to determine whether a given list is empty;

and we shall need to know how to make insertions in a list and deletions from it.

Since we have it very much in mind that the lists we handle are to be constantly changing, it is appropriate when we come to implement lists in Pascal that we should use the dynamic capabilities of Pascal's **pointer** types. We think informally of a list as a sequence of nodes, each with two cells, one containing an element of E, the other giving the address of (i.e. a pointer to) the next node on the list. Formally, we make the declarations

> **Type** $T = Element\_type$;
> $List\_pointer = \uparrow Node$;
> $Node =$ **Record**
> $Info : T$;
> $Next : List\_pointer$
> **end**;

We recall that Pascal allows us to use $\uparrow Node$ as the definition of the type *List_pointer* even before the type *Node* itself has been defined. The reason for this is that the values of a pointer variable of any type are addresses: so to store any pointer variable requires only enough space to store an address. If p is a pointer variable of type $\uparrow Node$ it is conventional to represent the address which is the current value of p by an arrow to the object $p\uparrow$ of type *Node* which is actually stored at that address.

Having made these declarations we shall implement a list of elements of type T by an object of type *List_pointer* : we think of representing a list by a pointer to its head node whose *Next* field contains a pointer to the rest of the list. We begin by making the declaration

> **Var** $head : List\_pointer$;

and the assignment

> $head :=$ **nil** ;

which of course provides us with a list which has no members. To build up a list which actually does contain some members we have to consider the problem of making insertions in a list. We look first at the general situation where we want to insert a new item after an existing one; we think of gaining access to the item after which the insertion is to be made by means of a pointer to the node containing it. Suppose, then, that we want to insert an item a of type T after the node $p\uparrow$ pointed to by a (non-**nil**) pointer p, as in the diagram

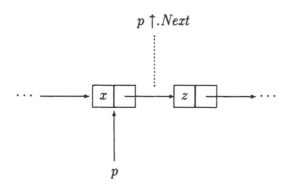

We must create a new node (by the standard Pascal device of introducing a local *List_pointer* variable q, say, and giving the command **new** (q) which sets q to point to the new node $q\uparrow$); the *Info* field of $q\uparrow$ is given the value a (the new item) and its *Next* field is given the value of the *Next* field of $p\uparrow$, which is then set equal to q, so that it points to the new node. Summing this up we have the Pascal procedure:

```
Procedure insert_after (a : T; Var p : List_pointer);
Var q : List_pointer;
Begin
   if p <> nil then begin
      new (q);
      with q↑ do begin
           Info := a ; Next := p↑.Next end ;
      p↑.Next := q end
   End ;
```

The operation of this procedure is illustrated by the diagram

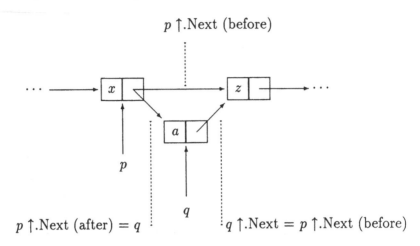

It is important to notice that the procedure insert_after is not applicable when we want to insert a new item at the head of the list, in particular when we want to insert the first item in a list initialised to nil—in these cases there is no node after which to make the insertion. We deal with this situation by means of the following procedure:

Procedure insert_at_head ($a : T$; **Var** *head* : *List_pointer*)
Var $q :$ *List_pointer*;
Begin
        new (q);
        with $q\uparrow$ **do begin**
                Info := a ; *Next* := *head* **end**;
        head := q
End;

We illustrate the operation of this procedure in the diagram

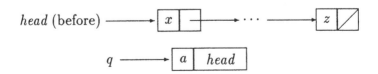

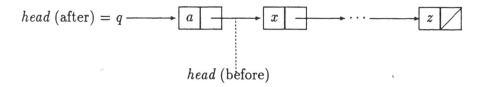

$head$ (after) $= q$ — a — x — $\cdots$ — z

$head$ (before)

(We use the diagonal line in the box representing the *Next* field of the last node to indicate that its *Next* pointer is **nil**.)

From the operation of inserting new items in a list we turn to the operation of deleting existing items. Here again it is convenient to make our approach to the item which is to be removed by means of a pointer p to the node which contains the item (if there is one) preceding the item to be deleted. The deletion is carried out by setting the *Next* field of the predecessor node to be the *Next* field of the node to be deleted; we can then use the built-in procedure *dispose* to return the unwanted node to the store of available memory locations. Of course the deletion procedure just described will not work if p is **nil**, nor if $p\uparrow.Next$ is **nil** (in that case there is no node to delete). Summing this up we have

```
Procedure delete_after (Var p :List_pointer) ;
Var q :List_pointer;
Begin
    if (p <> nil) and (p ↑.Next <> nil) then begin
        q := p↑.Next ;
        p↑.Next := q↑.Next;
        dispose(q) end
End ;
```

As in the case of insertion we notice also here that our procedure is not applicable at the head of the list: to deal with the operation of deleting the first element of a list we use the following procedure:

Procedure delete_at_head (**Var** *head* :*List_pointer*);
Var *q* :*List_pointer*;
Begin
    if (*head* <> nil) **then begin**
        q := *head* ;
        head := *q*↑.*Next* ;
        dispose(*q*) **end**
  End ;

Although we have used pointers to implement linked lists this is not the only way available to us: we may also implement linked lists by means of arrays. Since we need to know for each member of a list the location of the next member it will not be adequate to use an array of *Element_type* ; the array entries should be records with an information field of *Element_type* and a *Next* field containing the array index of the next element of the list. So we decide on an array size N and declare

Const $N = \ldots$

Type *Node* = **Record**
          Info : T;
          Next : $0 .. N$
      end ;

Var *list* : **Array** $[1 .. N]$ **of** *Node* ;

The reason we use $0 .. N$ as the range of values for the *Next* field is that we need to have a way of indicating that there is no next entry and it seems appropriate to use 0 for this purpose.

    This array approach to representing lists of course raises problems of programming—how are we to represent an empty list? how are we to gain access to a non-empty list? how do we handle insertions and deletions? These are not difficult questions to answer and we leave them to the reader as simple exercises. But there is another question to be considered if we decide to use arrays to implement lists: this is the choice of N, the size of the array. Two possible difficulties arise. On the one hand we may choose N too small for the number of items which we shall eventually want to include in the list (this number may well not be known in advance); in this case we shall have to start all over again with a new value for N. On the other hand, if we try to avoid the first difficulty by choosing N very large, we may end up with a situation where much of the storage set aside when the array is declared is never used. These difficulties are avoided when we use pointers, for there is (at least in theory) no limit to the number of insertions we can make, though each insertion requires the execution of the **new** operation.

1.5 Exercises 1

1. Suppose we declare

> **Var** A : **array** [1 .. 10] **of integer**;
> B : **array** [5 .. 20, −3 .. 3] **of real**;
> C : **array** [3 .. 7, 1 .. 10] **of real**;
> D : **array** [5 .. 16, 6 .. 10, 3 .. 12] **of boolean**;

Find the array mapping functions

(a) for A, where the base address is 995 and the component length is 4;

(b) for B, stored in row major order, where the base address is 1005 and the component length is 8;

(c) for C, stored in column major order, where the base address is 3716 and the component length is 8;

(d) for D, stored in dictionary order, where the base address is 643 and the component length is 1.

2. An $N \times N$ matrix A with real number entries a_{ij} is said to be **symmetric** if for all indices i, j we have $a_{ij} = a_{ji}$. To represent such a matrix we think first of declaring

> **Var** A : **array** [1 .. N, 1 .. N] **of real**;

As soon as we do this the computer reserves N^2 locations, one for each array entry. This is not an error, but it is extravagant of space, since once we know the entries on and below the main diagonal (the entries a_{ij} for which $i \leq j$) we know all the entries—for if $i > j$ we have $a_{ij} = a_{ji}$. There are only

$$1 + 2 + 3 + \ldots + N = \tfrac{1}{2}N(N+1)$$

entries a_{ij} with $i \leq j$, so we need actually store only this number of entries, not all N^2. So suppose $M = \tfrac{1}{2}N(N+1)$ and declare

Var $A1$: **array** $[1 .. M]$ **of real**;

Then we store
a_{11} in $A1[1]$,
a_{21} and a_{22} in $A1[2]$ and $A1[3]$ respectively,
a_{31}, a_{32} and a_{33} in $A1[4]$, $A1[5]$ and $A1[6]$ respectively

and so on. Show that a_{ij} with $i \leq j$ is stored in $A1[\tfrac{1}{2}i(i-1)+j]$.

If the entries of A are stored in the one-dimensional array $A1$ in this way then we can no longer access the entry a_{ij} as $A[i,j]$ and instead we get our hands on it by means of

Function extract $(i, j : 1 .. N)$: **real**;
Begin if $i \leq j$ **then** extract $:= A1[(i * (i-1))$ **div** $2 + j]$
                               else extract $:=$ extract(j, i) **End**;

In an analogous way define

Procedure update $(i, j : 1 .. N; x : $ **real**$)$;

which will have the effect of changing the current value of a_{ij} to x.

3. An $N \times N$ matrix S with real number entries is said to be **skew-symmetric** if for all indices i, j we have $s_{ij} = -s_{ji}$. Notice that for the diagonal elements s_{ii} we have $s_{ii} = -s_{ii}$ and so these elements are all zero. Thus when we store a skew-symmetric matrix we need only store the

$$0 + 1 + 2 + \ldots + (N-1) = \tfrac{1}{2}(N-1)N$$

elements s_{ij} below the main diagonal, i.e. the elements s_{ij} with $i < j$.

Show that if we do this in a one-dimensional array $S1$ with index set $1 .. \tfrac{1}{2}(N-1)N$ then each s_{ij} with $i < j$ is stored as the array entry $S1[((i-2) * (i-1))$ **div** $2 + j]$.

Define **Function** extract and **Procedure** update as in Exercise 2. (Remember that it would be an error to try to update a diagonal entry to a non-zero value.)

4. An $N \times N$ matrix T with real number entries is called a **tridiagonal** matrix if the only non-zero entries t_{ij} lie on the main diagonal $(i = j)$, the superdiagonal $(i = j - 1)$ and the subdiagonal $(i = j + 1)$. (Notice that we are not saying that the elements of these three diagonals are all non-zero, just that the elements *not* on these diagonals *are* zero.) Clearly we need store only the elements of the three diagonals, which are $3N - 2$ in number (N on the main diagonal and $(N - 1)$ on each of the super- and subdiagonals).

Show that if we store the elements of the three diagonals in row major order—i.e.

$$a_{11}, a_{12}, a_{21}, a_{22}, a_{23}, a_{32}, a_{33}, a_{34}, \ldots, a_{N,N-1}, a_{NN}$$

in a one-dimensional array $T1$ indexed by $1 \ldots 3N - 2$ then each a_{ij} with $|i - j| \leq 1$ is stored in $T1[2 * i + j - 2]$.

Define **Function** extract and **Procedure** update as in the previous exercises.

5. Suppose we declare

```
Type T = Record
            Key : integer;
            Info : array[1 .. 20] of char
         end;

     T1 = Record
            List : array [1 .. 15] of T;
            Season : (spring, summer, autumn, winter)
          end;

     Var a : T1 ;
```

Explain how to determine the addresses of the locations of the first bytes of

$$a.List[4].Info[13] \quad \text{and} \quad a.Season.$$

(Your answers will involve the base address and the component lengths of the types **integer** and **char**.)

6. Suppose we have made the usual declarations for handling linked lists using Pascal pointers, i.e.

> **Type** $T =$ *Element_type* ;
>   *List_pointer* $= \uparrow$ *Node* ;
>   *Node* = **Record**
>   *Info* : T;
>   *Next* : *List_pointer*
>   **end** ;

Write Pascal subprograms as follows:

(a) **Function** length (l : *List_pointer*) : **integer**;
such that length(l) is 0 if l is the **nil** list and otherwise is the number of nodes in the list headed by $l \uparrow$.

(b) **Procedure** print (l : *List_pointer*);
such that print(l) prints out the *Info* fields of the nodes in the list headed by $l \uparrow$. (We may suppose that elements a of type T can be output by the commands Write(a) and Writeln(a).)

(c) **Function** concatenate (p, q : *List_pointer*) : *List_pointer*;
such that concatenate(p,q) is a pointer to the head of the list formed by the list headed by $p \uparrow$ followed by the list headed by $q \uparrow$: thus if

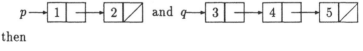

then

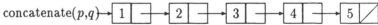

(Here and in future we adopt the convention that the diagonal line in the box representing the *Next* field of a node indicates that the *Next* pointer is **nil**.)

(d) **Procedure** dock (**Var** l : *List_pointer*);
Such that after the execution of dock(l) the list headed by $l \uparrow$ has its last entry removed.

(e) **Function** search (l : *List_pointer* ; x : T) : *List_pointer*;
such that search(l,x) is a pointer to the first node in the list

headed by $l \uparrow$ with x as its *Info* field (if there is such a node) and **nil** otherwise.

(f) **Function** reverse (l : *List_pointer*) : *List_pointer*; such that reverse (l) is a pointer to the list obtained by writing the entries of the list headed by $l \uparrow$ in reverse order.

(g) **Procedure** remove (x : T; **Var** l : *List_pointer*); such that after the execution of remove(x,l) all the nodes with x as *Info* field have been removed from the list headed by $l \uparrow$.

(h) **Procedure** interchange (m, n : 1 .. maxint; **Var** l : *List_pointer*); such that after the execution of interchange(m, n, l) the *Info* fields of the m-th and n-th nodes in the list headed by $l \uparrow$ are interchanged.

(i) **Function** compare ($l1, l2$: *List_pointer*) : **boolean**; such that compare ($l1, l2$) is **true** if $l1$ and $l2$ are the same length and have the same *Info* fields in corresponding nodes and **false** otherwise.

7. Suppose we have a polynomial such as

$$f(x) = 3x^4 + 7x^2 - 4x + 2.$$

We may declare

> **Type** *Polynomial_pointer* = $\uparrow$ *Term_Node*;
>   *Term_Node* = **Record**
>   *Coefficient* : **real**;
>   *Exponent* : 0 .. maxint;
>   *Next* : *Polynomial_pointer*
>   **end**;

Then we may declare

> **Var** f : *Polynomial_pointer*;

and initialise f so that we have

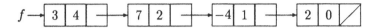

Define

Function derivative $(p : Polynomial\_pointer)$: $Polynomial\_pointer$;

such that derivative(f) is a pointer to the list representation of the derivative of the polynomial represented by the pointer p; for example with f as above we would have

derivative(f) ——→ 12 | 3 | ——→ 14 | 1 | ——→ −4 | 0 | ⧄

8. Make the **Type** declarations which we would need to work with *doubly* linked lists in which each node has an information field and two pointer fields, one containing a pointer to the successor of the node in the list, the other to its predecessor. Describe procedures to carry out insertions in and deletions from a doubly linked list.

9. If we have an $m \times n$ matrix A with integer or real number entries it is natural to represent it in a Pascal program by declaring

   Var A : **array** $[1 .. m, 1 .. n]$ **of integer** (or **real**);

   whereupon the computer reserves mn locations, one for each array entry. A matrix of numbers is said to be **sparse** if a large proportion of its entries is zero. (This is a pretty imprecise definition; in practice a large matrix is considered sparse if no more than 10% of its entries are nonzero.) For such a matrix it is a waste of space to set aside a location for each of the zero entries: clearly what is important for us to know is the values of the nonzero entries and their positions in the matrix. This information can be conveniently stored in a list of triples (i, j, a_{ij}) giving the row index, column index and value of each of the nonzero entries a_{ij}. So we might declare

   Type $Row\_index = 1 .. m$;
   $\quad\quad\quad Column\_index = 1 .. n$;

$$Number = \textbf{integer or real};$$
$$Matrix\_pointer = \uparrow Entry\_Node;$$
$$Entry\_Node = \textbf{Record}$$
$$\qquad\qquad Row : Row\_index;$$
$$\qquad\qquad Column : Column\_index;$$
$$\qquad\qquad Entry : Number;$$
$$\qquad\qquad Next : Matrix\_pointer$$
$$\qquad \textbf{end};$$

and form a list having one node for each nonzero entry of the matrix. It is convenient to organise the list in "dictionary" order, so that if a_{ij} and a_{kl} are nonzero entries of the matrix the node corresponding to a_{ij} precedes the node corresponding to a_{kl} if either $i < k$ or $i = k$ and $j < l$. For example the sparse matrix

$$\begin{bmatrix} 0 & 0 & 2 & 0 & 1 & 0 \\ 0 & 0 & 0 & 0 & 0 & 1 \\ 0 & 4 & 0 & 0 & 0 & 0 \end{bmatrix}$$

would be represented by the list

Define

> **Function** extract (s : $Matrix\_pointer$; i : Row_index;
> j : $Column\_index$) : $Number$;

which returns the (i, j)-th entry of the sparse matrix represented by (the dictionary-ordered list pointed to by) the *Matrix_pointer s*. Define also

> **Procedure** update (**Var** s : $Matrix\_pointer$; i : Row_index;
> j : $Column\_index$; x : $Number$);

which changes the (i, j)-th entry of the sparse matrix represented by s to x.

Chapter 2

STACKS AND QUEUES

2.1 Stacks

When we were dealing with linked lists in the last chapter we allowed the possibility of carrying out insertions and deletions at arbitrary positions in a list. We consider now a more restricted type of list in which insertions and deletions may be made at one end only, namely at the head; a list of this kind is called a **stack**. The requirement that insertions and deletions may be made at one end only implies that at any point of time the only element which can be removed or retrieved from a stack is the one which was most recently inserted: we say therefore that a stack exhibits last-in-first-out behaviour, or that it is a *LIFO* structure. Perhaps the most familiar example of a stack in everyday life is the pile of trays in a cafeteria, where newly washed trays are placed on the top of the pile and customers remove trays also from the top of the pile.

If E is any set the collection of all stacks with elements drawn from E, **stack**(E), is the same as the collection **list**(E); but the fundamental operations associated with **stack**(E) are more restricted. As in the case of linked lists we need to have an operation to create a stack and we have to be able to determine whether a given stack is full (because then no further insertion can be made) or empty (in which case no deletion can be made); but in place of the unrestricted insertions and deletions we allowed when we studied **list**(E) we require only the operation of

27

inserting an element of type E at the head—we call this operation
push—and the operation of removing the element at the head, which
we call **pop**.

When we come to look at examples of the use of stacks in computer
science we shall see that the stacks involved are constantly changing;
so it is natural to use the same kind of implementation using pointers
which we described for linked lists. Thus we make the declarations

> **Type** $T = Element\_type$;
> $Stack\_pointer = \uparrow Node$;
> $Node = $ **Record**
> $Info : T$;
> $Next : Stack\_pointer$
>   **end** ;
> **Var** $stack : Stack\_pointer$;

and, to create an initially empty stack, the assignment

> $stack :=$ **nil** ;

To determine whether the stack with head $stack$ is empty we clearly
have only to check whether the pointer $stack$ is **nil**; thus we define the
Pascal function

> **Function** empty ($stack : Stack\_pointer$) : **boolean**;
> **Begin** empty $:= (stack = $ **nil**) **End**;

Since insertion in a list implemented in Pascal using pointers will be
made using the operation **new** which (theoretically at least) can always
be applied to produce a new node, a stack implemented in this way will
never be full; so we might define the Pascal function

> **Function** full ($stack : Stack\_pointer$) : **boolean**;
> **Begin** full $:= $ **false** **End**;

The operation of pushing an element onto a stack is identical with that
of insertion at the head of a list; so we implement it by means of an
analogous procedure:

Procedure push (*a* : *T*; **Var** *stack* : *Stack_pointer*);
Var *q* : *Stack_pointer* ;
Begin if full(*stack*) **then** ... (⋆ take some appropriate action ⋆)
         else begin
              new(*q*);
              with *q*↑ **do begin**
                  Info := *a*; *Next* := *stack* **end**;
              stack := *q* **end**
End;

In the same way we may think of the operation of popping a stack as identical with that of deleting the element at the head of a list; but when we want to pop a stack we frequently want to use the element which is popped. So as formal parameters for the procedure which implements *pop* we use not only a *Stack_pointer* parameter (which must be a **Var** parameter since the stack is to be altered by the operation) but also a **Var** parameter of type *T* which, after the execution of the procedure, will hold the element which was at the stack head. Thus we define

Procedure pop (**Var** *stack* : *Stack_pointer*; **Var** *top* : *T*);
Var *q* : *Stack_pointer*;
Begin if empty(*stack*) **then** ... (⋆ take some appropriate action ⋆)
         else begin
              top := *stack*↑.*Info*;
              q := *stack*;
              stack := *stack*↑.*Next*;
              dispose(*q*) **end**
End;

The operation of this procedure in the case of a non-empty stack is shown in the diagram

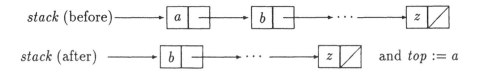

(As in the case of general linked lists we use a diagonal line in the box representing the *Next* field of a node to indicate that the *Next* pointer is **nil**.)

Although it seems most natural to use pointers to implement stacks, here also, as in the case of linked lists, it is possible to use arrays. As usual we must decide on the size of the array before we start using it (with the attendant dangers of running out of space to hold stack entries if we choose the size too small or of setting aside space which is never used if we choose it too large). At any rate we begin by estimating the largest size *maxsize* which we expect the stack to attain and then declare

   Const $N = maxsize$;

We think of inserting stack elements into the 1st, 2nd, ... positions of an array indexed by $1 .. N$. We shall also have to keep a note of the position of the top of the stack, i.e. the highest array index used to hold the current elements of the stack—to take account of the possibility that the stack is empty we shall use $0 .. N$ as range of values for the top index. So we declare

   Type *Stack* = **Record**
                   Stack_array : **array** $[1 .. N]$ **of** T;
                   Top : $0 .. N$
                 end ;

It is now clear how we should define the **boolean** functions which test whether a stack is empty or full.

   Function empty (s : *Stack*) : **boolean**;
   Begin empty := ($s.Top = 0$) **End**;

   Function full (s : *Stack*) : **boolean**;
   Begin full := ($s.Top = N$) **End**;

The operations of pushing and popping can now be implemented as follows:

Procedure push (*a* : *T*; **Var** *s* : *Stack*);
Begin if full(*s*) **then** ... (⋆ take some appropriate action ⋆)
        else with *s* **do begin**
                Top := *Top* + 1;
                Stack_array [*Top*] := *a* **end**
End;

Procedure pop (**Var** *s* : *Stack*; **Var** *top* : *T*);
Begin if empty(*s*) **then** ... (⋆ take some appropriate action ⋆)
        else with *s* **do begin**
                top := *Stack_array*[*Top*];
                Top := *Top* − 1 **end**
End;

2.2 Applications of stacks

As a first illustration of the use of stacks in computer science we describe how they are implicitly involved in the execution of computer programs. To do this we examine the following Pascal program:

```
1:      Program P;
2:          Var m, n : integer;

3:              Procedure Q (M : integer);
4:                  Var m : integer;

5:                      Procedure R (N : integer);
6:                          Var n : integer;
7:                      Begin (⋆ R ⋆)
8:                          n := 2 * N;
9:                          Writeln(m + n)
10:                     End; (⋆ R ⋆)

11:             Begin (⋆ Q ⋆)
12:                 m := 3 * M;
13:                 R(n);
14:                 Writeln(m + n)
15:             End; (⋆ Q ⋆)

16:         Begin (⋆ Main Program P ⋆)
17:             m := 1; n := 2;
18:             Q(m);
19:             Writeln(m + n)
20:         End. (⋆ Main Program ⋆)
```

where we have framed the procedures Q and R to emphasize their
relation to one another and to the main program P and have numbered
the lines for ease of reference (of course neither the frames nor the line
numbers form part of the program).

We recall the Pascal *scope rule* that for any occurrence of an
identifier the declaration which applies to it is the one at the head
of the smallest block containing both that occurrence and a declaration of the identifier. Thus on lines 8 and 9 n is the **integer** variable
declared on line 6 at the head of procedure R, while on line 9 m is
the **integer** variable declared on line 4 at the head of procedure Q.

On lines 12 and 14 m is the **integer** variable declared on line 4 at the head of procedure Q, while on lines 13 and 14 n is the **integer** variable declared on line 2 at the head of the main program P. Finally, on lines 17-19 m and n are the **integer** variables declared on line 2 at the head of P.

When the compiler first processes the program it marks each identifier occurrence for which there is no corresponding declaration in the smallest block containing the occurrence with an indicator of the larger block which contains the declaration applying to the occurrence. Thus on line 9 we mark m with a Q (writing it as $m.Q$ say) and on lines 13 and 14 we rewrite n as $n.P$.

When a procedure is called we form what is known as its **activation record** in which we collect various pieces of information which are required in order to run the procedure. Among these are the addresses of the locations set aside for the formal parameters of the procedure and for the local variables declared at the head of the procedure. In addition the activation record will hold the so-called **return address**: this is the address of the location containing the next command in the calling procedure to be executed after the execution of the called procedure is complete.

We can now describe how we use a stack, called the **run-time stack**, to organise the running of the program. The elements of our stack are activation records. Initially the stack is empty, but as soon as execution of the program starts with the **Begin** on line 16 we push on to the stack the activation record of P:

| Main Program P |
| Local variable m : **integer**, stored in location 1 |
| Local variable n : **integer**, stored in location 2 |

(There is no return address for the main program.) Line 17 assigns to locations 1 and 2 the values of the local variables m and n (1 and 2 respectively).

Line 18 calls procedure Q with actual parameter m, which we see (by consulting the activation record of P) is the local variable stored in location 1 with current value 1. The activation record of Q is pushed onto the stack which now becomes

> Procedure Q
> Formal parameter M : **integer**, stored in location 3
> Local variable m : **integer**, stored in location 4
> Return address: address of location holding line 19

> Main Program P
> Local variable m : **integer**, stored in location 1
> Local variable n : **integer**, stored in location 2

The activation record of Q shows that the formal parameter M is allocated to location 3; so location 3 is assigned the current value (1) of the actual parameter m.

In line 12 ($m := 3 * M$) we search in the activation record of Q (which is at the top of the stack) for identifiers m and M and find they have been allocated to locations 4 and 3 respectively. So location 4 is updated to $3 *$ (contents of location 3) = 3.

Line 13 calls procedure R with actual parameter n. Now n was marked as $n.P$, so we move down the stack till we reach the activation record of P; searching there we discover that n is allocated to location 2, which currently contains the value 2. The activation record of R is pushed onto the stack which is now

> Procedure R
> Formal parameter N : **integer**, stored in location 5
> Local variable n : **integer**, stored in location 6
> Return address: address of location holding line 14

> Procedure Q
> Formal parameter M : **integer**, stored in location 3
> Local variable m : **integer**, stored in location 4
> Return address: address of location holding line 19

> Main Program P
> Local variable m : **integer**, stored in location 1
> Local variable n : **integer**, stored in location 2

The activation record of R shows that the formal parameter N is allocated to location 5. So location 5 is assigned the current value (2) of the actual parameter n.

On line 8 ($n := 2 * N$) we search in the activation record of R, which is now at the top of the stack, for the identifiers n and N. Both appear in the activation record, where they are allocated to locations 5 and 6 respectively. Thus location 6 is updated to contain 2 $*$ (contents of location 5) = 4.

On line 9 m has been marked as $m.Q$; so we must move down the stack to the activation record of Q where we find that m is allocated to location 4, which currently contains 3. n appears in the activation record of R; it is allocated to location 6, which currently contains 4. So line 9 writes out 7.

When we reach line 10 we have completed the execution of procedure R; so we look in the activation record of R for the return address (line 14) and then pop the stack which now becomes

```
Procedure Q
Formal parameter M : integer, stored in location 3
Local variable m : integer, stored in location 4
Return address: address of location holding line 19
```

```
Main Program P
Local variable m : integer, stored in location 1
Local variable n : integer, stored in location 2
```

On line 14 we search the activation record of Q, which is now at the top of the stack, and find that m has been allocated to location 4, with current contents 3; n has been marked $n.P$ and by moving down the stack to the activation record of P we find that n corresponds to location 2, which contains the value 2. So line 14 writes out 5.

On line 15 we complete the execution of the procedure Q, so we look in its activation record for the return address (line 19) and pop the stack which becomes

Main Program P
Local variable m : **integer**, stored in location 1
Local variable n : **integer**, stored in location 2

On line 19 we search the activation record for P and find that m and n are allocated to locations 1 and 2, which currently contain 1 and 2 respectively. So line 19 writes out 3.

Line 20 concludes the execution of the program.

As a second application of stacks in computer science we mention that they occur implicitly also when we work with recursive procedures and functions. We illustrate this very informally by looking at everyone's favourite example of a recursively defined function, the factorial function. The definition is given by

Function factorial(n : **integer**) : **integer**;
Begin if $n = 0$ **then** factorial := 1
                else factorial := $n *$ factorial($n - 1$)
End;

We see that if, for example, a program in which this function is declared calls for the evaluation of factorial(3) then the function body will call for the evaluation of factorial(2); this evaluation will call for the evaluation of factorial(1), which calls in turn for the evaluation of factorial(0); this, however, is given explicitly to be 1. Having obtained the value of factorial(0) we can plug it into the evaluation of factorial(1), which can then be used to evaluate factorial(2) and hence eventually to give factorial(3). We can think of this process as forming a stack of function calls, pushing first factorial(3), then factorial(2), factorial(1), factorial(0) in order. Then factorial(0) can be immediately evaluated and the stack popped; the value of factorial(0) can be used to evaluate factorial(1) and the stack popped; proceeding in this way we eventually obtain the value of factorial(3).

The next application of stacks in computer science (again mostly concealed from the user by the friendly machine) concerns the representation of arithmetic expressions.

If a and b are numbers then we have long been used to representing their sum as

$$a + b.$$

We call this the **infix** notation. The Polish logician Łukasiewicz introduced an alternative notation for the sum of a and b; he wrote

$$+ \, a \, b.$$

This is called the **prefix** or (in more easily spelt reference to Łukasiewicz) the **Polish** notation. The third notation is called **postfix** or **reverse Polish** notation; here the sum of a and b is represented as

$$a \, b \, +.$$

Most computers use postfix notation for their internal representation of arithmetic expressions; both prefix and postfix notations have the great advantage that expressions can be written without parentheses.

Consider the following expression in standard infix form

$$a + b * c.$$

In order to evaluate this expression we have to know which of the operations $+$ and $*$ is to be performed first. The long-standing convention which we learned in our schooldays is that multiplication is done before addition or, as we say, multiplication has higher precedence than addition. To convert the given expression to postfix form we proceed as follows:

$$a + b * c \longrightarrow a + (b * c)$$
$$\text{(inserting parentheses to emphasize precedence)}$$
$$\longrightarrow a + (bc*) \text{ (converting product to postfix)}$$
$$\longrightarrow a(bc*)+ \text{ (converting sum to postfix)}$$
$$\longrightarrow abc * +$$

Notice that operations where the operator has higher precedence are converted first and that after a conversion of part of the expression to postfix form the converted form is treated as a single operand.

Consider now the same expression with the precedence changed by inserting parentheses:

$$(a + b) * c$$

Here the conversion proceeds as follows:

$$(a + b) * c \longrightarrow (ab+) * c$$
$$\longrightarrow (ab+)c*$$
$$\longrightarrow ab + c*$$

We now describe a systematic method, using a stack, for converting an arithmetic expression given in infix form to postfix form. First we lay down explicitly the rules of precedence: the conventional order of precedence of arithmetic operators, highest first, is:

Exponentiation ($\wedge$),
Multiplication ($*$) and Division ($/$) (with the same precedence),
Addition ($+$) and Subtraction ($-$) (with the same precedence).

There is a further convention that (unless this is over-ridden by bracketing) operators of the same precedence "associate to the left" except for exponentiation which "associates to the right". This means, for example, that

$$a - b + c \quad \text{is to be interpreted as} \quad (a - b) + c$$

while

$$a \wedge b \wedge c \quad \text{is interpreted as} \quad a \wedge (b \wedge c).$$

To take account of the convention about exponentiation we sometimes find it convenient to say that $\wedge$ has higher precedence than $\wedge$. There is, of course, underlying all these conventions the rule that a subexpression enclosed in parentheses (or square or curly brackets) is always to be considered as a single operand and so must be processed before any larger expression of which it forms a part.

To convert an arithmetic expression given in infix form to the equivalent postfix form we proceed as follows: we set up an (initially empty) stack whose entries are characters and enclose the whole given infix expression between an opening symbol $\vdash$ and a closing symbol $\dashv$ which do not otherwise appear in the expression. The whole expression is then read character by character and processed according to the following instructions:

1. The opening symbol ⊢ is pushed onto the stack;

2. Left parentheses or left brackets of any kind are pushed onto the stack;

3. Operands are added immediately to the output stream containing the postfix form;

4. An operator is compared with the character currently at the head of the stack. Then

    a. if this head character is the opening symbol ⊢ or a left parenthesis or bracket the incoming operator is pushed onto the stack;

    b. if the head character is an operator of lower precedence than the incoming operator, then the incoming operator is pushed onto the stack (it is here that we have to remember the convention about exponentiation: an incoming ∧ has higher precedence than an existing ∧ and so is pushed onto the stack);

    c. if the head character is an operator of higher precedence than the incoming operator or the same precedence, the head character is popped and added to the output stream and the incoming character is compared with the character which is now at the head of the stack and dealt with according to whichever of *a*, *b* or *c* is appropriate;

5. A right parenthesis or bracket is not added to the stack; all operators on the stack down to the first matching left parenthesis or bracket are popped and added to the output stream; both parentheses disappear;

6. When the closing symbol ⊣ is reached the stack is cleared, i.e. all entries are popped in turn and added to the output stream; both ⊣ and ⊢ disappear.

Example 1. Consider the expression we examined earlier, $a + b * c$. We introduce the opening and closing symbols, obtaining

$$\vdash \ a + b * c \ \dashv.$$

Let us write our stacks horizontally, with head to the left. Then we have

Input	Stack	Output
⊢	⊢	
a	⊢	a
$+$	$+\vdash$	
b	$+\vdash$	b
$*$	$*+\vdash$	
c	$*+\vdash$	c
⊣		$*+$

So the postfix form is $a\ b\ c\ *\ +$, as we found earlier.

Example 2. Consider now the bracketed expression $(a\ +\ b)\ *\ c$. Here we have

Input	Stack	Output
⊢	⊢	
$($	$(\ \vdash$	
a	$(\ \vdash$	a
$+$	$+\ (\ \vdash$	
b	$+\ (\ \vdash$	b
$)$	⊢	$+$
$*$	$*\ \vdash$	
c	$*\ \vdash$	c
⊣		$*$

Thus the postfix form is $a\ b\ +\ c\ *$.

Although we have now seen how to transform arithmetic expressions from their familiar infix form to the unfamiliar postfix form we still have to answer the question "Why bother?". We do this by describing an automatic procedure (using a stack—surprise, surprise!) for the evaluation of expressions in postfix form. The principle underlying the procedure is the observation that the operands of any operator in a postfix expression are the values of the preceding two subexpressions.

We set up a stack whose entries are to be operands, i.e. numbers. Then we read our postfix expression character by character and proceed as follows:

a. if the incoming character is an operand we push it onto the stack;

b. if the incoming character is an operator we pop the top two elements of the stack, combine them by applying the operator (being careful about the order) and push the result of this operation onto the stack so that it is available as an operand for a later operator.

When we have read the whole expression there is only one number left in the stack and this is the value of the expression.

Example 1. Evaluate 6 3 4 * + (which is the postfix form of the infix expression 6 + (3 * 4)).

When we read 6, then 3, then 4 the stack is successively

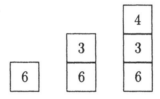

When we read * we pop 4, then 3 and form 3 * 4 = 12; then we push 12; the stack is now

```
┌────┐
│ 12 │
├────┤
│ 6  │
└────┘
```

When we read + we pop 12, then 6 and form 6 + 12 = 18; we push 18; the stack now contains 18 alone. Thus 18 is the required value.

Example 2. Evaluate 6 3 + 4 *, which is the postfix form of the expression (6 + 3) * 4.

When we read 6, then 3 the stack is successively

```
┌───┐   ┌───┐
│   │   │ 3 │
│ 6 │   ├───┤
│   │   │ 6 │
└───┘   └───┘
```

When we read + we pop 3, then 6 and form $6 + 3 = 9$; then we push 9, so that the stack consists of 9 alone.

When we read 4 we push it, so that the stack becomes

4
9

When we read * we pop 4, then 9 and form $9 * 4 = 36$; we push 36, and this is now the required value.

We should perhaps say a word about the parenthetical phrase above about "being careful about the order". We recall that a postfix expression of the form

$$(Operand1)\ (Operand2)\ (Operator)$$

is a representation of the infix expression

$$(Operand1)\ (Operator)\ (Operand2)$$

In our evaluation procedure Operand1 will be pushed onto the stack before Operand2; so Operand2 will be popped before Operand1. Thus the second operand to be popped is the first operand of the operator. This observation is crucial for the non-commutative operators $-$, $/$, $\wedge$ where changing the order of the two operands may change the value of the expression.

2.3 Queues

In spite of all we have seen about the usefulness of stacks in computer science we cannot, if we have been carefully brought up, avoid the uneasy feeling that the last-in-first-out behaviour of stacks is somehow unfair: in many situations of everyday life we much prefer to see *first*-in-first-out behaviour. There are also in computer science many situations where the first-in-first-out protocol is the one to use; so we study next a data structure which is subject to this protocol. Such a data structure is called a **queue** in obvious reference to queues in our everyday experience. Formally, a queue is a list in which deletions may be made at one end only, which we call the **front**, and insertions may be made only at the other end, which we call the **rear**; a queue is also referred to as a *FIFO* (first-in-first-out) structure.

If E is any set then the collection of all queues with elements drawn from the set E, **queue**(E), is the same as the collection **list**(E); but, as in the case of **stack**(E), the collection **queue**(E) has its own fundamental operations associated with it. As in the case of general linked lists we shall need an operation which creates a queue, and, as in the case of stacks (and for the same reasons), we shall need to be able to check whether a given queue is full or empty. In the case of queues we require the operation of removing an element from the front of the queue—we call this operation **serve**—and the operation of inserting an element at the rear, which we call **enqueue**.

The characteristic of queues which we join day by day, in the post office or cafeteria or booking office, is that they are always changing—customers at the front of the queue are gradually served and depart, while new customers join the rear of the queue. This suggests that for the computer implementation of queues we might again use pointers as we did for linked lists and stacks. So we declare

> **Type** $T = Element\_type$;
> $\qquad Queue\_pointer = \uparrow Node$;
> $\qquad Node = $ **Record**
> $\qquad\qquad\quad Info : T$;
> $\qquad\qquad\quad Next : Queue\_pointer$
> $\qquad\qquad$ **end**;
> $\qquad Queue = $ **Record**
> $\qquad\qquad\quad Front, Rear : Queue\_pointer$
> $\qquad\qquad$ **end**;
> **Var** $Q : Queue$;

and create an initially empty queue by making the assignments

$$Q.Front := \text{nil}; \ Q.Rear := \text{nil};$$

As in the case of stacks, insertions in queues will be carried out by using the operation **new** which (at least in theory) can be invoked indefinitely often; so queues implemented in this way will never be full. We may thus define the Pascal function

    Function full (Q: *Queue*) : **boolean**;
    Begin full := **false End**;

The analogy for queues of the test for an empty stack is

    Function empty (Q : *Queue*) : **boolean**;
    Begin empty := (*Queue.Front* = **nil**) **and**
                    (*Queue.Rear* = **nil**) **End**;

When an element of type T is added to a queue Q it is put in the *Info* field of a new node, which becomes the new rear node. This new node has to be tacked on to the end of Q; we do this by setting the *Next* field of the former rear node to point to the new node—unless, of course, Q is originally empty, in which case the new node becomes both the front and rear node of a one-node queue. Both cases are covered by the following procedure:

    Procedure enqueue (a : T; **Var** Q : *Queue*);
    Var p : *Queue_pointer*;
    Begin if full(Q) **then** ... (⋆ take some appropriate action ⋆)
                else begin
                      new(p);
                      with p↑ **do begin**
                          Info := a; *Next* := **nil end**;
                      if $Q.Rear$ = **nil then** $Q.Front$ = p;
                        else $Q.Rear$↑.*Next* := p;
                      $Q.Rear$:= p **end**
    End;

We illustrate the operation of this procedure in the case where Q is non-empty by the diagram

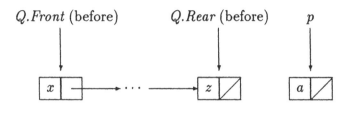

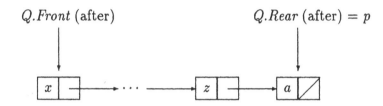

When we remove the element at the front of the queue we certainly change the queue; and we often want to work with the element which is removed. So we take as formal parameters for the procedure which implements *serve* a **Var** parameter of type *Queue* and another **Var** parameter of type T which, after the execution of the procedure, holds the element which was at the front of the queue. When we remove the front node of a queue the new front node is the node pointed to by the *Next* field of the original front node; if this pointer is **nil** then the original front node was also the rear node and after it is removed both front and rear pointers are **nil**. We sum this up in the following procedure:

```
Procedure serve (Var Q : Queue; Var first : T);
Var p : Queue_pointer;
Begin if empty(Q) then ... (* take some appropriate action *)
          else begin
                   p := Q.Front;
                   first := p↑.Info;
                   Q.Front := Q.Front↑.Next ;
                   if Q.Front = nil then Q.Rear := nil;
                   dispose(p) end
     End;
```

We illustrate the operation of the procedure (in the case where the queue is non-empty) in the following diagram

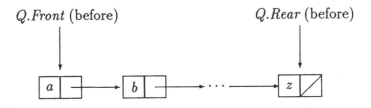

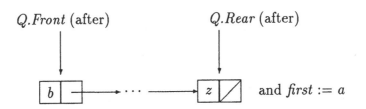

When we were studying linked lists and stacks we saw that it was possible to implement them not only by means of pointers but also using arrays; so we naturally ask whether we can implement queues also by means of arrays. The answer is that we can, but the details are not altogether straightforward. We begin, as in the case of lists and arrays, by guessing what will be the largest size *maxsize* which the queue will reach and then declare

Const $N = maxsize$;

We think of the queue entries at each moment of time as occupying successive positions, say from l to r in an array indexed by 1 .. N; we shall have to keep a record of the array indices which hold the front and rear of the queue. Thus we declare

Type *Queue* = **Record**
                   Queue_array : **array** [1 .. N] **of** T;
                   Front, Rear : 0 .. N
          end ;

(where we use 0 .. N as range for the front and rear indices to help us deal with the case of an empty queue). It turns out to be convenient also to let *Front* be the index of the position *just before* the one holding the first element of the queue (i.e. *Front* = $l - 1$); *Rear* will be the index of the position holding the last (most recently added) element of the queue, so that *Rear* = r. If we declare

Var Q : *Queue*;

then we initialise Q to an empty queue by making the assignments

$$Q.Front := 0; \; Q.Rear := 0;$$

Our first naïve idea about the way to handle the serving and enqueuing operations when the queue members are stored in the subarray indexed from l = *Front* + 1 to r = *Rear* is as follows. To serve the queue we remove the l-th entry of the array; the remaining members are stored in the subarray indexed from $l + 1$ to r, so *Front* is increased by 1. To enqueue a new element a of type T we assign a to the $(r + 1)$-st entry of the array; the queue now extends from the position l to the position $r + 1$, i.e. *Rear* has been increased by 1. If we use this approach we notice that when *Rear* has the value N it will not be possible to enqueue any further elements of T since increasing *Rear* by 1 would take it outside the permitted index range. This situation might arise even if all the "customers" had been served (when *Front* = *Rear* = N). Clearly this is undesirable, since even though *Rear* = N there may still be many vacant locations in the lower part of the array.

What are we to do to avoid this situation? We might think of imitating what happens in real-life queues, in which whenever a customer is served from the front of the queue all the remaining customers move up one place. If we did this the queue members would always reside in a subarray with lowest index 1 (so that *Front* would always be

0). To achieve this in a Pascal procedure would require an assignment
of the form

$$Queue\_array[\,i-1\,] := Queue\_array[\,i\,]$$

for each of the remaining queue members. Each of these assignments
takes time to execute. To reduce the time involved in this "moving up" performance we might decide to let the queue grow without
such movement until the rear got to the right hand end of the array
($Rear = N$) and then to move the queue to the left if there are any
unoccupied locations. This still requires an assignment operation for
each remaining member.

To avoid all this movement we think of letting the array "wrap
around". The difficulty we have been facing stems from the fact that
there is no array entry after the N-th; we can get round this by imagin-
ing that the first entry of the array follows immediately after the N-th,
so that instead of increasing *Front* by 1 when we serve the queue and
increasing *Rear* by 1 when we enqueue a new element we make this
increase **mod** N. We are not out of the wood yet though, for, as we
shall see, it is now hard to decide, using only *Front* and *Rear*, when a
queue is full or empty.

Consider the queue originally represented by the array

| a | b | c | | | with *Front* = 0 and *Rear* = 3

If we carry out three *serve* operations we obtain successively

| | b | c | | | with *Front* = 1 and *Rear* = 3

| | | c | | | with *Front* = 2 and *Rear* = 3

| | | | | | with *Front* = 3 and *Rear* = 3

The queue is now empty and we have *Front* = *Rear*. But consider the queue represented by

$$\boxed{}\ \boxed{b}\ \boxed{c}\ \boxed{d}\ \boxed{}\qquad \text{with } Front = 1 \text{ and } Rear = 4$$

If we enqueue *e* and then *a* we obtain successively

$$\boxed{}\ \boxed{b}\ \boxed{c}\ \boxed{d}\ \boxed{e}\qquad \text{with } Front = 1 \text{ and } Rear = 5$$

$$\boxed{a}\ \boxed{b}\ \boxed{c}\ \boxed{d}\ \boxed{e}\qquad \text{with } Front = 1 \text{ and } Rear = 1$$

This time the queue is full and again *Front* = *Rear*.

One way out of this difficulty is to introduce a further field

$$Count : 1 \mathrel{..} N$$

in the **Record** type *Queue* and to increase *Count* by 1 whenever a new element in enqueued and to decrease it by 1 whenever the queue is served. The queue would then be full when *Count* = *N* and empty when *Count* = 0. This approach is easy to understand and to implement, but it involves an assignment to *Count* for each application of *serve* or *enqueue* in addition to the inevitable assignments from or to *Queue_array* and to either *Front* or *Rear*, and each assignment takes time.

A widely favoured way to handle the difficulty we have been describing is to agree that the array holding a queue will be counted as full when all positions but one in the array are occupied by queue elements. An examination of the following examples

$$\boxed{b}\ \boxed{c}\ \boxed{d}\ \boxed{}\ \boxed{a}\qquad \text{with } Front = 4 \text{ and } Rear = 3$$

| | a | b | c | d | with $Front = 1$ and $Rear = 5$ |

| a | b | c | d | | with $Front = 0$ and $Rear = 4$ |

will show that in each case we have $Front = (Rear + 1) \bmod 5$.

So we are now able to implement the queue operations in the array representation as follows:

Function full (Q : *Queue*) : **boolean**;
Begin full := (($Q.Rear + 1$) **mod** N = $Q.Front$) **End**;

Function empty (Q : *Queue*) : **boolean**;
Begin empty := ($Q.Front = Q.Rear$) **End**;

Procedure enqueue (a : T; **Var** Q : *Queue*);
Begin if full(Q) **then** ... ($\star$ take some appropriate action $\star$)
            else with Q **do begin**
                  $Rear := (Rear + 1)$ **mod** N;
                  $Queue\_array[\, Rear\,] := a$ **end**
End;

Procedure serve (**Var** Q : *Queue*; **Var** *customer* : T);
Var *front* : $1 .. N$;
Begin if empty(Q) **then** ... ($\star$ take some appropriate action $\star$)
            else with Q **do begin**
                  front := ($Front + 1$) **mod** N;
                  customer := $Queue\_array[\, front\,]$;
                  $Front := front$ **end**
End;

The keen-eyed whizz-kid programmer will have noticed that in the enqueue procedure above we may have to calculate the number ($Q.Rear + 1$) **mod** N twice—once in evaluating full(Q) in the **if** part and possibly also in the **else** part. It is an easy exercise, left to the reader, to eliminate this possible duplication of effort.

The idea used in the array implementation we have just described—of making the array "wrap around" as we called it—suggests a third possible implementation of queues, using circular lists. We think of forming a circular list from an ordinary linked list by replacing the **nil** *Next* pointer from the rear node by a pointer to the front node. This has the advantage that it is no longer necessary to maintain both *Front* and *Rear* pointers, since *Front* may be replaced by *Rear↑.Next*. So for this implementation we would declare *T*, *Queue_pointer* and *Node* as before and then introduce

> **Var** *queue* : *Queue_pointer*;

and initialise *queue* to be **nil**.

The **boolean** functions to test if a pointer represents a full or an empty queue are defined in the obvious way:

> **Function** full (*queue* : *Queue_pointer*) : **boolean**;
> **Begin** full := **false End**;

> **Function** empty (*queue* : *Queue_pointer*) : **boolean**;
> **Begin** empty := (*queue* = **nil**) **End**;

To implement the operation of enqueuing an element *a* at the end of a queue whose rear node is pointed to by a pointer *queue* we shall form a new node and put *a* in its *Info* field. We have now to integrate the new node into its proper place in the circular list to which we have access by a pointer to the original rear node. If this pointer is **nil** then the new node will be the only node in the resulting queue, so it will be both front and rear node; its *Next* pointer must therefore point to itself. Otherwise, if the pointer to the original rear node is not **nil**, the *Next* pointer of the new node must point to the front node (which was previously pointed to by the *Next* field of the original rear node); this *Next* field must be altered to contain a pointer to the new node. Finally the access pointer to the list must be altered to point to the new node. This is illustrated in the diagram

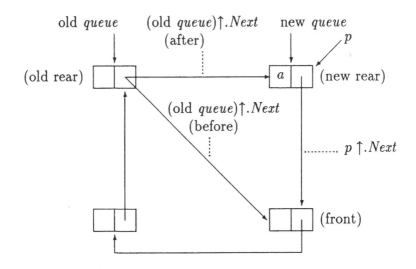

and summed up in the following procedure:

Procedure enqueue (*a* : *T*; **Var** *queue* : *Queue_pointer*);
Var *p* : *Queue_pointer;*
Begin if full(*Q*) **then** ... (⋆ take some appropriate action ⋆)
            else begin
                new(*p*);
                p↑.*Info* := *a*;
                if empty(*queue*) **then** *queue* := *p*
                    else *queue*↑.*Next* := *p*;
                queue↑.*Next* := *p*;
                queue := *p* **end**
End;

Serving a queue represented as a circular list to which we have access by
a pointer to the rear node involves first moving to the front node, which
is pointed to by the *Next* pointer of the rear node. We then retrieve the
element stored in the *Info* field of the front node and discard the front
node. We have now to decide what to do about the *Next* pointer of
the rear node. Notice first that if the queue originally consisted of one
node only (which would be the case if and only if *queue*↑.*Next* = *queue*)
then after a *serve* operation the queue will be empty and so we set the

pointer *queue* to be **nil**; but otherwise the *Next* pointer of the rear node must point to the node previously pointed to by the *Next* pointer of the original front node (which we had better get hold of before we dispose of the node). Summing up we have the following procedure:

Procedure serve (**Var** *queue* : *Queue_pointer*; **Var** *customer* : *T*);
Var *p* : *Queue_pointer*;
Begin if empty(*queue*) **then** ... (⋆ take some appropriate action ⋆)
          else begin
                  p := *queue*↑.*Next*;
                  customer := *p*↑.*Info*;
                  if *p* = *queue* **then** *queue* := **nil**
                      else *queue*↑.*Next* := *p* ↑.*Next*;
                  dispose(*p*) **end**
End;

2.4   Exercises 2

1. Suppose we have a stack X of characters; let out(X) be an abbreviation for

$$\textbf{begin } \text{pop}(X, x); \text{ Write}(x) \textbf{ end};$$

Suppose we have an input stream of letters, say S, T, A, R, which we push onto the stack X in that order. By introducing four applications of out at various places between the push operations we obtain output streams which are anagrams of STAR: for example

push('S',X); push('T',X); push('A',X); out(X); push('R',X);
                out(X); out(X); out(X);

produces ARTS.

Now consider the input stream A, B, C, D, E, F. By suitably interleaving push and out operations can the following anagrams of ABCDEF be produced as output streams?

(*a*) BDCFEA, (*b*) DBACEF, (*c*) ABCDEF,
(*d*) EBFCDA, (*e*) FEDCBA.

2. Suppose we have defined

> **Procedure** push (*a* : *T*; **Var** *s* : *P*);
> **Procedure** pop (**Var** *a* : *T*; **Var** *s* : *T*);
> **Function** full (*s* : *P*) : **boolean**;
> **Function** empty (*s* : *P*) : **boolean**;

where *P* is the type we are using to represent stacks (*Stack_pointer* or *Stack*). Using these, write functions and procedures as follows:

(a) **Function** stack_top (*s* : *P*) : *T*;
such that stack_top(*s*) is the most recently added element of the stack *s*, which is left unchanged.

(b) **Function** second (*s* : *P*) : *T*;
such that second(*s*) is the second top element of *s* and *s* itself is left unchanged;

(c) **Procedure** two_off (**Var** *s* : *P*; **Var** *a* : *T*);
such that after the execution of two_off(*s*, *a*) the value of *a* is the second top element of the stack *s* and *s* is left without its top two elements;

(d) **Procedure** bottom (**Var** *s* : *P*; **Var** *a* : *T*);
such that after the execution of bottom(*s*, *a*) the stack *s* is empty and the value of *a* is the bottom element of the stack (the one least recently added);

(e) **Function** last (*s* : *P*) : *T*;
such that last(*s*) is the bottom element of the stack *s* and *s* is left unchanged.

3. Show how to use a stack of characters to determine whether a given input stream of characters has the form xAx^*, where x is a character string and x^* is its reverse (e.g. *abcAcba*).

4. In a complicated mathematical expression we often have several sets of nested brackets of various kinds. How would you use a stack to test whether there is an equal number of opening and closing brackets,

that each closing bracket is preceded by a matching opening bracket
and that the types of opening and closing brackets match? Apply any
method you devise to test the expression

$$\{x + (y - [a + b]) * c - [(d + e)]\}/(h - (j - (k - [m - n]))).$$

5. Transform each of the following infix arithmetic expressions to postfix
   form:

   (a) $a/(b * c)$

   (b) $a/b * c$

   (c) $a \wedge b \wedge c$

   (d) $(a \wedge b) \wedge c$

   (e) $a - b - c$

   (f) $a - (b - c)$

   (g) $a^5 + 4a^3 - 3a^2 + 7$

   (h) $(a + b) * (c - d)$

   (i) S^{a+b^n}

6. If a, b, c have the values 3, 4, 5 respectively, use stacks to evaluate the
   following postfix expressions:

   (a) $a\,b\,+\,c\,*$

   (b) $a\,b\,c\,+\,*$

   (c) $a\,b \wedge c\,a\,+\,*$

7. Suppose we have declared a queue Q of type **char** and initialised it to
   be empty. Describe the composition of Q after each of the following
   operations, giving the value of *first* after each *serve* operation:

   (1) enqueue(’A’, Q);
   (2) enqueue(’B’, Q);
   (3) enqueue(’C’, Q);
   (4) serve(Q, *first*);
   (5) enqueue(’D’, Q);
   (6) enqueue(’E’, Q);

(7) serve(Q, *first*);
(8) serve(Q, *first*);
(9) enqueue('F', Q);
(10) serve(Q, *first*).

8. Suppose we have defined

> **Procedure** enqueue ($a : T$; **Var** $q : Q$);
> **Procedure** serve (**Var** $q : Q$; **Var** $a : T$);
> **Function** full ($q : Q$) : **boolean**;
> **Function** empty ($q : Q$) : **boolean**;

where Q is the type we are using to represent queues (either of the types *Queue* or *Queue_pointer*). Using these, write procedures which will write out the elements in a queue (a) from front to rear and (b) from rear to front, in each case leaving the queue unaltered.

9. A **deque** (double-ended queue) is a list in which insertion and deletion can take place at both ends of the list but nowhere else. How would you implement deques (a) using arrays, (b) using pointers?

Chapter 3

BINARY TREES

3.1 Binary trees

We begin with an informal and incomplete description of the kind of structure we are going to study in this section. Roughly speaking, a binary tree T with elements from a set E consists of a single distinguished element a of E called the root of E together with an ordered pair (L, R) of binary trees with elements from E; L and R are called respectively the left and right subtrees of T. We think of T pictorially as

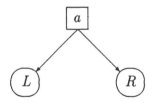

It is clear why the description we have just given is unsatisfactory: it is, of course, recursive, since it defines the binary tree T in terms of the binary trees L and R; but we have given no explicit example of a binary tree on which to found our recursive definition. The way out of this difficulty is not hard to seek: we simply lay it down that for every set E the empty set is a binary tree with elements from E. Now we can be a little more formal and say that a **binary tree** T with elements in E is a list which is either empty or else consists of three members, the first being an element of E, called the **root** of T, while the second and third are binary trees with elements in E, called respectively the **left** and **right subtrees** of T. Readers who have some knowledge of Prolog may like to think of what we have been saying as an indication of the way to define a Prolog predicate **is_E_tree**: namely, we write

   is_E_tree([ ]).
   is_E_tree([A, L, R]) :- **is_in_E**(A), **is_E_tree**(L), **is_E_tree**(R).

Although we have given a (more or less) formal definition of the binary tree structure it has to be admitted that most people think of binary trees pictorially. This is entirely reasonable since, for example, the diagram

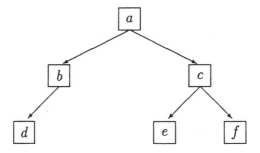

gives an immediately accessible description of the binary tree with root a and left and right subtrees represented by the diagrams

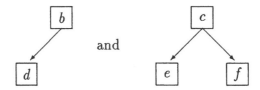

respectively. The left subtree has root b, left subtree represented by d (with root d and left and right subtrees empty) and empty right subtree. The right subtree has root c, left and right subtrees represented by e and f respectively, with e and f as roots and empty left and right subtrees. The two-dimensional representation in the diagram is much more transparent than the one-dimensional list form:

$$[\,a,[\,b,[\,d,[\ ],[\ ]\,],[\ ]\,],[\,c,[\,e,[\ ],[\ ]\,],[\,f,[\ ],[\ ]\,]\,]\,].$$

It is conventional to call the elements of a binary tree **nodes**. It is easy to convince ourselves by looking at the pictorial representation of a binary tree (and not very much harder if we stick to the formal list definition) that every node in a binary tree is the root of a binary subtree of the original tree. Let N be a node in a binary tree and look at the binary tree T_N with root N. If the left subtree of T_N is non-empty we call its root the **left child** of N; if the left subtree of T_N is empty we say that N has no left child. Similarly if the right subtree of T_N is non-empty its root is called the **right child** of N and if the right subtree of T_N is empty then N has no right child. A node which has no children at all is called a **leaf**. A node N is called the **parent** of its child or children if it has one or both; if N has both a left and a right child these children are called **siblings**. If $N1$ and $N2$ are nodes we say that $N1$ is an **ancestor** of $N2$ and $N2$ is a **descendant** of $N1$ if either (1) $N1$ is the parent of $N2$ or else (2) $N1$ is the parent of an ancestor of $N2$; here we have another example of a recursive definition since the clause (2) defines 'ancestor' in terms of 'ancestor' but clause (1) provides a firm foundation for the recursion.

We associate with each node in a binary tree a number called its **level**; the level of the root node is defined to be 0, while the level of any non-root node is defined to be 1 greater than the level of its parent. The **height** of a non-empty tree is the maximum level of any of its nodes; we define the height of the empty tree to be -1.

We show now that for every natural number n a binary tree of height n cannot have more than $2^{n+1} - 1$ nodes and not more than 2^n of these can be leaves. First of all it is clear that for each natural number k the maximum number of nodes at level k is 2^k and so, for a tree of height n the maximum number of nodes is

$$1 + 2 + 2^2 + \ldots + 2^n = 2^{n+1} - 1.$$

To prove the assertion about the maximum number of leaves we proceed by mathematical induction. First of all, if a tree has height 0 it must consist of the root node alone and this is the only leaf node: a tree of height 0 has exactly $1 = 2^0$ leaf. Now suppose that for some natural number k we have shown that every binary tree of height less than or equal to k has at most 2^k leaves (and note that we *have* done this for $k = 0$). Look at any binary tree T of height $k + 1$: both its left subtree and its right subtree must have height less than or equal to k. Thus the number of leaves of T, which is the number of leaves in the left subtree + the number of leaves in the right subtree $\leq 2^k + 2^k = 2^{k+1}$. Thus every binary tree of height less than or equal to $k + 1$ has at most 2^{k+1} leaves. This completes the inductive step.

When we think about how to implement binary trees in Pascal it is natural to think of the lines from the root to its left and right subtrees as pointers and so to make the declarations

Type $T = Element\_type$;
      $Tree\_pointer = \uparrow Node$;
      $Node = $ **Record**
              $Info : T$;
              $Left, Right : Tree\_pointer$
          end ;
    Var $tree : Tree\_pointer$;

Thus we think of representing a binary tree by a pointer to its root; for an empty tree the corresponding pointer is **nil**.

It is also possible to represent binary trees by means of arrays. As usual when we do this in Pascal we have to begin by fixing the size of the array; so, just as we did in the case of linked lists, stacks and queues, we have to guess in advance what will be the maximum number N of nodes which will ever occur in the tree. Then we declare an array indexed by $1 .. N$. The entries of the array correspond to the nodes of the tree; so each entry must contain the element of type T stored in the corresponding node, together with some way of accessing the left and right subtrees. The simplest way of getting to the subtrees is to give the indices of the array entries corresponding to the left and right children of the node; to allow for the possibility that one or both children may be absent we should extend the range of possible indices to be 0 .. N and use 0 to indicate the absence of a child. Thus we declare

Const $N = \ldots$
Type *Node* = **Record**
    Info : T;
    Left, Right : 0 .. N
  end ;
Var *tree* : **Array** [1 .. N] **of** *Node* ;

For example the tree we looked at earlier would be represented by the array

Index	Info	Left	Right
1	*a*	2	3
2	*b*	4	0
3	*c*	5	6
4	*d*	0	0
5	*e*	0	0
6	*f*	0	0

If we have a binary tree which is known to have height n then, as we have seen, the maximum number of nodes is $2^{n+1} - 1$. In this case we may represent the tree as an array indexed 1 .. $2^{n+1} - 1$, thus allocating an array entry for each possible tree node, whether it is actually present or not. This may be wasteful if the tree has far fewer than the maximum number of nodes; but, on the other hand, it avoids the necessity to have **record** entries for our array—we can get by with an **array** [1 .. $2^{n+1} - 1$] **of** T if we make the convention that the information stored at the root appears in the first position of the array while for each index i from 1 to $2^n - 1$ the information items held by the left and right children of the node represented by the i-th entry appear in the $2i$-th and $(2i + 1)$-th entries.

Suppose we have a collection of n objects and an operation, which we call *process*, which can be carried out on these objects. When we

apply the operation to each of the n objects exactly once we say that
we carry out a **traversal** of our collection. There are $n!$ arrangements
of n objects, so there are $n!$ possible traversals. Some of these $n!$
possible orders of processing the n objects seem more natural than
others, depending on the way we have stored them. For example, if
the objects are stored in a linked list it seems most natural to process
first the object stored at the head of the list, then to follow the *Next*
indicator and process the object stored in the location it indicates and
then to proceed in this way till we reach the end of the list.

It is not so obvious how to carry out a traversal if our objects are
stored in a binary tree. To get a clue about what we might do we
look a little more closely at the traversal of a linked list. In the informal (but surely understandable) description in the preceding paragraph
the phrase "proceed in this way" is a signal that we are describing a
recursive procedure. To bring out the recursion more explicitly we
might say that to traverse a list we process its head and then traverse
the remainder (the tail) of the list; of course this doesn't work for an
empty list, which doesn't have a head—but to traverse an empty list
we don't have to do anything: this observation provides the foundation
for our recursion. How can we adapt this recursive idea to the traversal
of a binary tree? Here, in place of a bipartite division into the head
which is processed and the tail of the list which is traversed, we have a
tripartite division into root, left subtree and right subtree. Clearly the
element at the root must be processed and the subtrees traversed—but
in what order? Three arrangements of the operations have proved important in computer science. They are as follows:

(1) **Preorder traversal**: here we first process the root, then
carry out the preorder traversal of the left subtree, followed by the preorder traversal of the right subtree;

(2) **Inorder traversal**: here we carry out the inorder traversal
of the left subtree, then process the root and finally make the inorder
traversal of the right subtree;

(3) **Postorder traversal**: in this case we carry out the postorder
traversal of the left subtree, followed by the postorder traversal of the
right subtree and then process the root.

The prefixes *pre-*, *in-* and *post-* indicate the position of the root-
processing operation. These descriptions of binary tree traversals are

of course recursive but, as they stand, they are incomplete unless we note explicitly that to traverse an empty tree we do nothing. The three traversals can be implemented by recursive Pascal procedures; we need only give one example:

Procedure preorder (*t* : *Tree_pointer*);
Begin
    If *t* <> **nil then with** *t* ↑ **do begin**
                process(*Info*);
                preorder(*Left*);
                preorder(*Right*) **end**
End;

Consider the binary tree

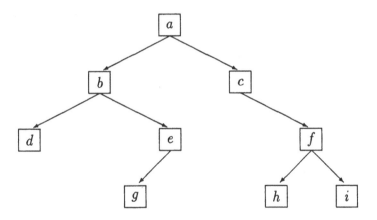

Then the order in which we process the information fields in the preorder traversal is

$$a\ b\ d\ e\ g\ c\ f\ h\ i.$$

For the inorder traversal the order is

$$d\ b\ g\ e\ a\ c\ h\ f\ i$$

and for the postorder traversal

$$d\ g\ e\ b\ h\ i\ f\ c\ a.$$

We have met the prefixes *pre-*, *in-* and *post-* earlier in connexion with the representation of arithmetic expressions in prefix, infix and postfix forms; we shall now see how these are tied up with binary tree traversals. Suppose we are given an arithmetic expression in infix form. The rules of precedence allow us to put the expression in the form

(subexpression 1) (operator) (subexpression 2).

We represent this by a binary tree which has the operator in the *Info* field of its root and whose left and right subtrees are the binary tree representations of subexpression 1 and subexpression 2 respectively. As usual we are giving a recursive definition, so we must ensure that it is well-founded. Our recursive description certainly doesn't work when the arithmetic expression just consists of a single operand: in this case we represent the expression by a tree consisting of a single node with the operand in its *Info* field and its *Left* and *Right* fields **nil**—this prescription provides a base for our recursion.

Consider for example the expression

$$b \uparrow 2 - 4 * a * c$$

Recalling that $*$ associates to the left, so that $4 * a * c$ has to be interpreted as $(4 * a) * c$, we have the binary tree representation

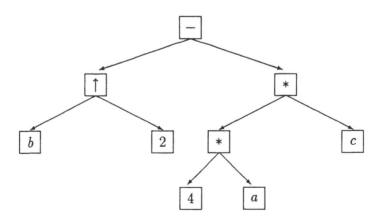

If we now carry out the preorder and postorder traversals of this tree we obtain

$$- \uparrow b \, 2 * * 4 \, a \, c$$

and

$$b \, 2 \uparrow 4 \, a * c * -$$

which we recognise as the prefix and postfix forms of the original infix expression.

3.2   Binary search trees

When we were studying binary trees in complete generality in the last section we laid no restriction at all on the type E to which the information fields of the tree nodes belong. We now specialise to the situation where the type E of the information field is either itself ordered or (more usually) a **record** type one of whose fields, usually called the *key field*, is of an ordered type. (We recall that if E is an ordered type there is a relation $<$ (less than) defined on E such that if a and b are distinct members of E then either $a < b$ or $b < a$.) A binary tree with elements of such a type E is called a **binary search tree** if for every node in the tree the key field of its information field is greater than that for every node in its left subtree and less than that for every node in its right subtree. When we give examples to illustrate binary search trees we shall usually take the information field itself to be of ordered type, for example integers or character strings with dictionary order; but in the real world our main interest is seldom in the ordered key field but in all the other fields of the **record** type—the chief importance of the key field is to determine the location in which to store and later to find the associated information. As an example of a binary search tree with integer entries we have

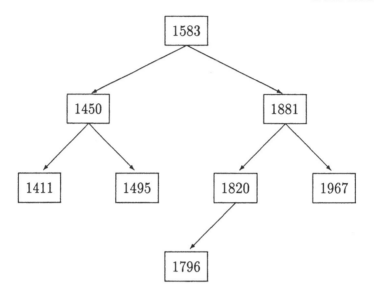

(Readers in the eight older Scottish universities will not need to be told the significance of the entries.)

To implement binary search trees using pointers we make the declarations

> **Type** *Key_type* = ... (⋆ some ordered type ⋆)
>   *Element_type* = **Record**
>   *Key* : *Key_type*;
>   ... (⋆ other information fields ⋆)
>   **end** ;
>   *Tree_pointer* = ↑ *Node*;
>   *Node* = **Record**
>   *Info* : *Element_type*;
>   *Left, Right* : *Tree_pointer*
>   **end** ;
> **Var** *tree* : *Tree_pointer*;

and initialise the variable *tree* by making it **nil**.

The fundamental operations associated with binary search trees are the insertion of new entries and the removal of existing entries; each of these operations has to be defined in such a way that when we apply it to a binary search tree the result is again a binary search tree.

It is easy to see how to carry out the insertion of a new record. First of all, if the given tree is empty we make a new node containing the new record in its *Info* field and **nil** pointers in its *Left* and *Right* fields; we then change the original **nil** *Tree_pointer* to point to the new node. This provides us with the basis for a recursive definition, for if the given tree is not empty we compare the key of the new record (the "new key") with the key of the record held in the *Info* field of the root node (the "root key"); if the new key is less than the root key the new record must be inserted in the left subtree, while if the new key is greater than the root key the new record must go in the right subtree. (An ultra-careful programmer might like to consider what action should be taken if the new key is the same as the root key.)

For example, to insert a record with key 5 in the binary search tree

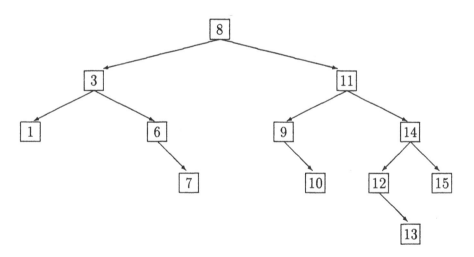

(in which we display only the keys of the entries) we argue as follows: 5 is less than 8 so it must be inserted in the left subtree of 8, which has root 3; 5 is greater than 3, so it must be inserted in the right subtree of 3, which has root 6; 5 is less than 6, so it must be inserted in the left subtree of 6, which is **nil**; so a new node must be created to contain 5 and inserted as left child of 6, producing the tree

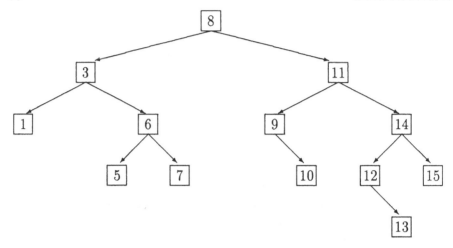

(Notice that we have referred in a slipshod way to "the left subtree of 8" for example when we should properly have spoken of "the left subtree of the tree with root 8".)

We sum up the general story in the following procedure:

> **Procedure** insert (*a* : *Element_type;* **Var** *t* : *Tree_pointer*);
> **Var** *p* : *Tree_pointer*;
> **Begin if** *t* = nil **then begin**
>   **new**(*p*);
>   **with** *p* **do begin**
>   *Info* := *a*;
>   *Left* := **nil**;
>   *Right* := **nil end**;
>   *t* := *p* **end**
>   **else if** (*a.Info.Key* < *t* ↑.*Info.Key*)
>   **then** insert(*a*, *t* ↑.*Left*)
>   **else if** (*a.Info.Key* > *t* ↑.*Info.Key*)
>   **then** insert(*a*, *t* ↑.*Right*)
>   **else** Writeln ('already present')
> **End**;

Next we consider the problem of deleting an entry from a binary search tree in such a way that after the deletion we are left with a binary search tree. There are three cases to consider:

(1) If the node *N* containing the element to be deleted has no child-

ren it may be removed without any further adjustment to the tree by reassigning the pointer to N to be **nil**. This is the situation when we delete 15 from the above tree, when we obtain

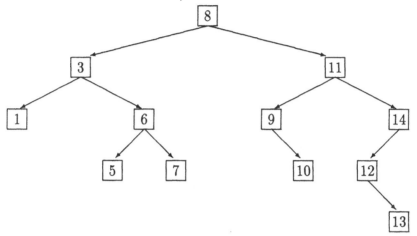

(2) If the node N containing the element to be deleted has one child we have to remove N from the tree while still leaving its child as a node of the tree. Suppose N is $p \uparrow$ where p is either the pointer to N from its parent or else (if N is the root node) the tree pointer by which we gain access to the binary search tree. Then we alter p to point to the single child of N. It is not hard to check that the binary search tree property is maintained. To illustrate consider what happens when we delete 9 from the tree we have just obtained:

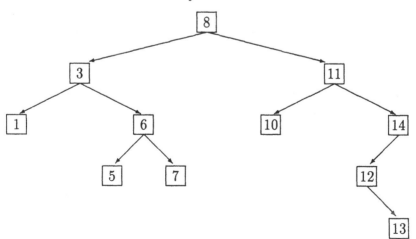

(3) Suppose finally that the node N to be deleted has two children (think of the node containing 11 in the above tree). In this case we look first at the node N' which comes immediately after N in the inorder traversal of the tree, its "immediate inorder successor"; N' is the farthest left node of the right subtree of N and so has key greater than the key of N. Notice that N' cannot have a left child: any such child would also be in the right subtree of N but would come before N' in the inorder traversal.

To delete N we replace the pointer to N by a pointer to N' and the pointer to N' by the *Right* pointer from N' (i.e. the pointer to its right child if it has one and **nil** if it doesn't). Again it is easy to check that the binary search tree property is maintained. When N is the node containing 11 the immediate inorder successor N' is the node containing 12. So when N is removed in the way just described the tree becomes

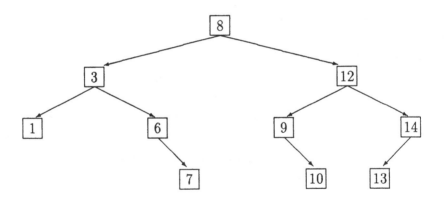

which is still a binary search tree.

It would of course be possible to replace N by its immediate inorder predecessor (the farthest right node in its left subtree) and that predecessor by its left child (it couldn't have a right child).

The following Pascal procedure implements the deletion operation as we described it:

Procedure delete (a : *Element_type;* **Var** t : *Tree_pointer*);
Var p, q : *Tree_pointer*;
Begin if t = nil **then** Writeln (a, 'is not present')
   else if a < $t \uparrow$.*Info.Key* **then** delete(a, $t \uparrow$.*Left*)
      else if a > $t \uparrow$.*Info.Key* **then** delete(a, $t \uparrow$.*Right*)
         else ($\star$ if a = $t \uparrow$.*Info.Key* $\star$)
           begin
              $q := t$;
              if $q \uparrow$.*Right* = nil **then** $t := q \uparrow$.*Left*
                  else if $q \uparrow$.*Left* = nil **then** $t := q \uparrow$.*Right*
                      else begin
                            $p := q \uparrow$.*Right*;
                            while $p \uparrow$.*Left* <> nil **do** $p := p \uparrow$.*Left*;
                            $t := p$;
                            $t \uparrow$.*Left* := $q \uparrow$.*Left*;
                            $p := p \uparrow$.*Right* **end end**
End;

Readers who are anxious to know what binary search trees have to do with searching must be patient until they reach Part III on Storing and Searching.

3.3 Exercises 3

1. Draw diagrams of all possible binary trees with 4 nodes.

2. How many ancestors does a node at level n in a binary tree have? Prove your answer using mathematical induction.

3. Write Pascal functions which will determine

   (a) the number of nodes in a binary tree;

   (b) the height of a binary tree;

   (c) the sum of the information fields (supposed to be of type **integer**) of all the nodes in a binary tree.

4. A binary tree is said to be **strictly binary** if every node which is not a leaf has two children. Write a Pascal function which will determine whether a given binary tree is strictly binary.

5. Carry out the preorder, inorder and postorder traversals of the binary tree

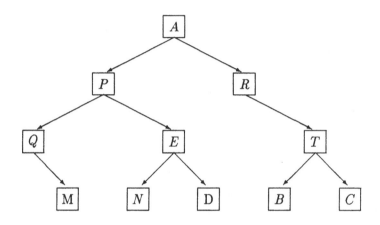

6. Find the binary tree whose preorder traversal is

$$A\ B\ C\ D\ E\ X\ Z\ U\ T\ Y$$

and whose inorder traversal is

$$D\ C\ E\ B\ A\ U\ Z\ T\ X\ Y.$$

7. Represent each of the following arithmetic expressions by means of a binary tree and hence derive the Polish and reverse Polish forms of each:

   (a) $a/(b*c)$
   (b) $a^5 + 4a^3 - 3a^2 + 7$
   (c) $(a+b)*(c-d)$
   (d) S^{a+b^n}

8. Build up binary search trees using the following input streams of key fields:

    (a) 1 2 3 4 5;

    (b) 5 4 3 2 1;

    (c) *fe cx jk ha gc ap aa by my da.*

(In (c) the order relation is dictionary order.)

9. Construct a binary search tree using the input stream:

$$8, 9, 11, 15, 19, 20, 21, 7, 3, 2, 1, 5, 6, 4, 13, 10, 12, 17, 16, 18$$

and then delete in order the nodes containing

$$2, 10, 19, 8, 20$$

so that at each stage the tree is still a binary search tree.

Chapter 4

HEAPS

4.1 Priority queues and heaps

Although most queues in everyday life follow the first-in-first-out protocol there are familiar situations where it is acceptable for people to "jump the queue": for example in a hospital casualty department patients may in general be treated in order of their arrival times, but a severely injured accident victim is certain to be dealt with before someone with a fishbone in the throat no matter at what times they arrived. It is natural to say that the accident victim has higher priority than the patient with the fishbone. There are also situations in the operation of a time-sharing computer system where requests are handled not in the order in which they are made in time but according to the priorities assigned to them by the operating system.

In these cases we are clearly dealing with a new kind of data structure, which we call a **priority queue** or **heap**. This is a collection of objects drawn from some set E each of which has a priority associated with it; the priorities of the objects are elements of some ordered type (so that we can talk of one object's priority as being higher or lower than that of another). At any stage in its existence the only object which can be removed from a priority queue is the one with highest priority.

It might appear at first sight that in order to implement a priority queue we should think of storing the elements in decreasing order of priority; but since at any moment we are interested only in the element which is currently of highest priority the order of the remaining elements is not really relevant—and of course it may change as soon as a new object is added to the queue.

It is best to begin by representing a heap as a special kind of binary tree, which we call a **heap-tree**. As in the case of binary search trees (which are *not* heap-trees) the information field type E of the nodes of the tree is either an ordered type or (more usually) a **record** type one of whose fields, the *key* field, is of an ordered type (when we use a heap-tree to implement a priority queue this would be an indicator of the priority). The defining characteristics which a binary tree must satisfy in order to qualify as a heap-tree are as follows:

(1) all the leaves of the tree are on one level or on two adjacent levels;

(2) all the levels, except possibly the one with highest level number (the lowest on the page in the usual way of displaying trees), have the largest possible number of nodes containing information items; and all the leaves in the "lowest" level are as far to the left as possible;

(3) for each non-leaf node the key of the information item which it holds is greater than the keys of the items held by its children.

Notice that condition (3) implies that the element stored in the root node has the greatest key of all the items in the whole tree.

As an example of a heap-tree, in which we take the information items to be just the integer keys, we have

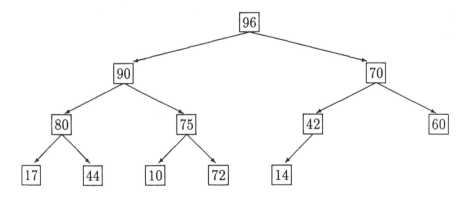

We can of course implement heap-trees using Pascal pointers in the

way we described when we introduced binary trees in Chapter 3; but since nearly all the nodes of a heap-tree are used to store information (all but possibly some at the right of the lowest level) it is not unreasonable to think of using an array implementation. Namely, if the height of the heap-tree is N, we set up an array H of type E (the type of the information items) indexed by $1 \ .. \ (2^{N+1} - 1)$; we store the element at the root in the array entry $H[1]$ and for each index i, if the node whose information is stored in $H[i]$ has one child then the child's information is stored in $H[2i]$, while if it has two children then their information is stored in $H[2i]$ and $H[2i+1]$. For example the heap-tree in the diagram above would be represented by the array

| 96 | 90 | 70 | 80 | 75 | 42 | 60 | 17 | 44 | 10 | 72 | 14 | | | |

(Notice that if a node has two children the one with the larger key may appear as either the left or right child.)

The basic operations to be carried out on a heap are (1) insertion of a new element in a given heap in such a way that the heap properties are still satisfied after the insertion and (2) removal of the element at the root of the heap (the element with largest key) and reorganisation of the remaining entries so that we still have a heap. We shall also need to have a method for creating a heap and (as in the case of stacks and ordinary queues) we should have methods for deciding whether a given heap is empty or full.

As we shall see in a moment the operation of insertion in a heap-tree requires us to compare the key of the information field of a node with that of its parent. So to implement the heap-tree structure using pointers would involve introducing an additional *Tree_pointer* field *Parent* in the definition of the type *Node*. In the array approach, however, where we store the children of $H[i]$ in $H[2i]$ and $H[2i + 1]$, then the parent of $H[j]$ is clearly $H[j \ \textbf{div} \ 2]$. So it is more convenient to use the array implementation.

We begin by guessing the greatest height, *maxheight*, to which the heap-tree will grow and then declare

Const $N = maxheight \ ; \ M = 2^{N+1} - 1;$

It follows from the definition of a heap-tree and our agreement about how to store its elements in an array that the elements occupy consecutive positions starting at position 1 in an array indexed by 1 .. M. It will be important for us to know how many positions are in use, so we declare

Type *Key_type* = ... (⋆ some ordered type ⋆)
         Element_type = **Record**
                                   Key : *Key_type*;
                                   ... (⋆ other information fields ⋆)
                             end ;
         Heap = **Record**
                       Heap_array : **array** [1 .. M] **of** *Element_type*;
                       Count : 0 .. M
                   end ;

If we declare

   Var H : *Heap*;

then we initialise H to an empty heap by making the assignment

$$H.Count := 0;$$

Clearly a heap is empty if its *Count* field has the value 0 and full if its *Count* field has the value M. Formally we define

   Function empty (H : *Heap*) : **boolean**;
   Begin empty := ($H.Count = 0$) **End**;

   Function full (H : *Heap*) : **boolean**;
   Begin full := ($H.Count = M$) **End**;

Now we examine the operation of inserting a new element in a heap H. This will of course not be possible if the heap is full; but if H is not full the existing elements will be stored in positions 1 to $H.Count$ of $H.Heap\_array$. The obvious place to put a new element is in the

(*H.Count* + 1)-th position of *H.Heap_array*; but if the key (of the *Info* field) of the new element is greater than that of its parent the heap condition will be violated. If this happens we try to retrieve the situation by interchanging the new element and its parent. Even when we have done this, however, the heap condition may not yet be satisfied, for the key of the new element may be greater than that of its new parent; obviously if this occurs we interchange the new element and the parent of its new position and keep on in the same way until either the new element reaches the root or has key less than its current parent. We talk of **bubbling up** the new element.

For example, suppose we have to insert 82 in the heap we considered above,

| 96 | 90 | 70 | 80 | 75 | 42 | 60 | 17 | 44 | 10 | 72 | 14 | | | |

We start by inserting 82 in a new node which is attached to the tree as right child of the node containing 42. The tree represented by the resulting array

| 96 | 90 | 70 | 80 | 75 | 42 | 60 | 17 | 44 | 10 | 72 | 14 | 82 | | |

is not a heap since the parent 42 is not greater than its new right child 82. We interchange 42 and 82, obtaining

| 96 | 90 | 70 | 80 | 75 | 82 | 60 | 17 | 44 | 10 | 72 | 14 | 42 | | |

which still does not represent a heap since the next parent 70 is not greater than its new left child 82. We interchange 70 and 82, obtaining

| 96 | 90 | 82 | 80 | 75 | 70 | 60 | 17 | 44 | 10 | 72 | 14 | 42 | | |

which does represent a heap.

The insertion operation can be handled by the following procedure:

```
Procedure insert (a : Element_type; Var H : Heap);
Type Table : array [1 .. M] of Element_type;
Var k : 1 .. M;
    Procedure bubble (l : 1 .. M; Var K : Table);
    Var i, j : 1 .. M; x, y : Key_type;
        Procedure swap (r, s : 1 .. M);
        Var temp : Element_type;
        Begin (* swap *)
            temp:= K[r]; K[r] := K[s]; K[s] := temp
        End; (* swap *)
    Begin (* bubble *)
        i := l; j := l div 2;
        x := K[i].Info.Key; y := K[j].Info.Key;
        if ((j <> 0) and (y < x)) then begin
                                       swap(i, j);
                                       bubble(l div 2, K) end
    End; (* bubble *)
Begin (* insert *)
    if full(H) then ... (* take some appropriate action *)
        else begin
                k := H.Count;
                H.Heap_array[k + 1] := a;
                bubble(k + 1, H.Heap_array);
                H.Count := H.Count + 1 end
End; (* insert *)
```

When we come to the operation of serving a non-empty heap, by which we mean removing the element with largest key (which is stored at the root node of the heap-tree representation or in the first entry of the heap-array representation), we shall do as we did in the case of popping stacks and serving queues—we shall return the element which is removed as the value of a **Var** parameter. If $H.Count = 1$ before the first element is removed then after the removal H will be empty. But if $H.Count > 1$ how are we to reorganise the remaining elements so that they form a heap? In particular, which element should become the first heap-array entry, corresponding to the root node of the heap-tree representation? We begin by trying the last element in the *Heap_array* field of *H*, that is *H.Heap_array[H.Count]*; this is the element of the farthest right node of the lowest level of *H*. If we are very lucky the key *k* (of the *Info* field) of this element will be greater than the keys of both children of the root node; for if this happens the heap condition is satisfied. Otherwise we interchange the new root element with whichever of its children has the larger key; then we compare its key with the keys of the children of its new position and proceed in this way until it reaches either a position with no children (a leaf) or a position where the key or keys of its child or children are less than *k*. We describe this process as **trickling down**.

Consider for example the heap

| 77 | 73 | 66 | 60 | 26 | 59 | 62 | 14 | 10 | 20 | 25 | 27 | | | |

When we remove the root entry 77 we replace it by 27; this produces

| 27 | 73 | 66 | 60 | 26 | 59 | 62 | 14 | 10 | 20 | 25 | | | | |

which does not represent a heap since 27 is less than both its children 73 and 66. We interchange 27 and its larger child 73, obtaining

| 73 | 27 | 66 | 60 | 26 | 59 | 62 | 14 | 10 | 20 | 25 | | | | |

This still does not represent a heap since although 27 is greater than one of its children (26) it is less than the other (60). So again we interchange 27 with the larger of its children. The resulting structure

| 73 | 60 | 66 | 27 | 26 | 59 | 62 | 14 | 10 | 20 | 25 | | | | |

does represent a heap.

Serving a heap can be handled by the following procedure:

Procedure serve (**Var** a : *Element_type*; **Var** H : *Heap*);
Type *Table* : **array** $[1 .. M]$ **of** *Element_type*;

   Procedure swap $(r, s : 1 .. M;$ **Var** K : *Table*$)$;
   Var *temp* : *Element_type*;
   Begin($\star$ swap $\star$)
     temp$:= K[r]; K[r] := K[s]; K[s] := temp$
   End; ($\star$ swap $\star$)

   Procedure trickle $(k, l : 1 .. M;$ **Var** K : *Table*$)$;
   Var $i : 1 .. M; x, y, z$: *Key_type*;
   Begin ($\star$ trickle $\star$)
     $i := k; x := K[i].Key$;
     while $(i <= l$ **div** $2)$ **do begin**
        if $2 * i = l$ **then begin** $y := K[l].Key$;
               if $y > x$ **then begin**
                    swap$(i, 2*i, K); i := l$ **end end**
                    else begin
                    $y := K[2 * i].Key$;
                    $z := K[2 * i + 1].Key$;
        if $(x < y)$ **and** $(y > z)$ **then begin**
               swap$(i, 2 * i, K); i := 2 * i$ **end**
            else if $(x < y)$ **and** $(y < z)$ **then begin**
               swap$(i, 2 * i + 1, K); i := 2 * i + 1$ **end**
            else $i := l$ **end end**
   End; ($\star$ trickle $\star$)

Begin ($\star$ serve $\star$)
   if empty(H) **then** ... ($\star$ take some appropriate action $\star$)
     else begin $a := H.Heap\_array[1]$;
        swap$(1, H.Count, H.Heap\_array)$;
        if $H.Count = 1$ **then** $H.Count := 0$
            else begin $H.Count := H.Count-1$;
                trickle$(1, H.Count, H.Heap\_array)$**end**
   End; ($\star$ serve $\star$)

At each stage of the procedure trickle at which the current position of the element x which is being trickled down has two children we need two key comparisons in order to find which of the three elements (x and its two children) has largest key and so should stay in or be promoted to the current position. There is an alternative version of trickle which on average involves fewer comparisons. In this version we *always* exchange the element x with its child if it has only one and otherwise with the larger of its two children (it needs only one comparison at each stage to find which is the larger), continuing until x reaches a leaf; then we bubble x up, i.e. we keep comparing it with its parent, grandparent, ... and exchanging it if its key is greater than that of its current parent.

For the example we looked at earlier when we were trickling down 27 in

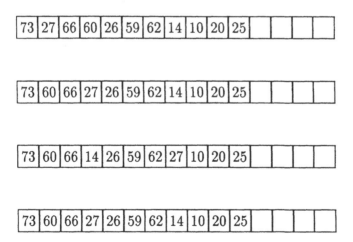

we needed 6 comparisons (2 to find the largest of 27, 73, 66; 2 to find the largest of 27, 26, 60; 2 to find the largest of 27, 14, 10). Using the alternative version of trickle we obtain successively

The result is the same as before but we needed only 4 comparisons (between 73 and 66, between 60 and 26, between 14 and 10, between 27 and 14).

The new version of trickle can be implemented as follows:

```
Procedure new_trickle (k, l : 1 .. M; Var K : Table);
Var i : 1 .. M; x, y : Key_type; temp, top : Element_type;
Begin i := k; top := K[i];
    while 2 * i <= l do begin
    if 2 * i = l then begin
                      K[i] := K[l]; i := l end
        else begin
                x := K[2 * i].Key; y := K[2 * i + 1].Key;
                if x >= y then begin
                    K[i] := K[2 * i]; i := 2 * i end
                    else if x < y then begin
                    K[i] := K[2 * i + 1]; i := 2 * i + 1 end
    end end;
    K[i] := top;
    while (i div 2) >= k do begin
                if K[i].Key > K[idiv 2].Key then
                                    swap(i, i div 2, K)
                    i := i div 2 end
    End;
```

If we are presented with an input stream of elements then we can of course make them into a heap by introducing an initially empty heap and invoking the insert procedure for each element in turn. There are situations, however, when we are given a collection of elements all at once and want to organise the collection as a heap. Suppose there are M elements altogether (M need no longer be of the form $2^{N+1} - 1$). We store the elements in an array A indexed by 1 .. M. For each index i greater than M **div** 2 we have $2i$ and $2i + 1$ greater than M; so the node represented by $A[i]$ has no children and hence the subarray indexed by (M **div** 2 + 1) .. M satisfies the heap property. We then move back to the beginning of the array trickling down $A[M\text{div } 2]$, $A[M$ **div** 2 – 1], ..., $A[1]$ in order.

For example, suppose we are given the **integer** array A

| 5 | 10 | 27 | 60 | 59 | 62 | 14 | 73 |

with $M = 8$. We begin by trickling down $A[M \text{ div } 2] = A[4] = 60$; this produces the array

| 5 | 10 | 27 | 73 | 59 | 62 | 14 | 60 |

Now we trickle down $A[3] = 27$, which gives

| 5 | 10 | 62 | 73 | 59 | 27 | 14 | 60 |

Trickling down $A[2] = 10$ gives first

| 5 | 73 | 62 | 10 | 59 | 27 | 14 | 60 |

and then

| 5 | 73 | 62 | 60 | 59 | 27 | 14 | 10 |

Finally we trickle down $A[1] = 5$, obtaining first

| 73 | 5 | 62 | 60 | 59 | 27 | 14 | 10 |

then

| 73 | 60 | 62 | 5 | 59 | 27 | 14 | 10 |

and at last the array

| 73 | 60 | 62 | 10 | 59 | 27 | 14 | 5 |

which does represent a heap.

Thus we construct a heap using

```
Procedure make_heap (Var A : Table);
Var i : 1 .. M;
Begin for i := M div 2 downto 1 do trickle(i, M, A) End;
```

4.2   Exercises 4

1. Check that the tree

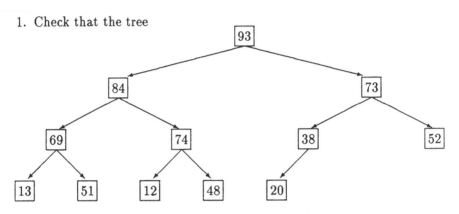

   is a heap-tree and give its array representation.

2. Insert 75 in the heap represented by the tree of Exercise 1.

3. Carry out the operation serve on the heap whose array representation
   is

93	69	67	54	53	64	61	48	41	51	47	39	25	59	34	30	32		

   using both versions of the trickle procedure.

4. Reorganise the entries of the arrays

43	12	94	17	55	19	68	73

   and

10	12	20	34	45	76	87	98

   to form arrays which represent heaps.

Chapter 5

GRAPHS

5.1   Graphs and their implementation

In the data structures we have been chiefly concerned with so far, linked
lists and binary trees and their variants, there is a kind of regularity to
be observed. Thus in a linked list each node except the last has a unique
successor and each node except the first has a unique predecessor; in
the case of a binary tree each node has at most two children and every
node except the root has a single parent. There are, however, many
collections of objects in the world in which the inter-relations are much
less regular. Consider, for example, the collection of civil airports in
Scotland. Some of them are linked by direct flights to many of the
others; but some are linked in this way to very few of the rest. It would
clearly be useful to have a way of imposing a structure on the set of
airports which would illustrate the direct connections (and possibly also
such associated information as the cost or distance or flying time for
each connection). There is, of course, a familiar way of representing
this information: we draw a rough sketch map, usually not to scale,
representing each airport by a dot; and if two airports are linked by a
direct flight then we join the dots representing them by a straight or
curved line; alongside each of these linking lines we may note the cost
or distance or flying time.

Such a picture is an example, quite familiar in everyday life, of a
pictorial representation of a structure called a graph, which we now

define formally as follows: a **graph** G is an ordered pair (V, E) consisting of a set V of **vertices** (in our example the vertices are the airports) and a set E of **edges**; each edge is a pair $\{v, w\}$ of distinct vertices (in the airport example the edges are the pairs of airports which have a direct connection). Two vertices v and w in a graph G are said to be **adjacent** and each is said to be a **neighbour** of the other if $\{v, w\}$ is one of the edges of G; an edge of G is said to be **incident** to each of the two vertices of which it is composed. A **weighted graph** is a graph $G = (V, E)$ equipped with a function W which associates to each edge e in E a number $W(e)$ which we call its **weight** (or length, or capacity according to the particular application). In the airport example distance, cost and flying times would be possible weights.

We represent a graph G pictorially just as we did in the airport example—each vertex v in V is represented by a dot and each edge e $= \{v, w\}$ by an arc (a straight line or curve) joining the dots which represent v and w. If the graph is weighted we may attach the weight of each edge to the arc representing it.

In our example of the airports linked by direct flights we took it for granted that if there is a direct flight from A_1 to A_2 then there is also a direct flight from A_2 to A_1. But if we come down to earth there are one-way traffic systems which provide a direct link in one direction between two places, say from A_1 to A_2 but require a very circuitous route to get from A_2 to A_1. Such a system would be represented by a **directed graph** or **digraph** D, which is an ordered pair (V, E) consisting of a set V of vertices and a set E of *directed* edges; in a digraph each directed edge is an *ordered* pair (v, w) of vertices. We call v the **tail** and w the **head** of the directed edge $e = (v, w)$, and we say that e is an edge **from** v **to** w. If v and w are vertices of a digraph and (v, w) is one of its edges we say that w is **adjacent** to or is a **neighbour** of v; we notice that even if w is adjacent to v it does not follow that v is adjacent to w—this will be the case only if (w, v) is also one of the directed edges of the digraph. A **weighted digraph** is a digraph $D = (V, E)$ equipped with a function W which associates to each directed edge e in E a number $W(e)$ called its weight.

We represent a digraph pictorially by using dots to represent the vertices and for each directed edge $e = (v, w)$ a directed arc from the dot representing v to the dot representing w, that is a straight line or curve with an arrow on it pointing from the dot representing v to the dot representing w.

We now describe how we implement graphs, with their possibly quite irregular structure, in the computer science environment. The two most widely-used methods are derived from the observation that if we are trying to describe a graph to someone we might begin by specifying its vertices and then either (1) for each pair $\{v, w\}$ of vertices saying whether or nor it is one of the edges of the graph or (2) for each vertex v giving a list of all the vertices w such that $\{v, w\}$ is an edge of the graph.

Let $G = (V, E)$ be a graph with vertex set $V = \{v_1, v_2, \ldots, v_N\}$. Then we may formalise the first way of describing G by means of its **adjacency matrix**. We declare

Var $adj :$ **array** $[1 .. N, 1 .. N]$ **of** $0 .. 1;$

and then initialise by the double loop

for $i := 1$ **to** N **do for** $j := 1$ **to** N **do**

$$adj[i, j] := \begin{cases} 1 \text{ if } \{v_i, v_j\} \text{ is one of the edges in } E \\ 0 \text{ if } \{v_i, v_j\} \text{ is not one of the edges in } E \end{cases}$$

If G is a weighted graph with weight function W taking real number values say, then we can modify our declaration of the adjacency matrix to

Var $adj\_W :$ **array** $[1 .. N, 1 .. N]$ **of real** ;

and the initialisation to

for $i := 1$ **to** N **do for** $j := 1$ **to** N **do**

$$adj\_W[i, j] := \begin{cases} W(\{v_i, v_j\}) \text{ if } \{v_i, v_j\} \text{ is one of the edges in } E \\ c \text{ if } \{v_i, v_j\} \text{ is not one of the edges in } E \end{cases}$$

where c is a constant which we choose depending on the particular problem for which our graph is being used—$adj\_W\,[i,j]$ might, for example, be taken as ∞ if the weights represent lengths of edges and there is no edge $\{v_i, v_j\}$; in other situations it may be more appropriate to choose c to be zero.

We notice that the adjacency matrix of a graph is symmetric, i.e. we have $adj\,[i,j] = adj\,[j,i]$ for all indices i, j: this is clear since the pairs $\{v_i, v_j\}$ and $\{v_j, v_i\}$ are the same and one is an edge if and only if the other is. Since the vertices constituting an edge are distinct it follows that all the diagonal elements $adj\,[i,i]$ are zero. Thus we need only store the

$$1 + 2 + \ldots + (N-1) = \tfrac{1}{2}N(N-1)$$

above-diagonal entries in the adjacency matrix. (For the details compare Exercise 1.2). If a graph has only a few edges then most of the entries in the adjacency matrix will be 0; thus the adjacency matrix is sparse and we can be even more economical of storage space (see Exercise 1.9).

Although we have defined the adjacency matrix to have entries in the subrange type $0\,..\,1$ it may sometimes be convenient to use **boolean** entries instead and to assign

$$adj[i, j] := \begin{cases} \textbf{true} \text{ if } \{v_i, v_j\} \text{ is one of the edges in } E \\ \textbf{false} \text{ if } \{v_i, v_j\} \text{ is not one of the edges in } E \end{cases}$$

If we use the first $(0\,..\,1)$ approach then the adjacency matrix for the graph

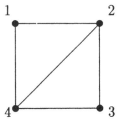

Figure 1

is easily seen to be

$$\begin{bmatrix} 0 & 1 & 0 & 1 \\ 1 & 0 & 1 & 1 \\ 0 & 1 & 0 & 1 \\ 1 & 1 & 1 & 0 \end{bmatrix}$$

It is not hard to see how to amend the definition of adjacency matrix to deal with digraphs. Namely, if $D = (V, E)$ is a digraph with vertex set $V = \{v_1, v_2, \ldots, v_N\}$ then we declare

Var adj : **array** $[1 \; .. \; N, 1 \; .. \; N]$ **of** $0 \; .. \; 1$ (or **boolean**)

and initialise adj by

for $i := 1$ **to** N **do for** $j := 1$ **to** N **do**

$$adj[i, j] := \begin{cases} 1 \; or \; \textbf{true} \; \text{if } (v_i, v_j) \text{ is one of the directed edges in } E \\ 0 \; or \; \textbf{false} \; \text{if } (v_i, v_j) \text{ is not one of the directed edges in } E \end{cases}$$

The amendment to deal with a weighted digraph is clear.

Using the 0 .. 1 approach we see that the adjacency matrix for the digraph

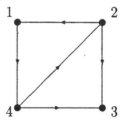

Figure 2

is

$$\begin{bmatrix} 0 & 0 & 0 & 1 \\ 1 & 0 & 1 & 0 \\ 0 & 0 & 0 & 0 \\ 0 & 1 & 1 & 0 \end{bmatrix}$$

We now turn to the second way of describing a graph by listing for each vertex all the vertices with which it forms an edge; this is the method of **adjacency lists**. Again let $G = (V, E)$ be a graph with vertex set $V = \{v_1, v_2, \ldots, v_N\}$. Then we declare

Type *Pointer* = ↑ *Node* ;
      Node = **Record**
               Vertex : 1 .. *N*;
               Next : *Pointer*
        end ;

Var *adj_list* : **array** [1 .. *N*] **of** *Pointer* ;

The idea here is that for $i = 1, 2, \ldots, N$ the array entry $adj\_list[i]$ points to the list of indices j of the vertices v_j such that $\{v_i, v_j\}$ is in E. For a digraph the i-th adjacency list would consist of the indices of the vertices v_j such that the directed edge (v_i, v_j) is in E.

In the case of the graph in Figure 1 the adjacency lists are given by

$adj\_list[1]$ ⟶ $\boxed{2\,|}$ ⟶ $\boxed{4\,\diagup}$

$adj\_list[2]$ ⟶ $\boxed{1\,|}$ ⟶ $\boxed{3\,|}$ ⟶ $\boxed{4\,\diagup}$

$adj\_list[3]$ ⟶ $\boxed{2\,|}$ ⟶ $\boxed{4\,\diagup}$

$adj\_list[4]$ ⟶ $\boxed{1\,|}$ ⟶ $\boxed{2\,|}$ ⟶ $\boxed{3\,\diagup}$

while for the digraph in Figure 2 the adjacency lists are

$adj\_list[1]$ ⟶ $\boxed{4\,\diagup}$

$adj\_list[2]$ ⟶ $\boxed{1\,|}$ ⟶ $\boxed{3\,\diagup}$

$adj\_list[3]$ = **nil**

$adj\_list[4]$ ⟶ $\boxed{2\,|}$ ⟶ $\boxed{3\,\diagup}$

In the case of a graph there will be two adjacency list entries corresponding to each edge $\{v_i, v_j\}$: for j will appear in the list $adj\_list[i] \uparrow$ and i in the list $adj\_list[j] \uparrow$. In the case of a digraph there will be only one adjacency list entry corresponding to each directed edge (v_i, v_j): namely j appears in the list $adj\_list[i] \uparrow$.

To adapt the adjacency list representation to deal with weighted graphs and digraphs the obvious approach is to redefine the type *Node* by introducing an additional *Weight* field, so that we would have

> **Type** *W_pointer* $= \uparrow$ *W_Node*;
> *W_Node* $=$ **Record**
> *Vertex* : 1 .. *N*;
> *Weight* : **real**;
> ($\star$ if the weight function *W* takes **real** values $\star$)
> *Next* : *W_pointer*
> **end** ;

> **Var** *W_adj_list* : **array** [1 .. *N*] **of** *W_pointer* ;

Then *W_adj_list*[*i*] will point to a list whose entries are the indices of the vertices v_j adjacent to v_i together with the weights $W(\{v_i, v_j\})$—or $W((v_i, v_j))$ in the case of a digraph—of the corresponding edges.

5.2 Graph traversals

When we were studying binary trees we introduced the notion of a *traversal* of a collection of objects. We recall the definition: we have a collection S of N objects and an operation called *process* which can be applied to the objects in S; then a **traversal** of S consists in applying *process* to each of the N objects in S exactly once. We described ways of carrying out traversals of a collection S when the objects of S are stored in a linked list or in a binary tree; now we examine how to make traversals of a collection of objects stored at the vertices of a graph or a digraph.

In the list and tree traversals which we described earlier we never visited a node more than once, so we never ran the risk of processing an object more than once (unless, of course, the same object was stored in more than one node, which ought not to happen). In a graph, however, the connections between the vertices may be much less regular than those between the nodes of a list or a binary tree, so we run the risk of returning to a vertex which we have already visited; if this happens we would clearly not wish to process again the element stored at that vertex, for that would contradict the 'exactly once' requirement in the definition of a traversal. To avoid the possibility of reprocessing an object we associate with each vertex of the graph a marker to indicate whether it has been visited. Thus if (V, E) is a graph or digraph, with vertex set $V = \{v_1, v_2, \ldots, v_N\}$ we might declare

Var *visited* : **array** $[1 .. N]$ **of boolean;**

and initialise this array by the loop

for $i :=$ 1 **to** N **do** *visited* $[i] :=$ **false;**

We describe two methods of traversal of a graph. The first, called **depth first traversal**, is an adaptation for general graphs of the preorder traversal of a binary tree. We begin by describing the depth first traversal **from a vertex** v—if v has already been visited no action is taken (the contents of v will already have been processed) but if v has not yet been visited we process its contents, mark it 'visited' and then (recursively) carry out depth first traversal from each of the vertices adjacent to v. The depth first traversal of the whole graph or digraph then consists in carrying out depth first traversal from all its vertices.

Suppose we have declared and initialised the array *visited* as above, and that we are using the adjacency list implementation, so that we have declared and initialised an array *adj_list* such that each entry *adj_list*$[i]$ points to the list of indices of the vertices v_j which are adjacent to v_i in the graph or digraph. Then the depth first traversal of the whole graph or digraph is carried out by

for $i := 1$ **to** N **do if not** *visited* $[i]$ **then** dft_from(i);

where we have declared

    Procedure deal_with $(i : 1 .. N)$;
    Begin ($\star$ apply *process* to object stored in v_i $\star$) **End**;

    Procedure dft_from $(i : 1 .. N)$;
    Var $k : 1 .. N$;
        $p : Pointer$;
    Begin
        visited $[i] :=$ **true**;
        deal_with (i);
        $p := adj\_list[i]$;
        while $p <>$ **nil do begin**
                    $k := p \uparrow . Vertex$;
                    if not *visited* $[k]$ **then** dft_from (k);
                    $p := p \uparrow . Next$ **end**
    End;

When executing our recursive procedure dft_from the computer will employ a stack, which we can think of as a stack of vertices waiting to be processed. When executing dft_from(i) we begin by pushing v_i onto an initially empty stack S; we then carry out the procedure informally described as follows:

Repeat
   pop(S,top):
   if not *visited*(top) **then begin**
        deal_with(top);
        visited$(top) :=$ **true**;
        push onto S all the unvisited vertices
               adjacent to the vertex just popped **end**
   until empty(S)

Consider for example the execution of dft_from (A) for the graph

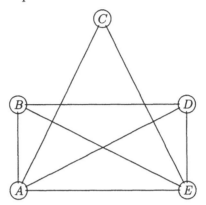

for which the adjacency lists are

$adj\_list[A] \longrightarrow \boxed{B}\!\!\longrightarrow\!\!\boxed{C}\!\!\longrightarrow\!\!\boxed{D}\!\!\longrightarrow\!\!\boxed{E}$

$adj\_list[B] \longrightarrow \boxed{A}\!\!\longrightarrow\!\!\boxed{D}\!\!\longrightarrow\!\!\boxed{E}$

$adj\_list[C] \longrightarrow \boxed{A}\!\!\longrightarrow\!\!\boxed{E}$

$adj\_list[D] \longrightarrow \boxed{A}\!\!\longrightarrow\!\!\boxed{B}\!\!\longrightarrow\!\!\boxed{E}$

$adj\_list[E] \longrightarrow \boxed{A}\!\!\longrightarrow\!\!\boxed{B}\!\!\longrightarrow\!\!\boxed{C}\!\!\longrightarrow\!\!\boxed{D}$

1. Initially we have *visited*$[X]$ = **false** for $X = A, \ldots, E$.
   The stack S is

   $S \longrightarrow \boxed{A}$

   pop(S,*top*) sets *top* to be A.
   Since *visited*$[A]$ = **false** we process the object stored at A, set
   visited$[A]$ to be **true** and push onto the stack the unvisited neighbours of A.

   The situation is now illustrated by the diagram

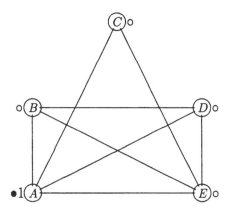

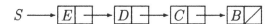

Here we use the symbol ∘ to indicate the vertices which have not yet been visited and the symbol •1 that A was dealt with at the first stage.

2. pop(S,*top*) sets *top* to be E.
   Since *visited*[E] = **false** we process the object stored at E, set *visited*[E] to be **true** and push onto the stack the unvisited neighbours of E. The situation is now

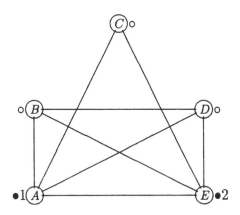

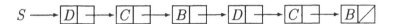

3. pop(S, *top*) sets *top* to be D.

   Since *visited*[D] = **false** we process the object stored at D, set *visited*[D] to be **true** and push onto the stack the unvisited neighbours of D.

   We have now reached the situation

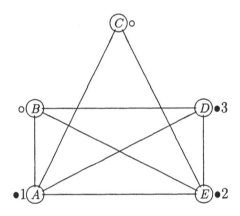

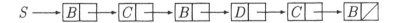

4. pop(S, *top*) sets *top* to B.

   Since *visited*[B] = **false** we process the object stored at B and set *visited*[B] to be **true**. Since B has no unvisited neighbours we leave the (popped) stack unaltered.

   We are now in the situation

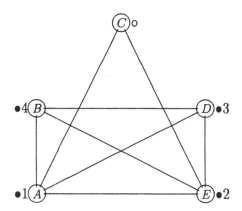

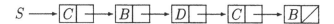

5. pop(S, *top*) sets *top* to C.

Since *visited*[C] = **false** we process the object stored at C, setting *visited*[C] to be **true**. Again the vertex just visited has no unvisited neighbours, so we leave the popped stack unaltered.

The situation is now

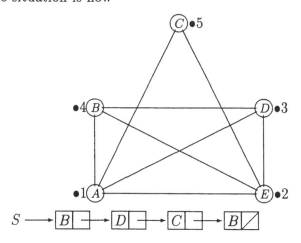

6. pop(S, *top*) sets *top* to B. Since *visited*[B] = **true** we take no action.

The stack is now

$$S \longrightarrow \boxed{D\ |\ } \longrightarrow \boxed{C\ |\ } \longrightarrow \boxed{B\ /}$$

pop(S, top) sets top to D. Since $visited[D]$ = **true** we take no action.

The stack is now

$$S \longrightarrow \boxed{C\ |\ } \longrightarrow \boxed{B\ /}$$

pop(S, top) sets top to C. Since $visited[C]$ = **true** we take no action.

Now the stack becomes

$$S \longrightarrow \boxed{B\ /}$$

pop(S, top) sets top to B. Since $visited[B]$ = **true** we take no action.

The stack S is now empty; so we have completed the execution of dft_from(A).

Thus the depth first traversal from A visits the vertices in the order

$$AEDBC.$$

To justify the statement we made earlier that depth first traversal of a graph is an adaptation of the preorder traversal of a binary tree, consider the graph

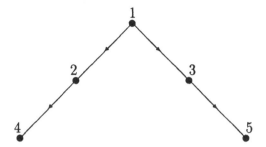

Suppose that on the adjacency list for each vertex its right child (if any) precedes , i.e. is nearer to the head of the list than its left child (if there is one). Then dft_from(1) proceeds as follows:

1. S consists of 1 alone; pop(S, *top*) sets *top* to 1. Since 1 is unvisited, process the contents of v_1; mark 1 'visited' and push the unvisited neighbours of 1—3 and then 2.

2. S now consists of 2 3 (we write our stacks with head to the left); pop(S, *top*) sets *top* to 2. Since 2 is unvisited, process the contents of v_2; mark 2 'visited' and push the unvisited neighbours of 2— there is only one, namely 4.

3. S now consists of 4 3; pop(S, *top*) sets *top* to 4. Since 4 is unvisited, process the contents of v_4; mark 4 'visited' and push the unvisited neighbours of 4—there are none.

4. S now consists of 3; pop(S, *top*) sets *top* to 3. Since 3 is unvisited, process the contents of v_3; mark 3 'visited' and push the unvisited neighbours of 3—there is only one, namely 5.

5. S now consists of 5; pop(S, *top*) sets *top* to 5. Since 5 is unvisited, process the contents of v_5; mark 5 'visited' and push the unvisited neighbours of 5—there are none.

The stack S is now empty, so dft_from(1) is complete. The order in which the vertices are visited is

$$1\ 2\ 4\ 3\ 5,$$

the same as in preorder traversal.

Perhaps the second example helps to explain the name *depth first*
traversal. In executing dft_from(i) we proceed from v_i to a neighbour,
then to a neighbour of that neighbour and so on, moving always further
away from v_i (distance being measured by the number of intermediate
edges) until there are no unvisited neighbours; only then do we retreat
towards v_i, and by the shortest distance possible, to the most recently
visited vertex which has unvisited neighbours.

In both the examples we have worked through we achieved a complete traversal of the graph by carrying out dft_from(1). But for the
digraph

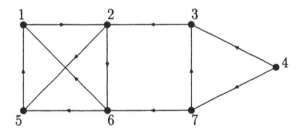

we see that

dft_from(1) visits only vertices 1, 2, 6 and 5;

dft_from(2) takes no action since 2 has been visited during the
execution of dft_from(1).

dft_from(3) visits only vertex 3.

dft_from(4) visits vertices 4 and 7 and the depth first traversal of
the graph is complete.

The second method of traversal of a graph which we describe is
known as **breadth first traversal**. As in the case of depth first traversal we begin by describing breadth first traversal **from a vertex** v—if
v has already been visited then no action is taken, but if v has not
yet been visited we process its contents, mark v 'visited' and visit all
its as yet unvisited neighbours, then all their unvisited neighbours and
proceed in this way. Thus breadth first traversal of a graph or digraph

is carried out by

for $i := 1$ **to** N **do if not** *visited* [i] **then** bft_from (i);

where we describe bft_from(i) informally as follows, using this time a queue Q of vertices waiting to be processed instead of the stack used in depth first traversal:

Begin enqueue(i,Q); *visited*[i] := **true**;
   while not empty(Q) **do**
                   begin serve(Q, *first*);
                        deal_with(*first*);
                        enqueue all the unvisited neighbours of *first*
                                 marking them 'visited' **end**
End;

Consider, for example, the breadth first traversal from A of the graph:

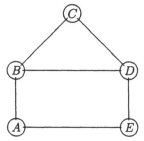

for which the adjacency lists are

$adj\_list[A] \longrightarrow \boxed{B} \!\!\!+\!\!\!\longrightarrow \boxed{E \diagup}$

$adj\_list[B] \longrightarrow \boxed{A} \!\!\!+\!\!\!\longrightarrow \boxed{C} \!\!\!+\!\!\!\longrightarrow \boxed{D \diagup}$

$adj\_list[C] \longrightarrow \boxed{B} \!\!\!+\!\!\!\longrightarrow \boxed{D \diagup}$

$adj\_list[D] \longrightarrow \boxed{B} \!\!\!+\!\!\!\longrightarrow \boxed{C} \!\!\!+\!\!\!\longrightarrow \boxed{E \diagup}$

$adj\_list[E] \longrightarrow \boxed{A} \!\!\!+\!\!\!\longrightarrow \boxed{D \diagup}$

1. Initially we have *visited*$[X]$ = **false** for $X = A, \ldots, E$.
   To start with the queue Q is illustrated by

   $$Q.Rear \quad \longrightarrow \boxed{A\diagup} \longleftarrow \quad Q.Front$$

   and we set *visited*$[A]$ to be **true**.
   Since Q is not empty we execute serve(Q, *first*), which sets *first*
   to A. We process the object stored at A. Then we enqueue the
   unvisited neighbours of A in the order in which they appear in
   the adjacency list of A (i.e. B, then E) and mark them 'visited'.

2. The situation is now

   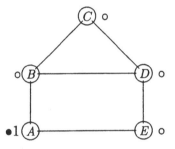

   (We use the symbol •1 to indicate that we have processed the
   object stored at A during stage 1 of the traversal; the symbol
   o marks vertices for which the stored objects have not yet been
   processed—even though they have been marked 'visited'.)

   $$Q.Rear \quad \longrightarrow \boxed{E\ \ } \longrightarrow \boxed{B\diagup} \longleftarrow \quad Q.Front$$

   Since Q is not empty we execute serve(Q, *first*) which sets *first* to
   B. We process the object stored at B and enqueue the unvisited
   neighbours C and D of B, marking them 'visited'.

3. Now we have

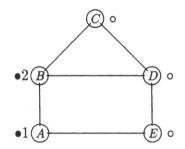

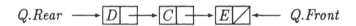

$Q.Rear \longrightarrow \boxed{D} \longrightarrow \boxed{C} \longrightarrow \boxed{E} \longleftarrow Q.Front$

Since Q is not empty we execute serve(Q, *first*), which sets *first* to
E. We process the object stored at E. Since E has no unvisited
neighbour the (served) queue is left unaltered.

4. Now we are in the situation

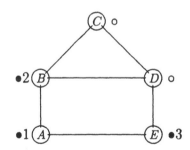

$Q.Rear \longrightarrow \boxed{D} \longrightarrow \boxed{C} \longleftarrow Q.Front$

Since Q is not empty we execute serve(Q, *first*), which sets *first* to
C. We process the object stored at C. Since C has no unvisited
neighbours no further vertices are added to the queue.

5. The situation is now illustrated by

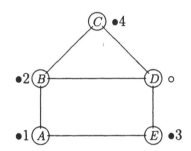

$$Q.Rear \longrightarrow \boxed{D\!\!\!\diagup} \longleftarrow Q.Front$$

Q is not empty. When we execute serve(Q, *first*) we set *first* to D. We process the object stored at D. Since D has no unvisited neighbours we add no vertices to the queue.

6. We have now reached the situation

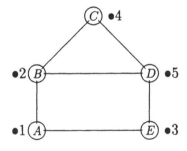

and

$$Q.Front = Q\,Rear = \textbf{nil}.$$

Since Q is now empty, execution terminates.

So breadth first traversal of the graph from A deals with the contents of the vertices in the order

$$ABECD$$

The name *breadth first traversal* possibly appears more natural if we apply it to the binary tree

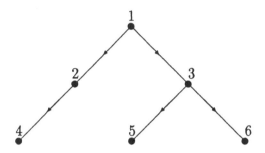

Let us agree that when we are enqueuing the children (which are the unvisited neighbours) of a node we shall enqueue the left child (if any) before the right child (if any). Then bft_from(1) proceeds as follows:

1. Mark 1 'visited'; Q consists of 1; serve Q and process the contents of v_1.
   Enqueue the unvisited neighbours of v_1 and mark them 'visited'.

2. Q consists of 3 2 (we write our queues with front to the right and rear to the left); serve Q and process the contents of v_2.
   Enqueue the unvisited neighbours of 2 and mark them 'visited'.

3. Q now consists of 5 4 3; serve Q and process the contents of v_3.
   Enqueue the unvisited neighbour of 3 and mark it 'visited'.

4. Q is now 6 5 4; serve Q and process the contents of v_4.
   4 has no unvisited neighbour.

5. Q is now 6 5; serve Q and process the contents of v_5.
   5 has no unvisited neighbour.

6. Q now consists of 6 alone; serve Q and process the contents of v_6. 6 has no unvisited neighbour.

The queue is now empty, so execution terminates.
    The vertices are visited in the order

$$1\ 2\ 3\ 4\ 5\ 6$$

so that we are visiting the vertices across the tree or 'breadthwise'.
    In both our examples we have obtained a complete traversal of the graph under consideration by carrying out bft_from(1). But, as in the case of depth first traversal, this is not always the case.

5.3   Exercises 5

1. Show how the graph

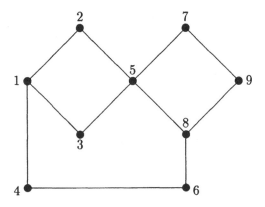

would be represented (a) by its adjacency matrix, (b) by means of adjacency lists.

How would these representations be changed if the graph were changed into a digraph by directing each edge from the endpoint with the smaller number to that with the larger number?

2. Carry out depth first and breadth first traversals for the graph in Exercise 1 and the digraph below, starting in each case at the vertex numbered 1:

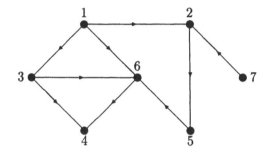

Part II

ALGORITHMS

Chapter 6

ALGORITHMS AND COMPLEXITY

6.1 Algorithms

In the ninth century of the Christian era, in a small town in Uzbekistan now called Khiva but then Khowarizm, there lived an Arab mathematician called Abu Ja'far Mohamed ben Musa, who was nicknamed al-Khowarizmi, the man from Khowarizm. He was the author of a book on arithmetic and algebra (*algebra* is actually derived from one of the Arabic words in his title) and it was through the translation of this book that the Arabic numerals and the decimal number system became known in Europe. The word *algorism*, derived from his nickname, was used to refer to the Arabic system and more generally to arithmetic. By what the Oxford English Dictionary calls 'learned confusion' with the Greek word *arithmos*, meaning 'number', it has been transformed into *algorithm*.

So much for its etymology: but what does it mean nowadays?

Before answering this question let us look at the kind of problems we are concerned with in computer science. Very roughly speaking these are problems in which we begin with some given information, data or input and try to produce from that input a result, an output which is related in some desired way to the input. We think, for example, of the following three problems:

1. Numerical multiplication. Here the input consists of two integers and the output is a single integer which is the product of the given integers.

2. Solution of simultaneous equations. In this case the input consists of six real numbers, $a_{11}, a_{12}, a_{21}, a_{22}, b_1, b_2$ subject to the condition that $a_{11}a_{22} - a_{12}a_{21} \neq 0$ and the desired output is a pair of real numbers x_1, x_2 such that

$$a_{11}x_1 + a_{12}x_2 = b_1$$
$$a_{21}x_1 + a_{22}x_2 = b_2$$

3. Sorting. Here the input might be an array of character strings and the desired output an array with entries the same as the given array but rearranged in dictionary order.

With these simple examples in mind we can agree that when we speak about solving a problem we mean finding a way to produce the desired output from the given input. We remark that, as in the examples, we are usually concerned not with single problems but with classes of problems; we are interested in finding solution methods which will work in a uniform way for all the problems of a given class—we don't want to have to develop a different solution method for each particular instance of a class of problems. Now there are many particular problems which can be solved by the use of intelligent guesswork or by the use of special properties of the input information. These special methods, these unexpected flashes of insight, are often very interesting; but, for all the fascination of clever ways to deal with special cases, it is important also to have general systematic methods of solution which will yield the desired output corresponding to *any* legitimate input. Such a general systematic method is what we mean by an *algorithm*.

As computer scientists we are inclined to think of formalising this idea of a general systematic method by that of a computer program; but attempts to give rigorous definitions of the notion of algorithm started in the 1930's before computers were invented.

Before we give a formal (or at least semiformal) definition of the term *algorithm* it is worth mentioning briefly some quite informal definitions which, with luck, will help to give us a rough notion of what is to be included in our formal definition. We begin by thinking of an algorithm as a concise description of a method for solving a problem— and we have at least at the back of our minds the idea that the method should be suitable for mechanical implementation. This leads us to describe an algorithm as a sequence of clearly described, well-understood steps taken to solve a problem; and we clearly have it in mind that the sequence is finite and that each step can be carried out with a finite amount of effort in a finite time. Since we are thinking of having the algorithm carried out in some sense mechanically, we would want to insist that none of the steps should include any subjective decision nor involve any use of intuition or creativity.

Putting these ideas together we arrive at the following semiformal definition: an **algorithm** is a finite sequence of instructions for solving a problem; the instructions must be carried out by a computing agent which reacts to them in a discrete stepwise fashion with no use of continuous methods or analogue devices; furthermore the execution of the instructions must proceed in a completely deterministic way, not subject to chance. We sometimes include in the definition the requirement that the computing agent should have facilities for making, storing and retrieving steps in the computation.

This definition has been described as semiformal: to make it completely formal we would have to give a formal definition of the computing agent—this can certainly be done, but to do so would lead us to a higher level of abstraction than is appropriate for an introductory book of this kind.

We cannot help noticing that, although the definition of algorithm which we have given essentially antedates the invention of modern electronic computers, we can probably most easily think of the definition when we relate it to computers. Thus the "finite sequence of instructions" corresponds roughly to a computer program; the "computing agent" to a computer; the "facilities for making, storing and retrieving steps in the computation" make us think of the memory of the computer; and the requirement that the computation should proceed in a discrete stepwise fashion is satisfied by a *digital* computer.

6.2   Complexity of algorithms

For a given problem or class of problems there may be many different algorithms which provide solutions; so the question arises: how are we to choose which of these algorithms to use? We may make our decision for human reasons—making our choice depend on how easy it is for a human user to understand the algorithm and/or how easy it is to implement the algorithm by a program; but we may also make our choice for machine reasons—on the basis of the efficiency of use of our computer resources (time and space, especially time). Neither viewpoint can be ignored, because the cost of using an algorithm to solve a problem can be split up as

$$\text{Cost} = (\text{Cost of understanding and programming})$$
$$+ (\text{Cost of running})$$
$$= \text{Software cost} + \text{Hardware cost}$$

Now the hardware cost is expressible as

Hardware cost =
    (Cost of running program once) $*$ (Number of executions)

If the algorithm is to be used once only or just a few times then the software costs predominate; so it is probably best in this case to use an easily understandable, easily programmable algorithm even if it is relatively expensive in its use of computer resources. But if the algorithm is to be used many times then it is probably worth the effort to understand and program a more complicated algorithm if it can be shown to use computer resources more efficiently.

So we are faced with the question: How do we compare the efficiency of two algorithms?

We might think of measuring the execution times of programs which implement the algorithms. But this is dependent on the particular machine we choose to run our programs on; and of course it requires us to implement both algorithms in order to compare the execution times. Again, we might compare the size of program required to implement the algorithms (the number of lines or the number of instructions, for example); but this measure depends on the skill of the programmer and on the particular language chosen for the program, and of course it again requires us to implement both algorithms. It would clearly be better to have some way of measuring the efficiency which depends on the algorithm itself, not on the machine, the programming language or the programmer.

No doubt if we had before us a completely formal, abstract definition of the computing device referred to in the definition of an algorithm we might measure the complexity of an algorithm by counting up the number of operations carried out by the abstract "machine". The difficulty here is that such an approach tends to be so abstract that it takes us very far from our intuitive understanding of how our algorithms work. (And again we would have to carry out the detailed formal analysis for each of the algorithms being compared.)

So in examining the efficiency or complexity of algorithms it is usual to concentrate our attention on what we think of as the "basic operations" involved in the kind of problem we happen to be considering. Different classes of problem will have different basic operations associated with them, for example

1. When we consider the problem of searching for a given object in a particular collection we might think of the basic operation as the comparison of the object we are searching for with an object in the collection.

2. When we are concerned with the problem of multiplying two matrices with numerical entries it is natural to think of the multiplication of two numbers as the fundamental operation.

3. When we deal with the problem of sorting a collection of records with keys from an ordered type then we might consider the comparison of two keys (to see which is the less) as the basic operation; we might also think of the exchange of two records as the basic operation.

If we have just a single problem for which there are several algorithms available we might count up for each algorithm the number of basic operations required to deal with the problem, and we would think of choosing the algorithm for which the number of fundamental operations is least.

But typically we are not concerned with single problems—we usually deal with classes of problems consisting of a large number of instances: these may not all be of the same size and we naturally expect that the amount of work (by which we mean the number of basic operations) required for an instance of large size will be greater than that for one of small size. We notice in passing that there is no reason to suppose that all problem instances of the same size will necessarily involve the same amount of work (think of the multiplication of single-digit numbers: it would probably require less work to multiply by 0 or 1 than by other multipliers).

We think of choosing a way to measure the size of a problem instance. For example, for a searching problem it would be natural to take the number of elements in the collection in which we are searching; for the problem of multiplying square matrices we would naturally take the size of the matrices; and for the problem of solving simultaneous equations we would take the number of equations in the system.

Now suppose that we have a class of problems for each of which the size can be given by an integer $n \geq 0$. We describe two ways of defining the notion of complexity of an algorithm designed to solve the class of problems.

(1) For each integer $n \geq 0$ we look at all instances of the problem which have size n. For each such instance I we work out the amount of work (the number of basic operations) required by the algorithm when applied to I: call this number $T(I)$. Then define

$W(n)$ = the maximum value of $T(I)$ for all instances I of size n.

Then the function W which assigns to each integer $n \geq 0$ the integer $W(n)$ is called the **worst case complexity** of the algorithm.

(2) Again for each integer $n \geq 0$ we look at all instances of the problem which have size n. Suppose that, from experience, or on the basis of some special information or by making some simplifying assumption we have been able to assign to each instance I of size n a measure $p(I)$ of the probability that the instance I will occur. Then we define

$A(n)$ = the sum of the numbers $p(I)T(I)$ for all instances I of size n.

Thus $A(n)$ is the expected number (in the sense of probability theory) of basic operations which will be carried out when the algorithm is applied to a problem instance of size n.

The function A which assigns to each integer $n \geq 0$ the number $A(n)$ is called the **average complexity** of the algorithm (corresponding to the probability assignments $p(I)$).

Suppose we have two algorithms P_1 and P_2 for the same problem class, with worst case complexities W_1 and W_2 given by $W_1(n) = 100n$ and $W_2(n) = 4n^2$ respectively.

For input sizes $n \leq 25$ we have $W_1(n) = 100n \geq 4n^2 = W_2(n)$; so for input sizes not exceeding 25 it is more economical to use algorithm P_2; but if $n > 25$ we have $W_2(n) > W_1(n)$ and so for input sizes greater than 25 it is more economical to use algorithm P_1. This simple example suggests that in comparing the complexity of different algorithms it is important to examine how they behave for large input sizes.

Now suppose we have a third algorithm P_3 for our problem class, with worst case complexity W_3 given by $W_3(n) = 10000n$. Clearly, if we implement them both on the same computer P_3 will always take longer on its worst case than P_1 does on its worst case (though the worst cases may be different) whatever the input size n, but if we implement P_3 on a computer which runs 1000 times faster than the one used for P_1 the time required for the worst case for P_3 will be less than that for the worst case for P_1. Notice also that if we run P_2 and P_3 on the same machine then P_2 will run faster than P_3 for all input sizes n less than 2500; but for input sizes greater than 2500 it is more economical of effort to use P_3.

These examples are intended to suggest that we ought not to distinguish between functions which are constant (positive) multiples of one another, but that we should distinguish between functions if one eventually outstrips the other.

We now introduce some technical notation and terminology which is useful when we talk about the rate of growth of real-valued functions.

We let f and g be two positive real-valued functions defined for all positive integers n. Then we say

1. g is $O(f)$ or $g(n)$ is $O(f(n))$ (read "g is big O of f") if $g(n)$ is eventually less than a constant multiple of $f(n)$, i.e. if there is a

positive real number K and an integer n_0 such that $g(n) \leq K f(n)$ for all integers $n \geq n_0$.

2. g is $\Omega(f)$ or $g(n)$ is $\Omega(f(n))$ (read "g is big omega of f") if $g(n)$ is eventually greater than a constant multiple of $f(n)$, i.e. if there is a positive real number K_1 and an integer n_1 such that $g(n) \geq K_1 f(n)$ for all integers $n \geq n_1$.

3. g is $\Theta(f)$ or $g(n)$ is $\Theta(f(n))$ (read "g is big theta of f") if $g(n)$ is eventually between two constant multiples of $f(n)$, i.e. if there are positive real numbers K and K_1 and an integer n_0 such that $K f(n) \leq g(n) \leq K_1 f(n)$ for all integers $n \geq n_0$.

If g is $O(f)$ but f is not $O(g)$ we say that $O(g)$ **is better than** $O(f)$. In this case an algorithm with worst case complexity g will eventually (that is for all sufficiently large input sizes) run faster than one with worst case complexity f. An algorithm is said to be **efficient** if its worst case complexity is $O(n^k)$ for some positive integer k.

For the sake of readers whose mathematical background includes the notion of *limit* of a sequence of real numbers we offer some useful methods of comparing the growth rates of two functions f and g.

1. If $\lim g(n)/f(n) = c$ where c is a non-negative real number (i.e. $c \geq 0$) then g is $O(f)$.

   We recall that when we say that $\lim g(n)/f(n) = c$ we mean that $g(n)/f(n)$ is eventually as close as we please to c. So we eventually have $g(n)/f(n)$ within 1 of c. That is to say there is an integer n_0 such that for all integers $n \geq n_0$ we have

   $$c - 1 < g(n)/f(n) < c + 1.$$

   So for all integers $n > n_0$ we have $g(n) < (c+1)f(n)$. Thus g is $O(f)$.

2. If $\lim g(n)/f(n) = c$ where c is a strictly positive real number (i.e. $c > 0$) or if $\lim g(n)/f(n) = \infty$ then g is $\Omega(f)$.

   Suppose first that $\lim g(n)/f(n) = c$ where c is a strictly positive real number. Then we eventually have $g(n)/f(n)$ within $\frac{1}{2}c$ of c.

That means there is an integer n_1 such that for all integers $n \geq n_1$ we have

$$\tfrac{1}{2}c < g(n)/f(n) < \tfrac{3}{2}c.$$

So for all integers n greater than n_1 we have $g(n) > \tfrac{1}{2}cf(n)$. Thus g is $\Omega(f)$.

Now suppose that $\lim g(n)/f(n) = \infty$. This means that $g(n)/f(n)$ is eventually as large as we please, say greater than 1; so there is an integer n_1 such that for all integers $n \geq n_1$ we have $g(n)/f(n) > 1$ and so $g(n) > f(n)$. So in this situation also we have that g is $\Omega(f)$.

3. If $\lim g(n)/f(n) = c$ where c is a positive real number (i.e. $0 < c < \infty$) then g is $\Theta(f)$.

By 2. above we see that g is $\Omega(f)$; so there is a positive real number K_1 and an integer n_1 such that $g(n) \geq K_1 f(n)$ for all integers n greater than n_1. Similarly, by 1. above, g is $O(f)$; so there is a positive real number K_2 and an integer n_2 such that $g(n) \leq K_2 f(n)$ for all integers n greater than n_2. Hence for all integers n greater than the larger of n_1 and n_2 we have

$$K_1 f(n) \leq g(n) \leq K_2 f(n).$$

So g is $\Theta(f)$.

Notice that if $\lim g(n)/f(n) = c$, where c is a positive real number, we have $\lim f(n)/g(n) = 1/c$, which is also a positive real number; so in this case we have both that g is $O(f)$ and that f is $O(g)$. But if $\lim g(n)/f(n) = 0$, although we have that g is $O(f)$, f is not $O(g)$; so in this case g is better than f.

(To see this, suppose that f *were* $O(g)$, so that $f(n)$ is eventually less than some positive constant multiple of $g(n)$, say

$$f(n) \leq Kg(n) \text{ for all integers } n \text{ greater than some integer } n_0$$

where K is a positive real number. It follows that for all integers n greater than n_0 we have $g(n)/f(n) \geq 1/K$; so we cannot have $g(n)/f(n)$ eventually closer to 0 than $1/K$ and so we cannot have $\lim g(n)/f(n) = 0$.)

Readers who have been introduced to elementary mathematical analysis may remember meeting the following results:

$$\lim(\log_2 n/n) = 0, \qquad \lim(n/n \log_2 n) = 0, \qquad \lim(n \log_2 n/n^2) = 0,$$

$$\lim(n^p/n^q) = 0 \text{ if } p < q, \qquad \lim(n^p/2^n) = 0 \text{ for all positive indices } p.$$

It is not important for non-mathematical readers to look at the details of the proofs of these results; but even for them it *is* important in studying the relative efficiency of algorithms to remember the following consequences:

1. $O(\log_2 n)$ is better than $O(n)$;

2. $O(n)$ is better than $O(n \log_2 n)$;

3. $O(n \log_2 n)$ is better than $O(n^2)$;

4. $O(n^p)$ is better than $O(n^q)$ if $p < q$;

5. $O(n^p)$ is better than $O(2^n)$ for all positive indices p.

Suppose we have an algorithm with worst case complexity $W(n)$; suppose that the time taken for a given machine to carry out one of the basic operations of the algorithm is τ. Then for a given time T the maximum size of input which we can be sure of being able to handle in time T is obtained by solving the equation $W(n)\tau = T$.

For example, if $\tau = 1$ ms, $W(n) = n^2$ and $T = 1$ hour we solve

$$n^2 \times 10^{-3} = 60 \times 60 \text{ (number of seconds in one hour)}$$

whence $n^2 = 6 \times 10^5$, so that $n = 600\sqrt{10} \approx 1897$.

Suppose we run the same algorithm on a machine which works at k times the speed of the first, so that the time taken to carry out a basic operation is τ/k. If the maximum sizes of input which we can be sure of handling in time T on the two machines are n_1 and n_2 then we have

$$W(n_1)\tau = T = W(n_2)\tau/k$$

so that n_1 and n_2 are related according to the equation

$$W(n_2) = kW(n_1).$$

For example, if $W(n) = 2^n$ we have $2^{n_2} = k\,2^{n_1}$, from which we deduce that $n_2 = n_1 + \log_2 k$.

When we develop an algorithm for the solution of a problem or class of problems it is interesting and important to analyse its complexity, worst case or average or both; we are particularly concerned to produce efficient algorithms, in the technical sense that their worst case complexity is $O(n^k)$ for some positive integer k, preferably quite small—only for such algorithms is the execution practically feasible when the problem size n is large.

But complexity is not the only factor to be considered. As we mentioned earlier, if a problem is to be solved only once, or a very small number of times, the cost of programming an algorithm is a significant part of the total cost; so it may be more economical to choose the algorithm which is easiest to implement rather than the one with slowest growth rate. Again, as we saw earlier in the chapter, if a problem is to be solved only for small input sizes, the algorithm which eventually (i.e. for sufficiently large input sizes) runs fastest may not necessarily be the best to choose. We have to recall also that algorithms whose complexity functions are of the same order do not all run at the same speed. There is also the sad and often-forgotten fact that complicated programs, however efficient, may not be easy to maintain, especially if the programmer is not the original author.

6.3 Exercises 6

1. Let p and q be real numbers such that $0 < p < q$. Prove that n^p is $O(n^q)$ but that n^q is not $O(n^p)$.

2. Consider the function f given by

$$f(n) = 4n^3 - 3n^2 + 2n - 1 \text{ for all positive integers } n.$$

For what positive integers k can we say that (1) f is $O(n^k)$; (2) f is $\Omega(n^k)$; (3) f is $\Theta(n^k)$?

3. Let f and g be positive real-valued functions defined for all positive integers n. Prove that (1) if f is $O(g)$ then g is $\Omega(f)$; (2) if f is $\Theta(g)$ then g is $\Theta(f)$.

4. Find the worst case complexity of the following program designed to multiply two $n \times n$ matrices A and B:

```
for i := 1 to n do
        for j := 1 to n do
            begin
                C[i, j] := 0;
                for k := 1 to n do
                    C[i, j] := C[i, j] + A[i, k] * B[k, j]
            end;
```

5. Find the worst case complexity of the following recursive algorithm for computing the value of a certain function F:

```
Function F (n : integer) : integer;
Begin
        If n = 1 then F := 1
                    else F := F(n − 1) + F(n − 1)
End;
```

How would your result be altered if we were to replace the **else** clause by

$$\textbf{else } F := 2 * F(n - 1) \ ?$$

6. Suppose we have a programming language in which **go to** commands are allowed. Consider a program which has a loop containing such a command (subject to some **boolean** condition C) to a point after the loop, as follows:

for $i := 1$ **to** n **do begin**

......

If C **then go to** L

......

end;

L : instruction;

How would you suggest estimating the complexity of this program?

7. Consider the program fragment

$$\textbf{if } C \textbf{ then } S_1 \textbf{ else } S_2$$

where C is a **boolean** condition and S_1 and S_2 are sequences of instructions. How would you estimate the complexity of this fragment?

Chapter 7

SORTING ALGORITHMS

Suppose we have a collection E of data items each of which consists of a number of pieces of information; suppose too that each of these items has a key belonging to an ordered set K. (We recall that an ordered set K is equipped with a relation which we denote by $<$ and call "is less than" or "precedes"; furthermore, if k_1 and k_2 are distinct members of K then we have either $k_1 < k_2$ or $k_2 < k_1$.) The key of a data item—think of a student's ID number—is not usually very interesting; its main use is to provide a means of access to the information components of the item.

It is the common experience of everyone that it is much easier to search for a number in a list arranged in increasing order or a word in a list arranged in dictionary order than to search in completely random lists. (We shall prove in Chapter 10 that if we have an ordered collection of N objects of an ordered set we can locate one of these objects in $O(\log N)$ time, while for an unordered collection we may require $O(N)$ time.) This familiar observation suggests that if we are to be searching for data items in our collection E by means of their keys it would be well worth while arranging the items in non-decreasing order of key—this is what we mean by **sorting** E according to key.

127

To fix our ideas let us suppose we have made the Pascal declarations

Type $K = (\star$ some ordered type $\star)$;
          $T = $ **Record**
                    Key : K;
                    ... ($\star$ other fields holding information $\star$)
              end;

and let E be a collection of items of type T.

The collection E may be small enough to fit into the internal memory of the computer we are using. In this case we would think of storing the elements of E in an array. If E is too large to be held all at once in the internal memory we would store E in a file held on an external storage device, probably on disk though possibly on magnetic tape. Algorithms for sorting collections stored in arrays are called **internal** sorting algorithms; those for sorting collections stored in files are called **external** sorting algorithms.

When we come to analyse the complexity of sorting algorithms it is clear that we should take as measure of the size of a problem instance simply the number of elements in the collection E. For the 'basic operations' which we are to count up to measure the complexity we have two choices: we may count either the number of comparisons of keys required by our algorithm or else the number of times we exchange two records in our collection.

We look for a moment at sorting methods which use only key comparisons. Such an algorithm can be represented by a binary tree, which we call a decision tree, in the following way: each non-leaf node of the tree corresponds to a comparison of two keys k_1 and k_2; we make the convention that if $k_1 \leq k_2$ we pass to the left child of the node while if $k_1 > k_2$ we pass to the right child. For example one method of sorting three keys a, b, c is represented by the tree

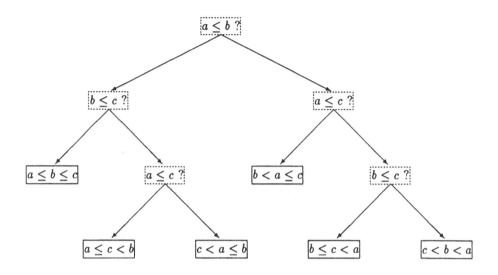

The worst case complexity of a sorting algorithm involving comparisons only which can be represented by a decision tree in this way is the maximum number of comparisons required to reach the sorted arrangement: this is clearly the height of the decision tree. If the collection E which is being sorted consists of N elements there are $N!$ possible outcomes, which will appear as leaves of the tree. We recall from Section 3.1 that a binary tree of height h has at most 2^h leaves. Hence, if h is the height of the decision tree, we have $2^h \geq N!$ and so the worst case complexity $W(N) = h \geq \log_2(N!)$.

Let n be any positive integer. If n is even, say $n = 2k$ where k is an integer, we have

$$n! \geq (2k)(2k-1)\ldots(k+1)k > k^{k+1} \geq k^k = (\tfrac{1}{2}n)^{\frac{1}{2}n}$$

while if n is odd, say $n = 2k+1$, we have

$$n! \geq (2k+1)(2k)(2k-1)\ldots(k+1) > (k+\tfrac{1}{2})^{k+1} > (k+\tfrac{1}{2})^{k+\frac{1}{2}} = (\tfrac{1}{2}n)^{\frac{1}{2}n}.$$

So for every positive integer n we have $n! > (\tfrac{1}{2}n)^{\frac{1}{2}n}$ and consequently $\log_2(n!) > \tfrac{1}{2}n\log_2(\tfrac{1}{2}n)$. If $n \geq 4$ we have $\tfrac{1}{2}\log_2 n \geq 1$, and so

$$\log_2(\tfrac{1}{2}n) = \log_2 n - 1 \geq \tfrac{1}{2}\log_2 n.$$

It follows that for $N \geq 4$ we have

$$W(N) \geq \log_2(N\,!) \geq \tfrac{1}{4}N\log_2 N$$

So the worst case complexity is $\Omega(N \log_2 N)$.

7.1   Internal sorting by comparisons

Throughout this section suppose we have declared

> **Const** $N = \ldots$ ($\star$ the size of the array to be sorted $\star$);
> **Type** $K = \ldots$ ($\star$ the ordered key type $\star$);
> $\quad$ $Index = 1 .. N$;
> $\quad$ $T =$ **Record**
> $\quad\quad\quad$ $Key : K$;
> $\quad\quad\quad$ $\ldots$ ($\star$ other information fields $\star$)
> $\quad\quad$ **end**;
> **Var** A : **array** $[Index]$ **of** T;
> **Procedure** swap (**Var** $x, y : T$);
> $\quad$ **Var** $temp : T$;
> $\quad$ **Begin** $temp := x$; $x := y$; $y := temp$ **End**;

We begin by describing three elementary methods of sorting the entries in an array. These methods are easy to understand and easy to program, but they are not very efficient, having worst case complexity $O(N^2)$.

(1) **Bubblesort.** Bubblesort of an array with N elements proceeds in $N - 1$ stages, which we call 'passes' through the array.

After the first pass the entry with the smallest key lands in the first place in the array; after the second pass the entries with the smallest and second smallest key fields are in the first and second places respectively; in general, after the k-th pass (for $k = 1, 2, \ldots, N-1$) the entries with the smallest, second smallest, $\ldots$, k-th smallest key fields are in the first, second, ... , k-th places respectively. Thus finally, after the $(N-1)$-th pass, the array is sorted.

To see how this works it is convenient to number the passes from 2 to N. Then, on the i-th pass, we start with $A[N]$ and compare it with $A[N-1]$; if they are in the wrong order, that is if we have $A[N].Key < A[N-1].Key$, we exchange them; we then compare the (possibly altered) $A[N-1]$ with $A[N-2]$, exchanging them if they are in the wrong order of key; and proceed in this way as far as the comparison of $A[i]$ and $A[i-1]$.

The whole process can be summed up in the program fragment

```
for i := 2 to N do
    begin
        for j := N downto i do
            if A[j].Key < A[j − 1].Key then swap(A[j − 1], A[j])
    end;
```

We illustrate the operation of Bubblesort by applying it to the array A of integers

$$\boxed{4 \mid 1 \mid 3 \mid 2}$$

Here $N = 4$. So the outer **for** loop runs from $i = 2$ to $i = N = 4$. When $i = 2$ the inner **for** loop runs from $j = 4$ down to $j = 2$ as follows.

$j = 4$: Consider

$$\boxed{4 \mid 1 \mid 3 \mid 2}$$

Compare $A[4] = 2$ and $A[3] = 3$; since $3 > 2$ we swap $A[3]$ and $A[4]$, obtaining

$$\boxed{4 \mid 1 \mid 2 \mid 3}$$

$j = 3$: Consider

$$\boxed{4}\ \boxed{1}\ \boxed{2}\ \boxed{3}$$

Compare the new $A[3] = 2$ and $A[2] = 1$; since $1 < 2$ we do nothing.

$j = 2$: Consider

$$\boxed{4}\ \boxed{1}\ \boxed{2}\ \boxed{3}$$

Compare $A[2] = 1$ and $A[1] = 4$; since $4 > 1$ we swap $A[1]$ and $A[2]$.

Thus at the end of the $i = 2$ stage A is

$$\boxed{1}\ \boxed{4}\ \boxed{2}\ \boxed{3}$$

Now when $i = 3$ the inner **for** loop runs from $j = 4$ down to $j = 3$ as follows.

$j = 4$: Consider

$$\boxed{1}\ \boxed{4}\ \boxed{2}\ \boxed{3}$$

Compare $A[4] = 3$ and $A[3] = 2$; since $2 < 3$ we do nothing.

$j = 3$: Consider

$$\boxed{1}\ \boxed{4}\ \boxed{2}\ \boxed{3}$$

Compare $A[3] = 2$ and $A[2] = 4$; since $4 > 2$ we swap $A[2]$ and $A[3]$.

So at the end of the $i = 3$ stage A is

$$\boxed{1\;|\;2\;|\;4\;|\;3}$$

When $i = 4$ the inner **for** loop is executed only for $j = 4$, where we consider

$$\boxed{1\;|\;2\;|\;4\;|\;3}$$

We compare $A[4] = 3$ and $A[3] = 4$; since $4 > 3$ we swap $A[3]$ and $A[4]$.

The final version of A is then

$$\boxed{1\;|\;2\;|\;3\;|\;4}$$

On the i-th pass of Bubblesort we make $N - i + 1$ comparisons. So the total number of comparisons is

$$(N - 1) + (N - 2) + \ldots + 3 + 2 + 1 = \tfrac{1}{2} N (N - 1).$$

Hence, counting comparisons, the worst case complexity of Bubblesort is $O(N^2)$.

(2) **Insertion Sort.** Insertion Sort proceeds by looking at the second, third, $\ldots$, N-th entries of the array A in turn and inserting each of them in its proper place among the (already sorted) preceding entries. To find the proper place for the entry in the i-th position we compare it with the $(i - 1)$-th, $(i - 2)$-th, $\ldots$ entries in turn until either we reach an entry with smaller key or else reach the left hand end of the array.

There is a temptation to describe Insertion Sort by means of the Pascal program fragment

```
for i := 2 to N do begin
              x := A[i]; j := i - 1;
                  while (j > 0) and (A[j].Key > x.Key)
                      do begin
                          swap(x, A[j]); j := j - 1 end end;
```

Unfortunately this will not work satisfactorily: before entering the
while loop Pascal will check both conditions ($j > 0$ and $A[j].Key >$
$x.Key$); if the previous execution of the loop has set $j = 0$, in which
case the loop should not be re-entered, Pascal tests whether $j > 0$ (and
finds this condition **false**) but then goes on to test if $A[0].Key < x.Key$
and this produces an error message since 0 does not belong to the index
set *Index* of the array A. To get round this difficulty we redeclare

Var A : **array** $[0 .. N]$ **of** T;

and store the elements to be sorted in the entries $A[1], \ldots, A[N]$. Then
we proceed according to the program fragment

```
for i := 2 to N do begin
        x := A[i]; A[0] := x; j := i - 1;
        while (A[j].Key > x.Key)
            do begin
                    A[j + 1] := A[j];
                    A[j] := x;
                    j := j - 1 end end;
```

To illustrate the operation of Insertion Sort we consider again the
array A of integers

4	1	3	2

and extend it by introducing a 0-th entry.

Again $N = 4$ and Insertion Sort consists of a **for** loop running from
$i = 2$ to $i = N = 4$

When $i = 2$ we begin by setting $A[0] = x = A[2] = 1$ and $j = 1$. We
compare $A[j] = A[1] = 4$ with $x = 1$:

1	4	1	3	2

Since $4 > 1$ we have satisfied the condition for entry to the body of the **while** loop, so we set $A[2] = 4$, $A[1] = x = 1$ (interchanging $A[1]$ and $A[2]$), obtaining

$$\boxed{1}\ \fbox{1}\ \fbox{4}\ \fbox{3}\ \fbox{2}$$

Now j becomes 0 and we compare $A[j] = A[0] = 1$ with $x = 1$:

$$\boxed{1}\ \fbox{1}\ \fbox{4}\ \fbox{3}\ \fbox{2}$$

The loop condition $A[j] > x$, i.e. $1 > 1$ is false; so we exit from the **while** loop. Thus at the end of the $i = 2$ stage the original array is transformed to

$$\fbox{1}\ \fbox{4}\ \fbox{3}\ \fbox{2}$$

(with the first 2 entries in order).

When $i = 3$ we set $A[0] = x = A[3] = 3$ and $j = 2$. We compare $A[j] = A[2] = 4$ with $x = 3$:

$$\boxed{3}\ \fbox{1}\ \fbox{4}\ \fbox{3}\ \fbox{2}$$

Since $4 > 3$ we enter the body of the **while** loop; so we interchange $A[2]$ and $A[3]$, obtaining

$$\boxed{3}\ \fbox{1}\ \fbox{3}\ \fbox{4}\ \fbox{2}$$

We set $j = 1$ and compare $A[j] = A[1] = 1$ with $x = 3$:

$$\boxed{3}\ \fbox{1}\ \fbox{3}\ \fbox{4}\ \fbox{2}$$

The loop condition $A[j] > x$, i.e. $1 > 3$ is false, so we exit from the

while loop and see that at the end of the $i = 3$ stage the original array is

$$\boxed{1}\ \boxed{3}\ \boxed{4}\ \boxed{2}$$

(with the first 3 entries in order).

When $i = 4$ we set $A[0] = x = A[4] = 2$ and $j = 3$; we compare $A[j] = A[3] = 4$ with $x = 2$:

$$\boxed{2}\ \boxed{1}\ \boxed{3}\ \boxed{4}\ \boxed{2}$$

Since $4 > 2$ we enter the body of the **while** loop; so we interchange $A[3] = 4$ and $A[4]$, obtaining

$$\boxed{2}\ \boxed{1}\ \boxed{3}\ \boxed{2}\ \boxed{4}$$

and set $j = 2$. Next we compare $A[j] = A[2] = 3$ with $x = 2$:

$$\boxed{2}\ \boxed{1}\ \boxed{3}\ \boxed{2}\ \boxed{4}$$

Since $3 > 2$ we re-enter the body of the **while** loop; thus we interchange $A[2]$ and $A[3]$, obtaining

$$\boxed{2}\ \boxed{1}\ \boxed{2}\ \boxed{3}\ \boxed{4}$$

and set $j = 1$. Then we compare $A[j] = A[1] = 1$ with $x = 2$:

$$\boxed{2}\ \boxed{1}\ \boxed{2}\ \boxed{3}\ \boxed{4}$$

This time $A[j] > x$, i.e. $1 > 2$, is false, so we exit from the **while** loop. So at the end of the $i = 4$ stage the original array is

$$\boxed{1}\ \boxed{2}\ \boxed{3}\ \boxed{4}$$

We remark now that the program fragment we wrote to implement Insertion Sort and worked through in the example reflects faithfully our naïve idea of the working of the algorithm. But it is in fact rather inefficient: each execution of the body of the **while** loop involves three assignments $(A[j + 1] := A[j]; A[j] := x; j := j - 1)$; but we do not really need to overwrite successive array entries with x until we exit from the **while** loop, and the following fragment, with only two assignments in the body of the **while** loop and one on exit, will implement Insertion Sort more efficiently:

> **for** $i := 2$ **to** N **do begin**
> $\qquad x := A[i]; A[0] := x; j := i - 1;$
> $\qquad$ **while** $(A[j].Key > x.Key)$
> $\qquad\qquad$ **do begin**
> $\qquad\qquad\qquad A[j + 1] := A[j]; j := j - 1$ **end**;
> $\qquad A[j + 1] := x$ **end**;

On the i-th execution of the **for** loop of Insertion Sort the maximum number of comparisons we have to make in order to find the proper place for the i-th entry is $i - 1$ (this occurs in the case where the i-th entry is less than all the preceding $i - 1$ entries). So we see that in the worst possible case the total number of comparisons is

$$(N - 1) + (N - 2) + \ldots + 3 + 2 + 1 = \tfrac{1}{2} N(N - 1)$$

So, counting by comparisons, the worst case complexity of Insertion Sort is $O(N^2)$.

(3) **Selection Sort.** Selection Sort proceeds in $N - 1$ stages. At the i-th stage $(i = 1, \ldots, N - 1)$ we find the entry with least key among the i-th, $(i + 1)$-th, $\ldots$, N-th entries of the array and put it in the i-th place.

The trick to find the entry with minimum key among $A[i], \ldots, A[N]$ is to introduce auxiliary variables k of type *Index* and x of type T, initialising k to i and x to $A[i]$. Then we execute the loop

> **for** $j := i + 1$ **to** N **do**
>   **if** $A[j].Key < x.Key$ **then begin** $k := j; x := A[j]$ **end**;

The entry with minimum key is the final value of x; its position in the array is given by the final value of k. We then exchange $A[i]$ and $A[k]$.

We illustrate the operation of Selection Sort on the integer array A

4	1	3	2

At the $i = 1$ stage the minimum entry among $A[i](= A[1]), \ldots, A[4]$ is 1, in position 2; so we exchange $A[2]$ and $A[1]$, changing A to

1	4	3	2

When $i = 2$ the minimum entry among $A[i](= A[2]), \ldots, A[4]$ is 2, in position 4; so we exchange $A[4]$ and $A[2]$, changing A to

1	2	3	4

Finally, when $i = 3$ the minimum entry among $A[i](= A[3]). \ldots, A[4]$ is 3, in position 3; no exchange is necessary and A is now

1	2	3	4

It is clear that there are $N - i$ comparisons involved in finding the entry with least key among $A[i], \ldots, A[N]$. So once again the total number of comparisons is

$$(N - 1) + (N - 2) + \ldots + 3 + 2 + 1 = \tfrac{1}{2} N (N - 1)$$

and the worst case complexity is $O(N^2)$.

Many experiments have been carried out to compare the efficiency of sorting methods. Table 1 shows the results of applying the three methods we have described to arrays of integers of length 128, 256, 512, 1024 and 2048 with "random" entries and also to two arrays of length 1024 whose entries are in sorted order and the reverse of sorted order, denoted in the table by O1024 and R1024 respectively.

	128	256	512	1024	O1024	R1024	2048
Bubblesort	54	221	881	3621	1285	5627	14497
Insertion Sort	15	69	276	1137	6	2200	4536
Selection Sort	12	45	164	634	643	833	2497

Table 1

It is not hard to explain why Selection Sort tends to run faster than Bubblesort and Insertion Sort—we remark that, although it always carries out $\frac{1}{2}N(N-1)$ comparisons whatever array it is applied to, Selection Sort involves at most $N-1$ exchanges of array elements, and exchanges (which are carried out by means of three assignments) take more time than comparisons. We also see easily why Insertion Sort does so well on an array which is already sorted—for such an array it makes only $N-1$ comparisons and no exchanges are required.

The moral to be drawn from all the experimental evidence is that although Bubblesort, Insertion Sort and Selection Sort all have worst case complexity $O(N^2)$ we should use Selection Sort in preference to Insertion Sort unless the data is very nearly sorted, and that *Bubblesort should never be used.*

We turn now to three internal sorting methods which, at least on average, perform better than the $O(N^2)$ methods we have just described.

(4) **Quicksort** is an example of what is known as a **divide-and-conquer** algorithm. The underlying philosophy of such an algorithm is easy to describe: to solve a large problem we split it into smaller subproblems, solve these (perhaps by means of further subdivisions, perhaps by some other method) and then obtain the solution to the original large problem by an appropriate combination of the solutions to the subproblems. It will not have escaped the eagle-eyed reader that

if we solve the subproblems by a further subdivision we are in effect using a technique which is very familiar, namely recursion.

Quicksort is indeed a recursive algorithm. Like every recursive algorithm it requires a basis, and this is provided by the observation that an array with just one component is certainly sorted. An application of Quicksort to an array with more than a single element consists of two stages. First we choose an object of the key type K, usually but not necessarily the key of one of the records stored in the array: we call this object the **pivot**. Once the pivot is chosen the array is partitioned into two subarrays in such a way that all the entries with key less than the pivot appear in the left hand subarray while those with key greater than or equal to the pivot appear in the right hand subarray.

Let us suppose, without giving details for the moment, that we have defined (1) a function

Function find_pivot $(i, j : Index) : K;$

such that find_pivot(i, j) is the object of key type to be used in partitioning the subarray indexed by $i .. j$ and (2) a procedure

Procedure partition $(i, j : Index;\ p : K;\ \textbf{Var}\ k : Index);$

such that the execution of partition(i, j, p, k) uses the pivot p to effect the required partition of the subarray indexed by $i..j$ and returns in the parameter k the left hand index of the right subarray of the partition. Then we define the recursive procedure quick as follows:

```
Procedure quick (i, j : Index);
Var p : K; k : Index;
Begin
      if i < j then begin
                  p := find_pivot(i, j);
                  partition(i, j, p, k);
                  quick(i, k − 1);
                  quick(k, j) end End;
```

We begin with the conditional clause "**if** $i < j$" because we ought never to have $j < i$ (perhaps we should output an appropriate error message if we do) and chiefly because if $j = i$ the subarray indexed by $i .. j$ has only one entry and so is sorted—thus no further action is required.

To sort the complete array A indexed by $1 .. N$ we make the procedure call quick$(1, N)$.

We turn now to the details of the function find_pivot and the procedure partition. Various suggestions have been made about how to choose a pivot to use for the partition of the subarray indexed by $i .. j$:

(1) Use a random number generator to produce an index k in the range $i .. j$ and then define find_pivot(i, j) to be the key of $A[k]$;

(2) Define find_pivot(i, j) to be the key of the "middle" element of the subarray, i.e. of $A[(i + j)$ **div** $2]$;

(3) Take a small sample of entries from the subarray and then define find_pivot(i, j) to be the median of the keys of the sample.

It is strongly advised on the basis of experience that we should not use the key of the first entry in the subarray, $A[i]$, as pivot.

Notice that if we follow any of the suggestions described above it may turn out that the pivot is the least key of all the entries in the array: *this is disastrous*, for with this choice of pivot the recursive procedure quick will never terminate—the left hand subarray produced by the partition procedure (which consists of entries with key less than the pivot) will be empty, while the right hand subarray will just be the original array. To ensure that we do not fall into this situation it is recommended that we examine the keys of $A[i]$, $A[i + 1]$, ..., $A[j]$ until we find two which are different and then choose the larger of these keys as our pivot; if all the entries in the subarray have the same key then we won't find a pivot by this method, but we don't need one, since in this case the entries are already ordered. To take account of this possibility it is convenient to introduce a new type

Type $Ext\_index = 0 .. N$;

and to define a function

Function pivot_index $(i, j : Index) : Ext\_index;$

which will return the index of the element whose key is to be used as pivot for partitioning the subarray indexed by $i..j$ unless all the entries have the same key, in which case it returns 0. This is done as follows:

```
Function pivot_index (i, j : Index) : Ext_index;
Var p, q : Integer;
    found : boolean;
Begin found := false;
      p := i − 1; q := i;
      Repeat
          p := p + 1; q := q + 1;
          if A[p].Key <> A[q].Key then found := true;
          if A[p].Key < A[q].Key then pivot_index := q
                 else pivot_index := p
      until (p = j − 1) or found;
      if not found then pivot_index := 0
End;
```

We then replace the procedure quick described above by

```
Procedure quick1 (i, j : Index);
Var p : K;
    k : Index;
    n : Ext_index;
Begin n := pivot_index(i, j);
      if (n <> 0) and (j > i) then begin
                                   p := A[n].Key;
                                   partition(i, j, p, k);
                                   quick1(i, k − 1);
                                   quick1(k, j) end End;
```

We describe next how to carry out the partitioning phase of Quicksort. We think of working with two pointers, *left* and *right* (not Pascal pointers, but our left and right forefingers); initially *left* points to $A[i]$

and *right* to $A[j]$. The pointer *left* moves gradually right, stopping when it reaches an array entry with key greater than or equal to the pivot; the pointer *right* moves gradually left, stopping when it reaches an entry with key less than the pivot; if both pointers come to a stop before crossing then the corresponding array entries are interchanged. We now repeat the performance until *left* and *right* do cross over. The final position of *left* is the left hand index of the right hand subarray of the partition. The Pascal version is as follows:

```
Procedure partition (i, j : Index; p : K; Var k : Index);
Var left, right : Index;
Begin left := i; right := j;
      Repeat
         while A[left].Key < p do left := left + 1;
         while A[right].Key ≥ p do right := right − 1;
         if left < right then swap(A[left], A[right])
      until left > right;
      k := left
End;
```

We illustrate the operation of Quicksort by looking at the problem of sorting into dictionary order the array of three-letter words

beg car sup and the bee sum pie

(where the words themselves are the keys).

Let us decide that for each subarray we shall choose as pivot the larger of the first two distinct keys. So we begin by choosing *car* as pivot and proceed to partition as follows, using < to mean "comes earlier in the dictionary than" with an obvious similar interpretation for ≥.

We have *beg < car*, so we move the *left* pointer to the right; then *car ≥ car*, so we stop. Starting at the right hand end we have *pie ≥ car*, so we move the *right* pointer to the left; next *sum ≥ car*, so we move *right* left again; then *bee < car*, so we stop in the situation

beg **car** *sup and the* **bee** *sum pie*

and interchange *car* and *bee*, obtaining

$$beg \textbf{ bee } sup \; and \; the \textbf{ car } sum \; pie$$

with the *left* and *right* pointers pointing to *bee* and *car* respectively.

Since *bee* < *car* we move the *left* pointer to the right; then since *sup* ≥ *car* we stop. Since *car* ≥ *car* we move the *right* pointer to the left; *the* > *car*, so we move *right* left again; *and* < *car*, so we stop in the situation

$$beg \; bee \textbf{ sup } \textbf{and} \; the \; car \; sum \; pie$$

Interchanging *sup* with *and* we obtain

$$beg \; bee \textbf{ and } \textbf{sup} \; the \; car \; sum \; pie$$

with the *left* and *right* pointers pointing to *and* and *sup* respectively.

Since *and* < *car* we move the *left* pointer to the right; since *sup* > *car* we stop. Since *sup* ≥ *car* we move the *right* pointer to the left; since *and* < *car* we stop; we have reached the partition

$$beg \; bee \; and \mid sup \; the \; car \; sum \; pie$$

in which all the words to the left of the vertical bar come before *car* in the dictionary and all those to the right of the bar other than *cur* itself come after it.

We now repeat the performance recursively on each of the subarrays so formed.

Next we examine the complexity of Quicksort. Notice first that in order to partition a subarray using a given pivot the keys of all the entries of the subarray must be compared with the pivot so that we know whether they should be assigned to the left or right subarray of the partition. Of course if the chosen pivot is the key of one of the array entries we need not carry out any comparison for that entry—we know it must be assigned to the right hand subarray. Thus the number of comparisons needed to partition an array of length l is either l or (if the pivot is the key of one of the entries) $l - 1$.

Suppose first that we apply Quicksort to an array indexed by $1 .. N$ in which the keys of the array entries are all distinct and *which is already sorted*; for each subarray let us use as pivot the larger of the keys of the first two entries with different keys—since the whole array is already sorted this will in each case be the key of the second entry of the subarray. The first application of the procedure partition will yield a 1-element left subarray and an $(N - 1)$-element right subarray. The 1-element left subarray needs no further manipulation, but we must apply the procedure partition to the right subarray. This produces a 1-element left subarray and an $(N - 2)$-element right subarray. Proceeding in this way we see that the number of comparisons required in an application of Quicksort to an array of length N which is already sorted is

$$(N - 1) + (N - 2) + \ldots + 3 + 2 + 1 = \tfrac{1}{2} N (N - 1);$$

The same number of comparisons would be required if the array were originally in the reverse of sorted order.

This discussion seems to suggest that Quicksort is no better than the $O(N^2)$ sorting algorithms described earlier in the chapter. But the situation we found ourselves in in the last paragraph is certainly not what we are hoping for when we apply Quicksort—what we would really like would be to have the procedure partition divide each subarray into roughly equal parts. Suppose we have $N = 2^m$ and suppose we are in the very best possible situation where each time we partition a subarray it is divided into exactly equal parts. Then, while the first partition of the original array of length 2^m will require 2^m comparisons, the partition of the two half-arrays of length 2^{m-1} will each require 2^{m-1} comparisons and so on. Thus the total number of comparisons is

$$2^m + 2(2^{m-1}) + 2^2(2^{m-2}) + \ldots + 2^{m-1} 2 = m2^m = N \log_2 N.$$

This is of course very much better than $O(N^2)$ and indeed, as we saw at the beginning of the Chapter, it is the best we can hope for from a sorting method based on comparisons. We would, however, be very lucky indeed to find ourselves in the "exact halving" situation. So we are led to ask not about the best nor the worst behaviour of Quicksort but about its *average* behaviour. We shall investigate this in the case where all the items to be sorted have different keys and where the pivot used to partition an array is always the key of one of its entries but never the least of these keys. If we have N items to be sorted, all with different keys, they may be stored in an array indexed by $1 \mathinner{..} N$ in $N!$ different ways; we make the further assumption that each of these $N!$ array representations is equally likely. It follows that it is equally likely that the left subarray of the partition of the array consists of $1, 2, \ldots, N-1$ items.

Let $A(l)$ be the average number of comparisons involved in the application of Quicksort to an array of length l. Then $A(1) = 0$ and if $N > 1$ we have

$$
\begin{aligned}
A(N) = {}& (N-1) \quad \text{(comparisons of ``non-pivot'' entries with the pivot)} \\
& + \text{(probability that left subarray has 1 entry)} \, (A(1) + A(N-1)) \\
& + \text{(probability that left subarray has 2 entries)} \, (A(2) + A(N-2)) \\
& \qquad \cdots \\
& + \text{(probability that left subarray has $(N-1)$ entries)} \, * \\
& \qquad\qquad\qquad\qquad\qquad\qquad\qquad\qquad * \, (A(N-1) + A(1))
\end{aligned}
$$

(The expressions $A(i) + A(N-i)$ represent the average number of comparisons involved in the application of Quicksort to the left and right subarrays.) Clearly the probabilities involved are all $1/(N-1)$. Thus

$$
A(N) = (N-1) + \frac{2(A(1) + \ldots + A(N-1))}{N-1} \tag{1}
$$

Replacing N in (1) by $N-1$ we obtain

$$
A(N-1) = (N-2) + \frac{2(A(1) + \ldots + A(N-2))}{N-2} \tag{2}
$$

Multiply (1) by $(N-1)$, (2) by $(N-2)$ and subtract: we obtain

$$
(N-1)A(N) - (N-2)A(N-1) = (N-1)^2 - (N-2)^2 + 2A(N-1)
$$

Rearranging and simplifying we have

$$
(N-1)A(N) - NA(N-1) = 2N - 3 \tag{3}
$$

Now divide (3) by $N(N-1)$; this gives

$$
\frac{A(N)}{N} - \frac{A(N-1)}{N-1} = \frac{2N-3}{N(N-1)} = \frac{3}{N} - \frac{1}{N-1}
$$

(the last equality being obtained by the technique of partial fractions). It is convenient to write $B(k)$ for $A(k)/k$ $(k = 1, \ldots, N)$. Then (3) becomes

$$B(N) - B(N-1) = \frac{3}{N} - \frac{1}{N-1}$$

Replace N in this equation by $N-1$, $N-2$, $\ldots$, 2 and add up; since $B(1) = 0$ we get

$$
\begin{aligned}
B(N) &= 3\left(\frac{1}{2} + \frac{1}{3} + \ldots + \frac{1}{N}\right) - \left(1 + \frac{1}{2} + \frac{1}{3} + \ldots + \frac{1}{N-1}\right) \\
&= 2\left(1 + \frac{1}{2} + \ldots + \frac{1}{N}\right) + \frac{1}{N} - 3
\end{aligned}
$$

Now it was discovered a long time ago by Euler (1707-1783) that when N is large the sum

$$1 + \frac{1}{2} + \frac{1}{3} + \ldots + \frac{1}{N}$$

is approximately equal to $\ln N$, the natural logarithm of N, which is approximately $0.693 \log_2 N$. We deduce finally that when N is large $A(N)$, the average complexity of Quicksort, is approximately $1.4 N \log_2 N$, which is certainly $O(N \log_2 N)$.

Table 2 allows us to compare the behaviour of Quicksort with the various $O(N^2)$ sorting algorithms we described earlier.

	128	256	512	1024	O1024	R1024	2048
Bubblesort	54	221	881	3621	1285	5627	14497
Insertion Sort	15	69	276	1137	6	2200	4536
Selection Sort	12	45	164	634	643	833	2497
Quicksort	12	27	55	112	1131	1200	230

Table 2

This shows clearly the unsatisfactory performance of Quicksort when dealing with arrays which are already sorted or in the reverse of sorted order. Table 2 also gives a very rough indication that the improvement in performance of Quicksort as compared with the $O(N^2)$ algorithms increases with the size of the input. Part of the reason for this is that for smaller arrays the computer overheads involved in successive recursive calls of the procedure quick (storing of return addresses, formal parameters and local variables) tend to outweigh the decrease in the number of comparisons. It seems sensible, therefore, to amend the procedure quick so that when $j - i$ is small (less than 16 is often suggested) quick(i, j) applies Selection Sort to the subarray indexed by $i .. j$. The results of this are shown in Table 3 in which we denote the modification of Quicksort by Quicksort1.

	128	256	512	1024	O1024	R1024	2048
Bubblesort	54	221	881	3621	1285	5627	14497
Insertion Sort	15	69	276	1137	6	2200	4536
Selection Sort	12	45	164	634	643	833	2497
Quicksort	12	27	55	112	1131	1200	230
Quicksort1	6	12	24	57	1115	1191	134

Table 3

(5) **Heapsort.** Although we often say informally that Quicksort is an $O(N \log_2 N)$ algorithm we ought never to forget that this is its *average* complexity and that its worst case behaviour is $O(N^2)$. We turn now to a sorting method, Heapsort, whose *worst case* complexity is $O(N \log_2 N)$.

We recall from Chapter 4 that an array A of records indexed by $1 .. N$ represents a heap or is a heap-array if for every index i such that $2i \leq N$ we have $A[i].Key > A[2i].Key$ and for every index i such that $2i + 1 \leq N$ we have $A[i].Key > A[2i + 1].Key$. It follows that in a heap-array the first entry has the largest key.

At the end of Chapter 4 we showed how to make a given array A into a heap by successive applications of the procedure trickle—we execute

for $i := N$ **div** 2 **downto** 1 **do** trickle(i, N, A).

The execution of trickle(i, N, A) consists of a succession of comparison-and-interchange stages. Each of these requires at most two comparisons to discover which of the array entries $A[j]$ (the current position of the element being trickled down) and its children $A[2j]$ and $A[2j + 1]$ has the largest key; there would, of course, be only one comparison if $2j = N$. The total number of comparisons is thus at most twice the number of comparison-and-interchange stages. After each stage in which an interchange takes place the index j is replaced by $2j$ or $2j+1$. Suppose there are k stages altogether involved in executing the instruction trickle(i, N, A); then the index of the entry containing the element which is being trickled down, originally set at i, is finally at least $2^k i$. But this index must of course be no greater than N, so we have $2^k i \leq N$ and hence $k \leq \log_2(N/i)$. It follows that the total number of comparisons involved in carrying out trickle(i, ,N, A) is not more than $2\log_2(N/i)$. Hence, if we write $m = N$ **div** 2, the total number of comparisons involved in making A into a heap-array is not more than

$$2\left(\log_2\left(\tfrac{N}{m}\right) + \log_2\left(\tfrac{N}{m-1}\right) + \ldots + \log_2\left(\tfrac{N}{1}\right)\right)$$

which is easily transformed into

$$2m\log_2 N - 2\log_2 m!$$

In 1730 the Scottish mathematician James Stirling found an approximation to the natural logarithm of $N!$ when N is large; from this we can deduce that when m is large then $\log_2 m!$ is approximately $m\log_2 m - 1.5m$. Thus the total number of comparisons required to form a heap-array from the array A is not greater than an upper bound which is approximately

$$2m\log_2 N - 2m\log_2 m + 3m = 2m\log_2(N/m) + 3m$$

and since N/m is approximately 2 this upper bound is approximately $5m$, which is approximately $2.5N$.

We recall once more that when the entries of an array have been rearranged to form a heap-array the entry with the largest key is in the first position. Heapsort proceeds by interchanging this entry with the one in the last position, for that is where the entry with the largest key ought to be. Once this is done we need never be concerned with this entry again: all that remains is to sort the first $N - 1$ entries. To do this we proceed by making the subarray indexed by $1 .. N - 1$ into a heap-array, whereupon the entry of the original array with the second largest key will be in the first position. We then interchange this entry with that in the $(N - 1)$-st position, which is where it ought to be when the array is sorted. Now only the first $N - 2$ entries have to be sorted and it should be clear how we proceed—we repeatedly form a heap-array from the remaining entries and then move the first entry to its proper position. Notice that since we are starting with a heap-array A all we have to do to transform a subarray $A[1 .. j]$ indexed by $1 .. j$ into a heap-array after the first entry is changed is to trickle down the new first entry. Thus we carry out

> **for** $i := N$ **downto** 2 **do begin**
>   swap($A[1]$, $A[i]$);
>   trickle($1, i - 1, A$) **end**;

We illustrate the operation of Heapsort using the array

5	10	27	60	59	62	14	73

which we looked at towards the end of Chapter 4 where we made it into a heap-array

73	60	62	10	59	27	14	5

We interchange the first and the last entries, obtaining

5	60	62	10	59	27	14		73

Now 73 is in its correct position (we have indicated this by offsetting it a little from the rest of the array) and we now proceed to make the first 7 elements into a heap-array by trickling down 5, obtaining first

62	60	5	10	59	27	14		73

and then

62	60	27	10	59	5	14		73

We interchange 62 and 14, producing

$$\boxed{14}\boxed{60}\boxed{27}\boxed{10}\boxed{59}\boxed{5}\;\;\boxed{62}\boxed{73}$$

and trickle down 14, getting first

$$\boxed{60}\boxed{14}\boxed{27}\boxed{10}\boxed{59}\boxed{5}\;\;\boxed{62}\boxed{73}$$

and then

$$\boxed{60}\boxed{59}\boxed{27}\boxed{10}\boxed{14}\boxed{5}\;\;\boxed{62}\boxed{73}$$

Now interchange 60 and 5; this gives

$$\boxed{5}\boxed{59}\boxed{27}\boxed{10}\boxed{14}\;\;\boxed{60}\boxed{62}\boxed{73}$$

Trickle down 5, producing in turn

$$\boxed{59}\boxed{5}\boxed{27}\boxed{10}\boxed{14}\;\;\boxed{60}\boxed{62}\boxed{73}$$

and then

$$\boxed{59}\boxed{14}\boxed{27}\boxed{10}\boxed{5}\;\;\boxed{60}\boxed{62}\boxed{73}$$

Interchange 59 and 5, getting

$$\boxed{5}\boxed{14}\boxed{27}\boxed{10}\;\;\boxed{59}\boxed{60}\boxed{62}\boxed{73}$$

Trickle down 5, so that we have

$$\boxed{27}\boxed{14}\boxed{5}\boxed{10}\;\;\boxed{59}\boxed{60}\boxed{62}\boxed{73}$$

Interchange 27 and 10; this gives

$$\boxed{10}\boxed{14}\boxed{5}\;\;\boxed{27}\boxed{59}\boxed{60}\boxed{62}\boxed{73}$$

Trickle down 10, getting

$$\boxed{14}\boxed{10}\boxed{5}\;\;\boxed{27}\boxed{59}\boxed{60}\boxed{62}\boxed{73}$$

Interchange 14 and 5; we obtain

| 5 | 10 | | 14 | 27 | 59 | 60 | 62 | 73 |

Trickle down 5, producing

| 10 | 5 | | 14 | 27 | 59 | 60 | 62 | 73 |

Finally interchange 10 and 5; we obtain the sorted version

| 5 | 10 | 14 | 27 | 59 | 60 | 62 | 73 |

To analyse the worst case complexity of Heapsort we recall first from our discussion earlier in this Section that the first phase of Heapsort, which transforms a given array indexed by $1 .. N$ into a heap-array, requires at most $2.5N$ comparisons. Next we extract from that earlier discussion an upper bound for the number of comparisons involved in carrying out trickle$(1, j, A)$, namely $2\log_2 j$. So the total number of comparisons required in the repeated interchange-and-trickle phase of Heapsort is at most

$$2\log_2(N-1) + 2\log_2(N-2) + \ldots + 2\log_2 1 = 2\log_2(N-1)! \leq 2\log_2 N!$$

which is approximately $2N\log_2 N - 3N$ when N is large.

The total number of comparisons involved in Heapsort is thus bounded above by $2N\log_2 N$; so the worst case complexity of Heapsort is $O(N\log_2 N)$.

(6) **Mergesort.** Let A and B be two sequences of records, both arranged in increasing order of keys. To **merge** A and B means to construct a new sequence C consisting of all the records in A and B arranged in increasing order of keys according to the following prescription—we keep looking at a record from A and a record from B, comparing their keys and moving the one with smaller key to C, until

one of the sequences A and B is exhausted, whereupon we copy to C the remaining records in the other sequence.

For example, if A is the sequence 1 3 4 and B is 2 5 6 we proceed as follows:

1. Compare 1 from A and 2 from B. Since $1 < 2$ we move 1 to C. So

   A is 3 4, B is 2 5 6 and C is 1.

2. Compare 3 from A and 2 from B. Since $2 < 3$ we move 2 to C. So

   A is 3 4, B is 5 6 and C is 1 2.

3. Compare 3 from A and 5 from B. Since $3 < 5$ we move 3 to C. So

   A is 4, B is 5 6 and C is 1 2 3.

4. Compare 4 from A and 5 from B. Since $4 < 5$ we move 4 to C. So

   A is empty, B is 5 6 and C is 1 2 3 4.

5. Since A is empty we copy the remainder of B to C so that

   A is empty, B is empty and C is 1 2 3 4 5 6.

In a computer situation the sequences A, B and C may be stored in arrays or in sequential files. If arrays are used then merging would be carried out by declaring

Type $Array1 = $ **array**$[1 .. M]$ **of** T;
$\quad Array2 = $ **array**$[1 .. N]$ **of** T;
$\quad Array3 = $ **array**$[1 .. M + N]$ **of** T;

(where M and N are the array sizes) and then using

Procedure merge $(A : Array1;\ B : Array2;$ **Var** $C : Array3)$;
Var $i : 1 .. M;\ j : 1 .. N;\ k : 1 .. M + N;\ l :$ **Integer**;
Begin $i := 1;\ j := 1;\ k := 1$;
$\quad\quad$ **while** $(i \leq M)$ **and** $(j \leq N)$ **do begin**
$\quad\quad\quad$ **if** $A[i].Key \leq B[j].Key$ **then begin**
$\quad\quad\quad\quad$ $C[k] := A[i];\ i := i + 1$ **end**

else begin $C[k] := B[j]$; $j := j + 1$ end;
    $k := k + 1$ end;
if $i > M$ then for $l := j$ to N do begin
    $C[k] := B[l]$; $k := k + 1$ end;
if $j > N$ then for $l := i$ to M do begin
    $C[k] := A[l]$; $k := k + 1$ end End;

The reader is invited to think about the appropriate analogue of this procedure for the case where the sequences are stored in files rather than arrays.

Mergesort is a divide-and-conquer internal sorting algorithm which proceeds by splitting the array to be sorted into two roughly equal subarrays, sorting the subarrays by recursive applications of Mergesort and then merging the sorted subarrays. The idea is expressed in the following quasi-Pascal procedure:

Procedure sort_by_merge (*low, high : Index*);
Var *mid : low .. high*;
    $B :$ **array** [*low .. high*] **of** T;
Begin if *low* < *high* **then begin**
        $mid := (low + high)$ **div** 2;
        sort_by_merge(*low, mid*);
        sort_by_merge(*mid* + 1, *high*);
        merge($A[low .. mid]$, $A[mid + 1 .. high]$, B);
        Copy B to $A[low .. high]$ **end End**;

In analysing the complexity of Mergesort we shall make the assumption that the time taken to merge two sorted sequences of lengths l_1 and l_2 is proportional to $l_1 + l_2$. Let W be the worst case complexity function for Mergesort. Then $W(1)$ is some constant, a say. Now suppose first that N is a power of 2, say $N = 2^k$. Then we have

$$W(N) = 2W(\tfrac{1}{2}N) + cN \text{ where } c \text{ is a constant}$$

(the right hand side of this equation is the maximum time to apply Mergesort to the two half-arrays + the time to merge the two sorted half-arrays). So we have

$$W(N) = 2W(\tfrac{1}{2}N) + cN$$

$$= 4W(\tfrac{1}{4}N) + 2cN$$

$$\ldots$$

$$= 2^k W(1) + kcN = aN + cN\log_2 N.$$

If $2^{k-1} < N \leq 2^k$ then we have

$$W(N) \leq W(2^k) = a.2^k + ck.2^k \leq a.2N + c(\log_2 N + 1)(2N)$$
$$= 2cN\log_2 N + 2(a+c)N$$

which is $O(N\log_2 N)$.

As in the case of Quicksort we can speed up Mergesort by refusing to carry out the subdivision of the array to be sorted (with the associated overheads of repeated recursive calls) right to the bitter end of one-element subarrays. Once $high - low$ is small, say less than 16, we make sort_by_merge(*low, high*) apply Selection Sort to the subarray $A[low .. high]$.

Table 4 displays the times achieved by all our sorting methods. (Mergesort1 is the modification of Mergesort which we have just described.)

	128	256	512	1024	O1024	R1024	2048
Bubblesort	54	221	881	3621	1285	5627	14497
Insertion Sort	15	69	276	1137	6	2200	4536
Selection Sort	12	45	164	634	643	833	2497
Quicksort	12	27	55	112	1131	1200	230
Quicksort1	6	12	24	57	1115	1191	134
Heapsort	21	45	103	236	215	249	527
Mergesort	18	36	88	188	166	170	409
Mergesort1	6	22	48	112	94	93	254

Table 4

7.2   Other internal sorting algorithms

The sorting methods we described in Section 1 can be applied to sort records whose keys are of any ordered type whatever since the only operation we carry out on the keys is comparison. But if we know more about the key type than just the simple fact that it is ordered we may perhaps be able to use the special properties of the key type to speed up the sorting process.

(1) To take a simple example, suppose first of all that we have an array A indexed by $1 \mathrel{..} N$ of records whose keys are known to be the integers from 1 to N in some order.

In this situation it is easy to obtain a sorted version of the entries of A by declaring a second array B, also indexed by $1 \mathrel{..} N$, and giving the instruction

$$\textbf{for } i := 1 \textbf{ to } N \textbf{ do } B[A[i].Key] := A[i];$$

Here we examine the records in the array A in increasing order of array index and put each entry of A in the position of B which in indexed by its key. So the record with key k lands in position $B[k]$ for $k = 1, \ldots, N$ and so the entries of B are those of A arranged in increasing order of key. Choosing the "basic operation" of this algorithm to be assignment we see that its complexity is $O(N)$. Notice, though, that this method needs extra space to accommodate the second array B.

It is possible, however, to apply the same basic idea without introducing a new array. It is clear that if the key of $A[i]$ is $j \neq i$ then, if we interchange $A[i]$ and $A[j]$ the new j-th entry (which has key j) is now correct. So we can sort A "in place" by means of the instruction

$$\textbf{for } i := 1 \textbf{ to } N \textbf{ do while } A[i].Key <> i \textbf{ do } \mathrm{swap}(A[i], A[A[i].Key]);$$

Choose the "basic operation" to be an interchange of array entries (a swap); then, since after each interchange at least one record is in its correct position, the maximum number of interchanges required is $N - 1$ (once $(N - 1)$ entries are in their correct positions the N-th must also be in its correct position) and hence the algorithm has worst case complexity $O(N)$.

(2) Suppose now that we have a collection of records whose keys are integers in the range 0 .. 99. We shall show how to sort this array by setting up an array of 10 queues. We make the declarations

Type *Queue_pointer* = ↑ Node;
       Node = **Record**
                Info : *T*;
                Next : *Queue_pointer*
          end;
       Queue = **Record**
                Front, Rear : *Queue_pointer*
          end;
   Var *Q* : *Queue*
     Qu : **array**[0 .. 9] **of** *Queue*;

It is convenient to store the records to be sorted in the queue Q. The first pass of **two-pass radix sorting** consists in taking the records from Q in turn, examining their keys and enqueuing each record in the queue in the array Qu indexed by the least significant digit of its key:

while not empty (Q) **do begin**
         serve (Q, x);
         $j := (x.Key)$ **mod** 10;
         enqueue $(x, Qu[j])$ **end**;

We now concatenate the queues $Qu[0]$, $Qu[1]$, ..., $Qu[9]$ into a single input stream, which we may as well call Q again. The second pass of radix sorting again takes the records from Q in turn and examines their keys, but this time enqueues each record in the queue in Qu which is indexed by the *most* significant digit of its key:

```
while not empty (Q) do begin
        serve (Q, x);
        j := (x.Key) div 10;
        enqueue (x,Qu[j]) end;
```

Again we concatenate the queues $Qu[0]$, $Qu[1]$, ..., $Qu[9]$ into a single output stream, which we claim is now in order. To see that this is indeed the case suppose that X and Y are the keys of two of the records to be sorted; let $X = 10a + b$, $Y = 10c + d$, where $0 \leq a, b, c, d < 10$.

If $X < Y$ then we must have $a \leq c$.

Suppose first that $a < c$. Then on the second pass of radix sorting the record with key X will be put in the queue $Qu[a]$ and the record with key Y in the queue $Qu[c]$. Since $a < c$ the queue $Qu[a]$ appears in the concatenated output stream before the queue $Qu[c]$; so the record with key X appears, as it should, before the record with key Y.

If $a = c$ then we must have $b < d$. In this case during the first pass of radix sorting the record with key X will be put in the queue $Qu[b]$ and the record with key Y in the queue $Qu[d]$. Since $b < d$ the queue $Qu[b]$ appears in the concatenated input stream for the second pass before $Qu[d]$. Thus, although on the second pass the records with keys X and Y are both put in $Qu[a] = Qu[c]$, the record with key X is added before the record with key Y and hence again appears first in the concatenated output stream.

We illustrate the two-pass radix sorting method using the input stream

$$73 \quad 29 \quad 92 \quad 14 \quad 74 \quad 45 \quad 54 \quad 18 \quad 3 \quad 97 \quad 9 \quad 61 \quad 11 \quad 63 \quad 35 \quad 37$$

After the first pass of radix sorting the queues $Qu[0]$, ..., $Qu[9]$ are as follows:

$Qu[0].Front = \textbf{nil} = Qu[0].Rear$

$Qu[1].Front \longrightarrow \boxed{61 \mid } \longrightarrow \boxed{11 \diagup} \longleftarrow Qu[1].Rear$

$Qu[2].Front \longrightarrow \boxed{92 \diagup} \longleftarrow Qu[2].Rear$

$Qu[3].Front \longrightarrow \boxed{73 \mid } \longrightarrow \boxed{3 \mid } \longrightarrow \boxed{63 \diagup} \longleftarrow Qu[3].Rear$

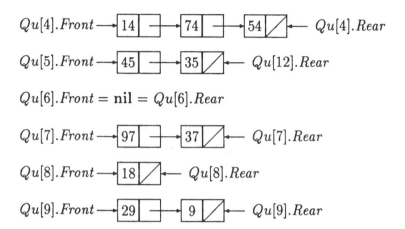

$Qu[4].Front \longrightarrow \boxed{14 \ |} \longrightarrow \boxed{74 \ |} \longrightarrow \boxed{54 \ /} \longleftarrow Qu[4].Rear$

$Qu[5].Front \longrightarrow \boxed{45 \ |} \longrightarrow \boxed{35 \ /} \longleftarrow Qu[12].Rear$

$Qu[6].Front = \mathbf{nil} = Qu[6].Rear$

$Qu[7].Front \longrightarrow \boxed{97 \ |} \longrightarrow \boxed{37 \ /} \longleftarrow Qu[7].Rear$

$Qu[8].Front \longrightarrow \boxed{18 \ /} \longleftarrow Qu[8].Rear$

$Qu[9].Front \longrightarrow \boxed{29 \ |} \longrightarrow \boxed{9 \ /} \longleftarrow Qu[9].Rear$

When we concatenate these queues the input stream for the second pass is

61 11 92 73 3 63 14 74 54 45 35 97 37 18 29 9

After the second pass the queues $Qu[0], \ldots, Qu[9]$ are

$Qu[0].Front \longrightarrow \boxed{3 \ |} \longrightarrow \boxed{9 \ /} \longleftarrow Qu[0].Rear$

$Qu[1].Front \longrightarrow \boxed{11 \ |} \longrightarrow \boxed{14 \ |} \longrightarrow \boxed{18 \ /} \longleftarrow Qu[1].Rear$

$Qu[2].Front \longrightarrow \boxed{29 \ /} \longleftarrow Qu[2].Rear$

$Qu[3].Front \longrightarrow \boxed{35 \ |} \longrightarrow \boxed{37 \ /} \longleftarrow Qu[3].Rear$

$Qu[4].Front \longrightarrow \boxed{45 \ /} \longleftarrow Qu[4].Rear$

$Qu[5].Front \longrightarrow \boxed{54 \ /} \longleftarrow Qu[5].Rear$

$Qu[6].Front \longrightarrow \boxed{61 \ |} \longrightarrow \boxed{63 \ /} \longleftarrow Qu[6].Rear$

$Qu[7].Front \longrightarrow \boxed{73 \ |} \longrightarrow \boxed{74 \ /} \longleftarrow Qu[7].Rear$

$Qu[8].Front = \mathbf{nil} = Qu[8].Rear$

$Qu[9].Front \longrightarrow \boxed{92 \mid \ \ } \longrightarrow \boxed{97 \mid /} \longleftarrow Qu[9].Rear$

When these queues are concatenated we obtain the sorted output stream

3 9 11 14 18 29 35 37 45 54 61 63 73 74 92 97

If we choose as fundamental operation for radix sorting the extraction of one of the digits of a key then it is clear that to apply two-pass radix sorting to a collection of N records requires $2N$ fundamental operations. There is, of course, more to be done in radix sorting than just the extraction of digits—each record has to be enqueued in the proper queue in each of the two passes, and the queues have to be concatenated after each pass. The effort required to enqueue the records is clearly proportional to N; and the concatenation involves only the adjustment of the *Next* fields of the *Rear* nodes of the queues $Qu[i]$. So the complexity of two-pass radix sorting is $O(N)$.

We have described *two*-pass radix sorting for the sake of simplicity, but it is surely clear how we would carry out m-pass radix sorting of a collection of records whose keys are m-digit numbers; the complexity here will still be $O(N)$.

7.3 External sorting algorithms

In this section we turn to the problem of sorting vast collections of records, that is collections which are too large to fit into the internal memory of the computer we are using. In such cases the records must be stored in secondary memory, possibly on magnetic tape or (as we shall assume in this section) in a file held on disk. We observe that the maximum number of records which can be held in internal memory depends on the size of the records—on the number and type of their fields. It might be possible to increase the number if corresponding to each of the records in the collection to be sorted we were to create a new record with just two fields, the key of the original record and its address (an indication of where it is stored on disk); but there might still be too many of these "key-address" pairs to fit at once into internal memory, so we may still have to resort to external sorting methods.

To describe these methods it is convenient to introduce the term **run** to mean a sequence of records, of arbitrary length, arranged in non-decreasing order of the key field. The sorting methods we consider proceed by identifying or constructing runs and then merging them to form successively longer runs until all the records to be sorted are included in a single run.

(1) **Balanced Mergesort.** We begin by declaring

Var F, $F1$, $F2$, $F3$, $F4$: **file of** T;

and suppose that a collection of N records to be sorted is held in the file F. Let M be the largest number of records which can be held in the internal memory of our computers (along with the program of an internal sorting method).

Balanced Mergesort now proceeds in two stages:

(a) The **Distribution Stage.** In this stage we construct runs of records, all (with possibly one exception) of length M, and distribute them between the files $F1$ and $F2$. We begin by opening F for reading and $F1$ and $F2$ for writing by giving the commands

Reset(F); Rewrite($F1$); Rewrite($F2$);

Then, so long as there are at least M records remaining in the file F we read exactly M into an array (in the internal memory) and sort the entries of this array using an internal sorting method. The elements of the sorted array constitute a run which we write to $F1$ or $F2$, using these files alternately. If we reach a situation in which there are fewer than M records (but at least one) remaining in F then we read the remaining records into an array, sort its entries into a run, again using an internal sorting method, and write the resulting run to whichever of $F1$, $F2$ was not used for the last run of length M.

(b) The **Merge Stage.** In this stage we merge the runs which were produced in the Distribution Stage and written to $F1$ and $F2$. We begin by opening $F1$ and $F2$ for reading and $F3$ and $F4$ for writing, using the commands

Reset($F1$); Reset($F2$); Rewrite($F3$); Rewrite($F4$);

Then, so long as both $F1$ and $F2$ are non-empty (i.e. **while not** eof($F1$) **and not** eof($F2$)) we read the leading runs on the two files and merge them into a single run which we write to $F3$ or $F4$, using these files alternately. If one of the files $F1$, $F2$ is exhausted before the other it is clear from the way the Distribution Stage works that the non-empty file contains just one run; in this case we copy the single run to whichever of $F3$, $F4$ was not used for the last merged run.

We now interchange the roles of $F1$, $F2$ and $F3$, $F4$ by giving the commands

Reset($F3$); Reset($F4$); Rewrite($F1$); Rewrite($F2$);

Then, so long as $F3$ and $F4$ are non-empty, we read the leading runs on these two files, merge them into a single run and write it to $F1$ or $F2$, using $F1$ and $F2$ alternately. Again, if one of the files $F3$, $F4$ is exhausted before the other we copy the single run remaining in the non-empty file to whichever of $F1$, $F2$ was not used for the last merged run.

We proceed in this way using the pairs $F1$, $F2$ and $F3$, $F4$ alternately for reading and writing until there is only one run and the sorting is complete.

To illustrate the working of Balanced Mergesort suppose we have a file F containing the letters

THEQUICKBROWNFOXJUMPSOVERTHELAZYDOG

which we want to sort into alphabetical order. Suppose that our computer can sort no more than four letters at a time. Then we read groups of four letters in turn from F, sort them, and write the resulting runs alternately to $F1$ and $F2$. This produces the following arrangement on $F1$ and $F2$:

$F1 : EHQT|BORW|JMPU|EHRT|DGO$
$F2 : CIKU|FNOX|EOSV|ALYZ$

(The vertical bars do not, of course, appear in the files but are introduced here to help the reader see the ends of the runs.)

The first round of the Merge Stage reads 4-member runs from $F1$ and $F2$ and merges them to form 8-member runs which it writes alternately to $F3$ and $F4$, producing the following arrangement:

$F3 : CEHIKQTU|EJMOPSUV|DGO$
$F4 : BFNOORWX|AEHLRTYZ$

The second round reads 8-member runs from $F3$ and $F4$, merges them to form 16-member runs and writes these alternately to $F1$ and $F2$, yielding the arrangement

$F1 : BCEFHIKNOOQRTUWX|DGO$
$F2 : AEEHJLMOPRSTUVYZ$

The third round produces

$F3 : ABCEEEFHHIJKLMNOOOPQRRSTTUUVWXYZ$
$F4 : DGO$

Finally we have

$F1 : ABCDEEEFGHHIJKLMNOOOOP$
$\qquad\qquad QRRSTTUUVWXYZ$
$F2 :$ empty

where the original collection is sorted into a single run on $F1$.

To analyse the complexity of Balanced Mergesort we suppose for simplicity that N, the number of records to be sorted, is an integer multiple of M, the run length at the Distribution Stage; so the number of runs formed at the Distribution Stage is $r = N/M$ (in general r is the least integer greater than or equal to N/M). To simplify the analysis still further let us assume that r is a power of 2, say $r = 2^k$. After each round of the Merge Stage the length of the runs is doubled and their number halved; so after k merge rounds sorting is complete.

Suppose that at the Distribution Stage we use an internal sorting algorithm whose complexity (counting by comparisons) is $O(X\log_2 X)$; thus when X is large the number of key comparisons involved in sorting X records is at most $AX\log_2 X$ where A is a constant. So the total number of comparisons involved in forming the r runs of length M will be at most $r(AM\log_2 M) = AN\log_2 M$.

On the first round of the Merge Stage we merge $r/2$ pairs of runs of length M; on the second round $r/4$ pairs of runs of length $2M$ and so on. We notice that when we merge two runs of length l the number of key comparisons is at least l and at most $2l - 1$. (Think first of merging the two runs 1 2 3 and 4 5 6, which requires only 3 comparisons, and then of merging 1 3 5 and 2 4 6, which requires 5 comparisons.) So the maximum number of comparisons required in the Merge Stage is

$$\tfrac{1}{2}r(2M - 1) + \tfrac{1}{4}r(4M - 1) + \ldots + \tfrac{1}{2^k}r(2^k M - 1)$$

$$= krM - r(\tfrac{1}{2} + \tfrac{1}{4} + \ldots + \tfrac{1}{2^k})$$

$$\leq krM = N\log_2 r$$

If B is the larger of 1 and A we deduce that the total number of key comparisons involved in the whole Balanced Mergesort operation is at most $BN\log_2 M + BN\log_2 r = BN\log_2 N$.

(2) **Natural Mergesort.** When we use Balanced Two-way Mergesort the Distribution Stage uses the input stream of the records to be sorted to produce runs all of which (except possibly the last) have the same length. It may happen, however, that the input stream is made up of quite long runs, possibly even longer than the maximum which can be held in internal memory; to read in such runs (even if it were possible) and sort them is pointless. It would be a particular waste of time if we were to use Quicksort for the internal sorting: as we

have seen, Quicksort does not work very efficiently on arrays which are already sorted. So, provided we can devise a procedure to test when the input stream comes to the end of a run, we may read successive runs *of arbitrary length* from the input file F, write them alternately to $F1$ and $F2$ and then carry out a Merge Stage similar to that described for the Balanced Mergesort.

Although the basic idea behind Natural Mergesort is essentially the same as that of Balanced Mergesort, some care has to be taken in implementing the Natural version. In the Balanced version we know at each stage the length of every run except possibly the last; so we know when to stop using a section of the input file for merging. Consider, however, the input stream of characters

$$ADGKMRBXSTUCYVWEFKLNPQ$$

The Distribution Stage produces the arrangement

$F1 : ADGKMR|STU|VW$
$F2 : BX|CY|EFKLNPQ$

where again the vertical bars indicate the ends of the runs. Notice here that the bars are not just (as in the Balanced version) an aid to the eye of the reader: some such indication is essential for the proper running of the algorithm—without them the three runs on $F1$ would coalesce to form a single run; but if we were to treat the entries on $F1$ as a single run it would not be clear what to do with the second and third runs on $F2$.

The first round of the Merge Stage reads successive pairs of runs from $F1$ and $F2$ and merges them to form single runs which are written to $F3$ and $F4$ alternately, producing

$F3 : ABDGKMRX|EFKLNPQVW$
$F4 : CSTUY$

The second round reads runs from $F3$ and $F4$, merges them and writes the merged runs to $F1$ and $F2$ alternately. This produces the arrangement

$F1 : ABCDGKMRSTUXY$
$F2 : EFKLNPQVW$

Finally we have

> $F3: ABCDEFGKKLMNPQRSTUVWXY$
> $F4:$ empty

(3) **Polyphase Sorting.** We begin this section by talking about the **Fibonacci numbers.** These are the numbers F_k $(k = 0, 1, \dots)$ defined by

$$F_0 = 0, F_1 = 1 \text{ and, for all integers } k \geq 2, F_k = F_{k-1} + F_{k-2}.$$

So the Fibonacci numbers are

$$0, 1, 1, 2, 3, 5, 8, 13, 21, 34, 55, \dots$$

Suppose that we have managed to organise the collection of records to be sorted into r runs, where r is one of the Fibonacci numbers, say $r = F_n$. How this is actually done is not important for the description of the Polyphase Sorting algorithm—the runs may be formed as in Balanced Mergesort by reading in large blocks of data and sorting by an internal sorting algorithm or as in Natural Mergesort by reading successive "naturally occurring" runs from the input stream. Suppose the r runs are stored in a file T with "end-of-run" markers.

Let $r = F_n$ where $n \geq 2$ (there is clearly no sorting to be done if $n = 0$ or 1); then we have $F_n = F_{n-1} + F_{n-2}$. We introduce three working files $T1, T2, T3$ and give the commands

$$\text{Rewrite}(T1); \text{Rewrite}(T2); \text{Reset}(T);$$

We then read F_{n-1} runs from T, writing them to $T1$, and write the remaining F_{n-2} runs to $T2$.

Now we give the commands

$$\text{Rewrite}(T3); \text{Reset}(T1); \text{Reset}(T2);$$

and merge the leading F_{n-2} pairs of runs on $T1$ and $T2$, writing all the merged runs to $T3$ and using "end-of-run" markers to separate successive runs. When this has been completed the file $T2$ is empty, but $T1$ still holds $F_{n-1} - F_{n-2}$ runs; by the definition of the Fibonacci numbers this is F_{n-3}. So we are again in the position we were in at the start—we have three files, one of which is empty and the other two hold runs which are in number two successive Fibonacci numbers. We can then repeat the process, using the empty file for writing and the other files for reading, carrying on in this way until there is only one run left, i.e. the collection is sorted.

Suppose, for example, the input file T holds $F_8 = 21$ runs. We distribute these runs by giving the commands

$$\text{Rewrite}(T1); \text{Rewrite}(T2); \text{Reset}(T);$$

sending $F_7 = 13$ runs to $T1$ and $F_6 = 8$ runs to $T2$. Thus we have the starting position

$T1$ holds $F_7 = 13$ runs, $T2$ holds $F_6 = 8$ runs, $T3$ is empty

Now we give the commands

$$\text{Rewrite}(T3); \text{Reset}(T1); \text{Reset}(T2);$$

and merge the first, second, ..., 8th runs on $T1$ with the corresponding runs on $T2$, writing the 8 merged runs in turn to $T3$. We now have the situation

$T1$ holds $F_5 = 5$ runs, $T2$ is empty, $T3$ holds $F_6 = 8$ runs

We give the commands

$$\text{Rewrite}(T2); \text{Reset}(T3);$$

and merge 5 pairs of runs from $T1$ and $T3$, writing the merged runs to $T2$, so that we have

$T1$ is empty, $T2$ holds $F_5 = 5$ runs, $F3$ holds $F_4 = 3$ runs

Next we give the commands

$$\text{Rewrite}(T1); \text{Reset}(T2);$$

and merge 3 pairs of runs from $T2$ and $T3$, writing the merged runs to $T1$, whereupon we obtain

$T1$ holds $F_4 = 3$ runs, $T2$ holds $F_3 = 2$ runs, $T3$ is empty

We proceed in this way for three more stages, resulting successively in the positions

$T1$ holds $F_2 = 1$ run, $T2$ is empty, $T3$ holds $F_3 = 2$ runs
$T1$ is empty, $T2$ holds $F_2 = 1$ run, $T3$ holds $F_1 = 1$ run
$T1$ holds $F_1 = 1$ run, $T2$ is empty, $T3$ is empty

Our description of Polyphase Sorting started with the assumption that the collection of records to be sorted has been organised into r runs, where r is a Fibonacci number. In the general situation, where the number of runs is not a Fibonacci number we introduce enough dummy (empty) runs to make the total number a Fibonacci number and proceed in the way described above. (Clearly when we merge two dummy runs the result is a dummy run; when we merge a dummy run with a non-empty run we simply copy the non-empty run.)

7.4 Exercises 7

1. Use Bubblesort, Insertion Sort and Selection Sort to sort the following character strings into dictionary order:

   dog egg rum gin and rye nog for

2. Use Quicksort and Heapsort to sort the following stream of integers into increasing order:

   66 36 79 45 13 62 16 76

3. Show that if we use the entries of an array of records as input stream to build a binary search tree then the inorder traversal of the resulting tree will display the entries in increasing order of key. Illustrate by sorting the array:

$$53 \ 29 \ 82 \ 44 \ 11 \ 54 \ 14 \ 75$$

What is the worst case complexity (counting comparisons) of the tree-building phase of this sorting method?

4. Use the pivot-and-partition idea of Quicksort to develop a recursive algorithm for finding the entry of an array of records whose key is k-th in order of size of key.

5. Sort the following array of integers into increasing order using Mergesort:

$$66 \ 22 \ 36 \ 6 \ 79 \ 26 \ 45 \ 75 \ 13 \ 31 \ 62 \ 27 \ 76 \ 33 \ 16 \ 47$$

6. Following the example of two-pass radix sorting design a three-pass sorting method to sort collections of three-digit numbers. Illustrate by sorting the following input stream:

$$131 \ 92 \ 325 \ 921 \ 444 \ 508 \ 135 \ 8 \ 900 \ 477 \ 83 \ 721 \ 698 \ 923 \ 42$$

7. Describe how to construct a radix-type sorting method to put in order an input stream of dates given in the form

Month Day Year

8. Write a function which takes as input a **Text** file F holding one integer per line and returns another **Text** file containing the entries of F one per line with a blank line introduced after each run.

9. Suppose we have a computer which can sort internally no more than 5 integers at a time. Apply Balanced Mergesort to a file F containing the following integers:

$$66 \ 31 \ 22 \ 97 \ 36 \ 15 \ 6 \ 32 \ 79 \ 44 \ 26 \ 19 \ 45 \ 46 \ 75 \ 8 \ 13 \ 17 \ 62 \ 88 \ 76 \ 33 \ 72.$$

10. Sort the same input file using Natural Mergesort.

11. Suppose we have N files F_1, F_2, ..., F_N with $N > 4$. Describe a mergesorting procedure along the lines of Balanced Mergesort using M and $N - M$ files, with both M and $N - M$ at least 2. Discuss how you would carry out the merging if the number of files containing runs to be merged exceeds 2.

Chapter 8

GRAPH ALGORITHMS

8.1 Shortest path algorithms

Let $G = (V, E)$ be a graph or digraph with vertex set V and edge set E. If a and b are vertices of G then we define a k-edge **path** from a to b to be a sequence

$$p : v_0 = a, \ v_1, \ v_2, \ \ldots, \ v_k = b$$

of $(k+1)$ vertices such that each vertex after the first is adjacent to its predecessor. We recall that this means, if G is a graph, that $\{v_i, v_{i+1}\}$ is an edge of G (is in E) for $i = 0, 1, \ldots, k - 1$, while if G is a digraph we have (v_i, v_{i+1}) a directed edge of G again for $i = 0, 1, \ldots, k - 1$. A **cycle** in G is a k-edge path p with k at least 3 in which no vertex occurs more than once except that $v_0 = v_k$.

If G is a *weighted* graph or digraph, with weight function W which takes real number values, then the **weight** or **length** of the path p is

$$W(p) = W(\{v_0, v_1\}) + W(\{v_1, v_2\}) + \ldots + W(\{v_{k-1}, v_k\})$$

if G is a graph and

$$W(p) = W((v_0, v_1)) + W((v_1, v_2)) + \ldots + W((v_{k-1}, v_k))$$

if G is a digraph. It is clear what is meant by a **shortest path** from a vertex a to a vertex b: it is a path p from a to b such that $W(p) \leq W(p')$ for all paths p' from a to b.

There are four shortest path problems which naturally suggest themselves for our consideration:

1. The single pair problem: find a shortest path from one given vertex a (the source) to another given vertex b (the sink);

2. The single source problem: given a source vertex a, find for every vertex v a shortest path from a to v;

3. The single sink problem: given a sink vertex b, find for every vertex v a shortest path from v to b;

4. The all pairs problem: for every ordered pair (a, b) of vertices find a shortest path from a to b.

Obviously problems (2) and (3) are essentially the same for an (undirected) graph; for a digraph they can be transformed into one another by the simple device of reversing the arrows on the directed edges (i.e. replacing each ordered pair (v, w) in E by the reversed pair (w, v) and giving it the same weight). Clearly also, if we can solve problem (2) then we can solve problem (4) by applying (2) to each vertex of G in turn. It might seem that problem (1) is the basic problem and that all the others would be deduced from that; but in fact all known approaches to solving problem (1) proceed by finding at least partial solutions to problem (2) or its equivalent, problem (3).

Although, as we said above, it is clear what is meant by a shortest path from one vertex to another, it is not so clear that there always exists such a path. To see what could prevent the existence of a shortest path we introduce the notion of a **negative cycle**: this is a cycle whose length is a negative number.

Suppose that a and b are vertices of a graph or digraph G such that there is at least one path from a to b. Then we claim that there actually exists a shortest path from a to b if and only if no path from a to b includes a negative cycle.

To see that this is so let us suppose first that some path from a to b does include a negative cycle and show that in this case there is no shortest path. This is clear, because if we start with a path which includes a negative cycle then we can produce a shorter path simply by going round the negative cycle again.

So, if there does exist a shortest path from a to b then no path from a to b can include a negative cycle.

Suppose conversely that there is no negative cycle included in any path from a to b. If a path from a to b has a repeated vertex v then the section of the path from the first occurrence of v to the second is a cycle whose length is non-negative; if we remove all the vertices of this cycle except one of the occurrences of v we produce a path from a to b whose length is less than or equal to the length of the original path. So we can confine our attention to paths from a to b with no repeated vertices. A shortest path from a to b is then one among these paths with least length.

We now confine our attention to weighted digraphs in which all the weights are non-negative; this implies, of course, that they have no negative cycles.

Dijkstra's algorithm solves the single source problem for such a digraph.

Dijkstra proceeds by building up a set S of vertices, initialised to consist of the source vertex alone, and adding one new vertex at a time until eventually all the vertices of the graph are in S. To decide at each stage which vertex is to be adjoined to S we work with an array d indexed by the vertices other than the source vertex; the array d is initialised by setting

$$d[w] := \begin{cases} W((a, w)) \text{ if } (a, w) \text{ is an edge of } G \\ \infty \text{ otherwise.} \end{cases}$$

Dijkstra's algorithm is most easily described by writing it as a loop:

for $i := 1$ **to** $n - 1$ **do begin**

    Choose a vertex v not in S for which $d[v]$ is least;

    $S := S \cup \{v\}$;

    For each vertex w not in S,

        $d[w] := \min\{d[w], d[v] + W((v, w))\}$ **end**;

(It might be worth while to replace the last line by

      begin $r := d[v] + W((v, w))$;

        if $r < d[w]$ **then** $d[w] := r$ **end end**;

We shall show that when the loop execution is complete then for each vertex w other than the initial vertex a the final value of the array entry $d[w]$ is the length of all shortest paths from a to w. The idea behind the algorithm can be seen by looking at the first iteration of the **for** loop. First, if v_1 is a vertex such that the edge from a to v_1 is no longer than any other edge from a, then clearly that edge consitutes a shortest path from a to v_1. (Any other path would have to start with the edge from a to some other vertex w, which would be at least as long as (a, v_1), followed by a path from w to v_1, so that the total length could not be less than the length of (a, v_1).) Then for each of the remaining vertices w we compare the lengths of the edge (a, w)—the "direct route" from a to w—and the sum of the lengths of the edges (a, v_1) and (v_1, w); in each case we update $d[w]$ to be the smaller of the lengths of the two possible paths from a to w. At the beginning of the second iteration of the **for** loop we choose a vertex v_2 for which the (updated) $d[v_2]$ is least, and it is not hard to convince ourselves that for this vertex v_2 the length of all shortest paths from a to v_2 is $d[v_2]$.

We illustrate the working of Dijkstra's algorithm by applying it to the graph shown below, with vertex 1 as source vertex.

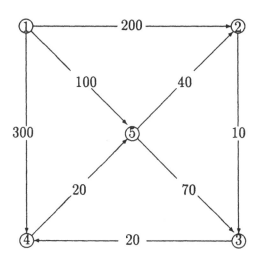

Initially $S = \{1\}$ and we have

$$d[2] = 200, \ d[3] = \infty, \ d[4] = 300, \ d[5] = 100.$$

The minimum entry in d is $d[5] = 100$, so we adjoin vertex 5 to S and then for $i = 2, 3, 4$ we change $d[i]$ to $\min\{d[i], d[5] + W((5, i))\}$. So we calculate

$$d[2] = \min\{d[2], d[5] + W((5,2))\} = \min\{200, 100 + 40\} = 140,$$
$$d[3] = \min\{d[3], d[5] + W((5,3))\} = \min\{\infty, 100 + 70\} = 170,$$
$$d[4] = \min\{d[4], d[5] + W((5,4))\} = \min\{300, 100 + \infty\} = 300.$$

So at this stage we have

$$d[2] = 140, \ d[3] = 170, \ d[4] = 300.$$

The minimum entry in d is now $d[2] = 140$, so we adjoin 2 to S and then for $i = 3, 4$ we change $d[i]$ to $\min\{d[i], d[2] + W((2,i))\}$. We calculate

$$d[3] = \min\{d[3], d[2] + W((2,3))\} = \min\{170, 140 + 10\} = 150,$$
$$d[4] = \min\{d[4], d[2] + W((2,4))\} = \min\{300, 140 + \infty\} = 300.$$

This time we have

$$d[3] = 150, \ d[4] = 300.$$

Now the minimum entry in d is $d[3] = 150$. We adjoin 3 to S and then change $d[4]$ to $\min\{d[4], d[3] + W((3,4))\} = \min\{300, 150 + 20\} = 170$.

So the lengths of the shortest paths from 1 to the remaining vertices are the final entries in d:

$$d[2] = 140, \ d[3] = 150, \ d[4] = 170, \ d[5] = 100.$$

We notice that vertices are added to S in increasing order of the lengths of their shortest paths from the source. Obviously if we are concerned only with the distance from the source to one particular vertex v we need only continue the execution of the algorithm until v is added to S.

To prove formally that Dijkstra's algorithm works it is useful to introduce the notion of a *special* path: a path from the source vertex a to a vertex v not in the set S is said to be S-**special** if all the vertices on the path except v itself are in S.

We are going to show that at each stage in the execution of the algorithm the following statements are true:

1. If w is a vertex in S other than the source vertex a then $d[w]$ is the length of all shortest paths from a to w;

2. If w is a vertex not in S then $d[w]$ is the length of all shortest *S-special* paths from a to w.

In proving these statements it will be helpful if we use S_{i-1} and S_i to represent the set S and d_{i-1} and d_i the array d before and after the i-th iteration of the **for** loop.

Statements (1) and (2) are certainly true before we enter the **for** loop, when $S = S_0$ consists of the source vertex a alone and $d[w]$ is either $W((a, w))$ if there is an edge from a to w or ∞ if not. (Statement (1) holds because there is no vertex w in S_0 other than a; statement (2) holds because at this stage an S_0-special path from a to any vertex w—that is a path all of whose intermediate vertices are in S_0—must be the edge (if there is one) from a, which is the only vertex in S_0, to w.)

Now we suppose that for some integer i ($i = 1, \ldots, n-1$) the statements (1) and (2) hold before we start the i-th iteration of the loop—we have just seen that this is certainly true when $i = 1$. We are going to prove that statements (1) and (2) hold *after* the i-th iteration, during which we adjoined a new vertex v_i to S_{i-1}.

The proof proceeds in two parts.

(*a*) For all the vertices w other than a which are contained in the set S_{i-1} (= S before the i-th iteration) the array entry $d_{i-1}[w]$ is not changed by the i-th iteration; so, since (1) holds before the i-th iteration, it follows that, for all vertices w in S_{i-1} other than a, $d_{i-1}[w]$ was then, and remains afterwards (as $d_i[w]$), the length of all shortest paths from a to w.

We have now to show that after the i-th iteration the entry $d[v_i]$, which also remains unaltered by this iteration, is the length of all shortest paths from a to v_i.

We recall that, since (2) holds before v_i is adjoined to S_{i-1}, $d_{i-1}[v_i]$ is the length of all shortest S_{i-1}-*special* paths from a to v_i. So if $d_i[v_i] = d_{i-1}[v_i]$ is not the length of all shortest paths from a to v_i there would have to be a shorter path p which is not S_{i-1}-special; such a path would have an intermediate vertex between a and v_i which is not in S_{i-1}. Follow the path p from a towards v_i and let x be the first vertex on it which is not in S_{i-1} (See Figure 1).

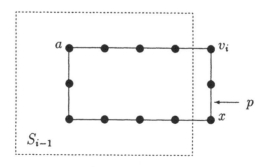

Figure 1

Clearly the section of p from a to x is an S_{i-1}-special path to x. Now we have

Total length of p
    $\geq$ length of section of p from a to x
    $=$ length of an S_{i-1}-special path from a to x
    $\geq d_{i-1}[x]$
(which is the length of the *shortest* S_{i-1}-special path from a to x)
    $\geq d_{i-1}[v_i]$
(since v_i was chosen because $d_{i-1}[v_i] \leq d_{i-1}[v]$ for all v not in S_{i-1})

But this is a contradiction since p was supposed to be a path of length less than $d_{i-1}[v_i]$. It follows that there is no shorter path from a to v_i than the S_{i-1}-special path corresponding to v_i. So $d_i[v_i]$ is the length of all shortest paths from a to v_i.

Thus (1) holds after the i-th iteration of the **for** loop.

(*b*) Now suppose w is a vertex not in $S_i = S_{i-1} \cup \{v_i\}$.
We recall that $d_i[w]$ is the smaller of $d_{i-1}[w]$ and $d_{i-1}[v_i]+W((v_i,w))$.
We want to show that the shortest length of any S_i-special path from a to w is $d_i[w]$.

There are two cases to consider: (*i*) there is a shortest S_i-special path from a to w not passing through v_i, (*ii*) all shortest S_i-special paths from a to w pass through v_i.

In case (*i*) any shortest S_i-special path p from a to w which does not pass through v_i is actually a shortest S_{i-1} special path from a to w and so has length $d_{i-1}[w]$. But in this case we have $d_i[w] = d_{i-1}[w]$; for if $d_{i-1}[v_i] + W((v_i,w)) < d_{i-1}[w]$ any shortest S_{i-1}-special path from a to v_i followed by the edge from v_i to w would be an S_i-special path from a to w shorter than p, which is impossible since p is a shortest such path.

In case (*ii*) let p be any shortest S_i-special path from a to w; by the hypothesis of case (*ii*) p must pass through v_i. We claim that v_i must be the last vertex on p which lies in S_i. If this is not the case let x be the last vertex on p which lies in S_i; since $x \neq v_i$ we must have $x \in S_{i-1}$. It follows that $d_{i-1}[x] \leq d_{i-1}[v_i]$ (otherwise v_i would have been adjoined to S_{i-1} before x). (See Figure 2.)

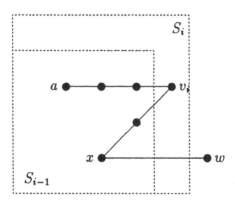

Figure 2

Now the total length of p

   = the length of the section of p from a to v_i
   + the length of the section of p from v_i to x
   + $W((x,w))$

Since p is a shortest S_i-special path from a to w, the section from a to v_i must be a shortest S_{i-1}-special path from a to v_i, so must have length $d_{i-1}[v_i]$. Thus we have

$$\text{Total length of } p > d_{i-1}[v_i] + W((x,w))$$
$$\geq d_{i-1}[x] + W((x,w))$$

i.e. we can produce an S_i-special path from a to w shorter than p by taking a shortest path to x followed by the edge from x to w.

So p has length $d_{i-1}[v_i] + W((v_i, w))$.

We claim that in this case we have $d_i[w] = d_{i-1}[v_i] + W((v_i, w))$. For, if we had $d_i[w] = d_{i-1}[w] < d_{i-1}[v_i] + W((v_i, w))$, we would have an S_{i-1}-special path from a to w shorter than p, which is not possible since, by the hypothesis of case (ii) all shortest S_i-special paths must pass through v_i.

We have thus shown in both cases (i) and (ii) that if w is a vertex not in S_i then $d_i[w]$ is the length of all shortest S_i-special paths from a to w, i.e. (2) holds after the i-th iteration of the **for** loop.

Since (1) and (2) hold before the first entry to the loop they hold on the first exit from the loop, which is the second entry; hence they hold on the second exit, which is the third entry, and so on until we reach the last exit, when all the vertices of the graph are in S. It follows that when the loop execution terminates $d[v]$ is the length of all shortest paths from a to v (for all vertices v other than the source), i.e. Dijkstra's algorithm works.

The reader may legitimately complain that all we have done so far is to find the *lengths* of all shortest paths from the source to the other vertices: we haven't actually produced the lists of vertices which form the shortest paths. We can do this by a simple modification of Dijkstra's algorithm. Namely, we introduce an array p indexed by the vertices other than the source and whose entries are vertices—what we have in mind is that if v is a vertex other than the source then $p[v]$ shall be the vertex immediately preceding v on the current shortest special path to v. We initialise p by setting $p[v] :=$ the source vertex for all vertices v other than the source. Then we would rewrite the Dijkstra **for** loop as follows:

```
for i := 1 to n − 1 do begin
        Choose a vertex v not in S for which d[v] is least;
        S := S ∪ {v};
        for each vertex w not in S do begin
                if d[v] + W((v, w)) < d[w] then begin
                        d[w] := d[v] + W((v, w));
                        p[w] := v end end;
```

It is then a simple programming exercise to produce the vertices in the shortest paths.

Dijkstra's algorithm is an example of a **greedy** algorithm. At each stage it makes what is currently the optimal choice, choosing for each vertex w not in S_i either the previously constructed shortest S_{i-1}-special path to w or else a new path going first to the newly added vertex v_i and then by the edge (v_i, w). This "greedy" strategy, proceeding in stages and making the best choice at each stage, cannot be guaranteed in every problem to produce a result which is best overall (see Exercise 1); but, as we have shown, it does succeed in the case of Dijkstra's algorithm.

We turn now to the fourth shortest path problem mentioned at the beginning of the section, the all pairs problem, that of finding for every ordered pair of vertices (a, b) a shortest path from a to b. We can certainly deal with this problem by applying Dijkstra's algorithm n times, using each of the n vertices in turn as source. There is, however, another way of dealing with the problem which gives an example of another interesting approach to algorithm construction. This is **Floyd's algorithm**. Like Dijkstra's algorithm this deals with a weighted digraph G in which all the weights are non-negative; we number the vertices from 1 to n.

Floyd's algorithm rests on the following simple observation: we consider a shortest path p from vertex i to vertex j and suppose that the intermediate vertex on this path with highest index is k. Then we easily convince ourselves that the section of p from i to k must be a shortest path from i to k having no intermediate vertex with index greater than $k - 1$ and the section of p from k to j must be a shortest path from k to j having no intermediate vertex greater than $k - 1$.

We begin by introducing an $n \times n$ matrix D whose entries are given by

$$D[i, j] := \begin{cases} W((i, j)) \text{ if } (i, j) \text{ is an edge of } G \\ \infty \text{ otherwise} \end{cases}$$

We now construct a sequence of matrices

$$D_0 = D, D_1, D_2, \ldots, D_n$$

where for $k = 1, 2, \ldots, n$ the entry $D_k[i, j]$ is the length of the shortest path from i to j having no intermediate vertex greater than k. Clearly the entries of D_n are the lengths of the absolutely shortest paths we are looking for.

We construct each matrix D_k ($k = 1, 2, \ldots, n$) from its predecessor D_{k-1} as follows.

Let us look at a shortest path from i to j which passes through no intermediate vertex greater than k: it is the length of such a path which is to appear as the matrix element $D_k[i, j]$. Two cases can occur. First, it may happen that the path we are considering has all its intermediate vertices less than k—so none is greater than $k - 1$. In this case we clearly have $D_k[i, j] = D_{k-1}[i, j]$. Alternatively, the path may pass through vertex k. In this case it is made up of two sections (a) a shortest path from i to k with no intermediate vertex greater than $k - 1$ followed by (b) a shortest path from k to j with no intermediate vertex greater than $k-1$. Thus in the second case its length is $D_k[i, j] = D_{k-1}[i, k] + D_{k-1}[k, j]$. Of course we don't know in advance which case will occur, but we can use D_{k-1} to calculate both possible lengths and then define

$$D_k[i, j] = \min\{D_{k-1}[i, j], D_{k-1}[i, k] + D_{k-1}[k, j]\}.$$

Notice that for each index i we have

$$D_k[i, k] = \min\{D_{k-1}[i, k], D_{k-1}[i, k] + D_{k-1}[k, k]\} = D_{k-1}[i, k]$$

and similarly for each index j we have

$$D_k[k, j] = \min\{D_{k-1}[k, j], D_{k-1}[k, k] + D_{k-1}[k, j]\} = D_{k-1}[k, j].$$

So as we move from D_{k-1} to D_k the k-th row and the k-th column are unchanged.

In programming Floyd's algorithm we need only a single matrix D declared as

Var D : **array** $[1 \mathinner{..} n, 1 \mathinner{..} n]$ **of real**;

(if the weights are real numbers) and initialised as described above. Then we carry out the triple loop

for $k := 1$ **to** n **do**
    for $i := 1$ **to** n **do**
        for $j := 1$ **to** n **do**
            $D[i,j] := \min\{D[i,j], D[i,k] + D[k,j]\};$

The final entries of D are the lengths of the required shortest paths.

(As we did in the case of Dijkstra's algorithm, we should consider replacing the last line by

$$\textbf{begin } r := D[i,k] + D[k,j];$$
$$\textbf{if } r < D[i,j] \textbf{ then } D[i,j] := r \textbf{ end;})$$

We illustrate Floyd's algorithm for the graph

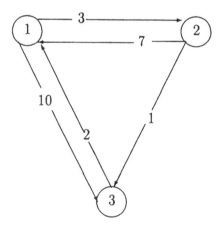

Here the initial version of the matrix D is

$$D = D_0 = \begin{bmatrix} 0 & 3 & 10 \\ 7 & 0 & 1 \\ 2 & \infty & 0 \end{bmatrix}$$

To form D_1 we have to make the assignments

$$D[i,j] := \min\{D[i,j], D[i,1] + D[1,j]\}.$$

As we saw above, the first row and first column remain unaltered; the diagonal entries $D[i, i]$ remain zero. So we compute

$$D[2, 3] := \min\{D[2, 3], D[2, 1] + D[1, 3]\} = \min\{1, 7 + 10\} = 1,$$
$$D[3, 2] := \min\{D[3, 2], D[3, 1] + D[1, 2]\} = \min\{\infty, 2 + 3\} = 5.$$

So we have

$$D = D_1 = \begin{bmatrix} 0 & 3 & 10 \\ 7 & 0 & 1 \\ 2 & 5 & 0 \end{bmatrix}$$

Now to form D_2 we make the assignments

$$D[i, j] := \min\{D[i, j], D[i, 2] + D[2, j]\}.$$

This time the second row and second column remain unchanged and the diagonal entries remain zero. We then compute

$$D[1, 3] := \min\{D[1, 3], D[1, 2] + D[2, 3]\} = \min\{10, 3 + 1\} = 4,$$
$$D[3, 1] := \min\{D[3, 1], D[3, 2] + D[2, 1]\} = \min\{2, 5 + 7\} = 2.$$

This gives

$$D = D_2 = \begin{bmatrix} 0 & 3 & 4 \\ 7 & 0 & 1 \\ 2 & 5 & 0 \end{bmatrix}$$

Finally we construct D_3 by making the assignments

$$D[i, j] := \min\{D[i, j], D[i, 3] + D[3, j]\}.$$

Here the third row and third column remain unaltered and the diagonal entries remain zero. So we calculate

$$D[1, 2] := \min\{D[1, 2], D[1, 3] + D[3, 2]\} = \min\{3, 4 + 5\} = 3,$$
$$D[2, 1] := \min\{D[2, 1], D[2, 3] + D[3, 1]\} = \min\{7, 1 + 2\} = 3.$$

So for each ordered pair (i, j) the length of the shortest paths from vertex i to vertex j is the (i, j)-th entry of

$$D = D_3 = \begin{bmatrix} 0 & 3 & 4 \\ 3 & 0 & 1 \\ 2 & 5 & 0 \end{bmatrix}$$

Like Dijkstra's algorithm, Floyd's may be modified to give the lists of vertices of the shortest paths, not just their lengths. We proceed by introducing a matrix P indexed by $1 .. n, 1 .. n$ whose entries are either 0 or vertices (and so are drawn from the range $0 .. n$). We initialise all the entries of P to 0. Then we amend Floyd's algorithm to read

for $k := 1$ **to** n **do**
    for $i := 1$ **to** n **do**
        for $j := 1$ **to** n **do**
            if $D[i, k] + D[k, j] < D[i, j]$ **then begin**
                $D[i, j] := D[i, k] + D[k, j]$;
                $P[i, j] := k$ **end**

Thus the current entry in $P[i, j]$ is the vertex of highest index on the current shortest path from i to j. To retrieve the list of vertices which constitute the shortest path from vertex v to vertex w we notice first that if $P(v, w) = 0$ then there are no intermediate vertices and the shortest path is the edge from v to w; but if $P[v, w] \neq 0$ we obtain the list of intermediate vertices by calling path(v, w) where path is the procedure defined as follows:

Procedure path $(i, j : 1 .. n)$;
Var $x : 0 .. n$;
Begin
    $x := P[i, j]$;
    if $x <> 0$ **then begin**
        path(i, x); Writeln (x); path(x, j) **end End**;

The next shortest path problem we consider has been traditionally known as the *Travelling Salesman Problem* and is often referred to as the TSP; but not all travelling salespeople are men, and this has led some authors to rename it the Travelling Sales*person* Problem. Unfortunately 'salesperson' is an unattractive word and so it is proposed here to call it the **Commercial Traveller Problem**. To describe the problem we are to think of a collection of customers all of whom the commercial traveller has to visit once each, using as little petrol, or taking the least time, or travelling the shortest distance possible. We naturally think of representing the customers by the vertices of a graph and the direct routes between the customers by its edges; to each edge we attach a number which is either the cost, the time or the distance involved in taking that route. So we reformulate the problem as follows. Let $G = (V, E)$ be a weighted digraph in which all the weights are non-negative; then the Commercial Traveller Problem is to find a tour of G of minimum cost, where by a **tour** of G we mean a cycle containing each vertex of G exactly once and the **cost** of the tour is the sum of the weights of all its edges.

Suppose $V = \{v_1, v_2, \ldots, v_n\}$.

We make the simple observation that if we have a cheapest tour starting and finishing at the vertex v_1 then, if the first edge is (v_1, v_k) the remainder of the tour must go from v_k back to v_1 passing through all the remaining vertices exactly once *and it must be the cheapest path to do so.*

For each index i $(1 \leq i \leq n)$ and each subset S of V we define $g(i, S)$ to be the cost of a cheapest path from v_i to v_1 passing exactly once through each of the vertices in S. Then the cost of a minimal cost tour of G starting and finishing at v_1 is $g(1, V \sim \{v_1\})$. To calculate this minimal cost we remark that if a cheapest tour starts with (v_1, v_k) then $g(1, V \sim \{v_1\}) = W((v_1, v_k)) + g(k, V \sim \{v_1, v_k\})$. Of course we don't know in advance which is the first edge; all we can say is that $g(1, V \sim \{v_1\})$ will be the minimum of all the $n - 1$ numbers $W((v_1, v_k)) + g(k, V \sim \{v_1, v_k\})$ for $k = 2, \ldots, n$. Thus if we could find $g(k, V \sim \{v_1, v_k\})$ for $k = 2, \ldots, n$ we would deduce at once the cost of the cheapest tour.

The same argument can be applied to show for every $i = 1, \ldots, n$ and every subset S of V that

$$g(i, S) = \min_{j \in S}\{W((v_i, v_j)) + g(j, S \sim \{v_j\})\} \quad \cdots \quad (*)$$

As a foundation for our calculations we remark that for each $i = 1, \ldots, n$ we have $g(i, \emptyset) =$ the cost of the cheapest path from v_i to v_1 passing through no intermediate vertex $= W((v_i, v_1))$.

To find the succession of vertices on the commercial traveller's tour all we have to do is to note at each stage along with the minimum $g(i, S)$ the index j which produces the minimum on the right hand side of the relation $(*)$.

To see how this line of attack works in practice we consider a digraph G with vertices numbered 1 to 5 whose adjacency matrix is

$$\begin{bmatrix} 0 & 4 & 3 & 5 & 8 \\ 3 & 0 & 5 & 5 & 4 \\ 5 & 4 & 0 & 8 & 5 \\ 2 & 7 & 5 & 0 & 5 \\ 7 & 4 & 9 & 4 & 0 \end{bmatrix}$$

Suppose we are looking for a shortest tour starting from and finishing at vertex 1.

For each vertex $i \neq 1$ we have

$$g(i, \emptyset) = \text{cost of cheapest path from } i \text{ to } 1 \text{ with no intermediate vertex}$$
$$= c_{i1}.$$

So

$$g(2, \emptyset) = c_{21} = 3,$$
$$g(3, \emptyset) = c_{31} = 5,$$
$$g(4, \emptyset) = c_{41} = 2,$$
$$g(5, \emptyset) = c_{51} = 7.$$

Next, for each $i \neq 1$ and each $k \neq 1, i$ we have

$$g(i, \{k\}) = \min_{j \in \{k\}}\{c_{ij} + g\{j, \emptyset\}\} = c_{ik} + g(k, \emptyset) = c_{ik} + c_{k1}.$$

So

$$g(2, \{3\}) = c_{23} + c_{31} = 5 + 5 = 10,$$
$$g(2, \{4\}) = c_{24} + c_{41} = 5 + 2 = 7,$$
$$g(2, \{5\}) = c_{25} + c_{51} = 4 + 7 = 11,$$
$$g(3, \{2\}) = c_{32} + c_{21} = 4 + 3 = 7,$$
$$g(3, \{4\}) = c_{34} + c_{41} = 8 + 2 = 10,$$
$$g(3, \{5\}) = c_{35} + c_{51} = 5 + 7 = 12,$$
$$g(4, \{2\}) = c_{42} + c_{21} = 7 + 3 = 10,$$
$$g(4, \{3\}) = c_{43} + c_{31} = 5 + 5 = 10,$$
$$g(4, \{5\}) = c_{45} + c_{51} = 5 + 7 = 12,$$
$$g(5, \{2\}) = c_{52} + c_{21} = 4 + 3 = 7,$$
$$g(5, \{3\}) = c_{53} + c_{31} = 9 + 5 = 14,$$
$$g(5, \{4\}) = c_{54} + c_{41} = 4 + 2 = 6.$$

Now for all appropriate i, j, k we have

$$g(i, \{j, k\}) = \min\{c_{ij} + g(j, \{k\}), c_{ik} + g(k, \{j\})\}.$$

Thus we have

$$g(2, \{3, 4\}) = \min\ \{c_{23} + g(3, \{4\}), c_{24} + g(4, \{3\})\}$$
$$= \min\ \{5 + 10, 5 + 10\} = 15,$$
$$\text{using either } 2 \to 3 \text{ or } 2 \to 4,$$
$$g(2, \{3, 5\}) = \min\ \{c_{23} + g(3, \{5\}), c_{25} + g(5, \{3\})\}$$
$$= \min\ \{5 + 12, 4 + 14\} = 17, \text{ using } 2 \to 3,$$
$$g(2, \{4, 5\}) = \min\ \{c_{24} + g(4, \{5\}), c_{25} + g(5, \{4\})\}$$
$$= \min\ \{5 + 12, 4 + 6\} = 10, \text{ using } 2 \to 5,$$
$$g(3, \{2, 4\}) = \min\ \{c_{32} + g(2, \{4\}), c_{34} + g(4, \{2\})\}$$
$$= \min\ \{4 + 7, 8 + 10\} = 11, \text{ using } 3 \to 2,$$
$$g(3, \{2, 5\}) = \min\ \{c_{32} + g(2, \{5\}), c_{35} + g(5, \{2\})\}$$
$$= \min\ \{4 + 11, 5 + 7\} = 12, \text{ using } 3 \to 5,$$
$$g(3, \{4, 5\}) = \min\ \{c_{34} + g(4, \{5\}), c_{35} + g(5, \{4\})\}$$
$$= \min\ \{8 + 12, 5 + 6\} = 11, \text{ using } 3 \to 5,$$
$$g(4, \{2, 3\}) = \min\ \{c_{42} + g(2, \{3\}), c_{43} + g(3, \{2\})\}$$
$$= \min\ \{7 + 10, 5 + 7\} = 12, \text{ using } 4 \to 3,$$
$$g(4, \{2, 5\}) = \min\ \{c_{42} + g(2, \{5\}), c_{45} + g(5, \{2\})\}$$
$$= \min\ \{7 + 11, 5 + 7\} = 12, \text{ using } 4 \to 5,$$

$$g(4, \{3,5\}) = \min \{c_{43} + g(3, \{5\}), c_{45} + g(5, \{3\})\}$$
$$= \min \{5 + 12, 5 + 14\} = 17, \text{ using } 4 \to 3,$$
$$g(5, \{2,3\}) = \min \{c_{52} + g(2, \{3\}), c_{53} + g(3, \{2\})\}$$
$$= \min \{4 + 10, 9 + 7\} = 14, \text{ using } 5 \to 2,$$
$$g(5, \{2,4\}) = \min \{c_{52} + g(2, \{4\}), c_{54} + g(4, \{2\})\}$$
$$= \min \{4 + 7, 4 + 10\} = 11, \text{ using } 5 \to 2,$$
$$g(5, \{3,4\}) = \min \{c_{53} + g(3, \{4\}), c_{54} + g(4, \{3\})\}$$
$$= \min \{9 + 10, 4 + 10\} = 14, \text{ using } 5 \to 4.$$

Next, for all appropriate i, j, k, l we have

$$g(i, \{j, k, l\}) = \min\{c_{ij} + g(j, \{k, l\}), c_{ik} + g(k, \{j, l\}), c_{il} + g(l, \{j, k\})\}.$$

So

$$g(2, \{3,4,5\}) = \min\{c_{23}+g(3, \{4,5\}), c_{24}+g(4, \{3,5\}), c_{25}+g(5, \{3,4\})\}$$
$$= \min\{5 + 11, 5 + 17, 4 + 14\} = 16, \text{ using } 2 \to 3,$$
$$g(3, \{2,4,5\}) = \min\{c_{32}+g(2, \{4,5\}), c_{34}+g(4, \{2,5\}), c_{35}+g(5, \{2,4\})\}$$
$$= \min\{4 + 10, 8 + 12, 5 + 11\} = 14, \text{ using } 3 \to 2,$$
$$g(4, \{2,3,5\}) = \min\{c_{42}+g(2, \{3,5\}), c_{43}+g(3, \{2,5\}), c_{45}+g(5, \{2,3\})\}$$
$$= \min\{7 + 17, 5 + 12, 5 + 14\} = 17, \text{ using } 4 \to 3,$$
$$g(5, \{2,3,4\}) = \min\{c_{52}+g(2, \{3,4\}), c_{53}+g(3, \{2,4\}), c_{54}+g(4, \{2,3\})\}$$
$$= \min\{4 + 15, 9 + 11, 4 + 12\} = 16, \text{ using } 5 \to 4.$$

Finally we have

$$g(1, \{2,3,4,5\}) = \min\{c_{12}+g(2, \{3,4,5\}), c_{13}+g(3, \{2,4,5\}),$$
$$c_{14}+g(4, \{2,3,5\}), c_{15}+g(5, \{2,3,4\})\}$$
$$= \min\{4 + 16, 3 + 14, 5 + 17, 8 + 16\}$$
$$= 17, \text{ using } 1 \to 3.$$

So the commercial traveller's tour is of length 17, going from 1 to 3 to 2 to 5 to 4 and back to 1.

To assess the complexity of the algorithm we have described for the solution of the Commercial Traveller Problem we count the number of comparisons involved in the calculation of the numbers $g(i, S)$. The index i can be chosen in $n - 1$ ways (it is one of the indices $2, 3, \dots, n$). For each choice of i the set S is a subset of $V \sim \{v_1, v_i\}$; the number of elements in S is thus between 0 and $n-2$ inclusive. For each such number k there are $\binom{n-2}{k}$ subsets with k elements.

If S has k elements with $k > 1$ the computation of $g(i, S)$, which involves finding the minimum of k numbers, requires $k-1$ comparisons. So the total number of comparisons for all possible subsets S of size k is $(k-1)\binom{n-2}{k}$. Thus for each $i = 2, 3, \ldots, n$ the number of comparisons for all subsets S of $V \sim \{v_1, v_i\}$ is

$$\sum_{k=1}^{n-2}(k-1)\binom{n-2}{k} = (n-4)2^{n-3} + 1 \ldots\ldots\ldots\ldots\ldots (1)$$

(See below for the justification of equation (1).) It follows that the total number of comparisons involved in calculating att the numbers $g(i, S)$ is

$$(n-1)\{(n-4)2^{n-3} + 1\}.$$

There are then a further $n-2$ comparisons involved in finding the number $g(1, V \sim \{v_1\})$. So the total number of comparisons is

$$(n-1)(n-4)2^{n-3} + 2n - 3$$

which is $O(n^2\, 2^n)$ and so very far from efficient; but at least it is better than the examination of all $n!$ possible tours.

To prove the result (1) above, we notice first that according to the binomial theorem we have

$$(1+X)^{n-2} = \sum_{k=0}^{n-2}\binom{n-2}{k}X^k.$$

So

$$\sum_{k=1}^{n-2}\binom{n-2}{k}X^k = (1+X)^{n-2} - 1 \ldots\ldots\ldots\ldots\ldots (2).$$

Setting $X = 1$ we have

$$\sum_{k=1}^{n-2}\binom{n-2}{k} = 2^{n-2} - 1 \ldots\ldots\ldots\ldots\ldots\ldots (3)$$

If we differentiate (2) we have

$$\sum_{k=1}^{n-2} k\binom{n-2}{k} X^{k-1} = (n-2)(1+X)^{n-3}$$

and putting $X = 1$ we have

$$\sum_{k=1}^{n-2} k\binom{n-2}{k} = (n-2)\, 2^{n-3}. \dots\dots\dots\dots\dots\dots\dots (4)$$

Subtracting (3) from (4) we obtain (1).

In introducing Floyd's algorithm we said that it offered another interesting approach to algorithm design, but we did not elaborate on this remark. Let us now consider the similarities between Floyd's algorithm and the algorithm we have just described for the Commercial Traveller Problem. Both problems are concerned with finding an *optimal* result—the shortest path between two vertices in a digraph, the cheapest tour of a digraph. In each case our thinking about the problem begins by asking a question to which we cannot immediately find the answer—we ask what is the largest index of the intermediate vertices on the shortest path from i to j and we ask what is the first vertex (after the starting vertex v_1) on a cheapest tour.

Although we don't know the answers to these questions we *do* know that if only an answer could be found then we would be able to solve our original optimisation problem provided we had the solution to a slightly simpler problem or problems of similar type. (If k were the intermediate vertex of highest index on a shortest path from i to j we would have to look for shortest paths from i to k and from k to j passing through no vertex with index greater than $k-1$; if v_k were the first vertex on a cheapest tour we would have to find a cheapest path from v_k back to the starting vertex passing through all the remaining vertices once only.)

The idea then is to find solutions to the simpler problem or problems corresponding to each possible answer to our original question—only one of them will be required as a constituent of the final solution, but we need to examine them all to decide which one it is. Of course the simpler problems are themselves of the same type and can be handled in the same way by finding optimal solutions to still simpler problems. We are thus led to a kind of 'bottom-up' approach in which we begin by noting the solutions to the very simplest problems (the shortest path from each vertex to every other passing through no intermediate vertex or the cheapest path from each vertex back to the starting vertex passing through no intermediate vertex) and we use these solutions to solve the second simplest and proceed in this way. Thus we build up a table of solutions to intermediate problems which lead eventually to a solution of the original problem.

This approach to algorithm design is known as **dynamic programming**; it may be tried in situations where the so-called *Optimality Principle* applies, that is when in an optimal sequence of decisions or choices each subsequence is also optimal.

8.2   Spanning tree algorithms

We begin with three definitions. First, a path

$$v_0, v_1, v_2, \ldots, v_k$$

(and, in particular, a cycle) in a graph is said to be **simple** if the vertices v_i are all distinct (except in the case of a cycle, where $v_0 = v_k$). Next, a graph is said to be **connected** if for all vertices v and w there is a simple path from v to w. Finally, a **tree** is a connected graph which has no simple cycle.

Although binary trees, which we met in Chapter 3, are defined in a completely different way, it is clear that our usual graphical representations of binary trees are trees in the sense we have just described.

We note two elementary facts about trees:

(1) If v and w are distinct vertices of a tree there is a unique simple path from v to w.

There is one such path because the tree is connected; if there were two, then the sequence formed by the first followed by the reverse of the second would be or would include a cycle.

(2) A tree with n vertices has $n - 1$ edges.

We think of building up the tree from one of its vertices: every time we add a new edge we must also add a new vertex (otherwise we would produce a cycle); so there must always be one more vertex than there are edges.

Let $G = (V, E)$ be a connected graph; a **spanning tree** of G is a tree whose vertex set is V and whose edge set is a subset of E—so it has all the vertices of G and just enough edges of G to form a tree. We may construct a spanning tree for a given connected graph by choosing a cycle and removing one of its edges, noting that after the removal we still have a connected graph; we then repeat the procedure with any cycle that remains, continuing until there are no cycles left. For example, starting with the connected graph

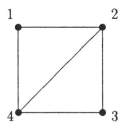

in which 1, 2, 3, 4, 1 is a cycle, we remove first the edge $\{1, 4\}$, obtaining

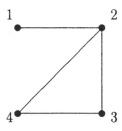

which is still connected but has a cycle 2, 3, 4, 2. If we remove the edge $\{3, 4\}$ from this cycle we obtain a spanning tree

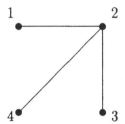

Now let $G = (V, E)$ be a weighted graph with n vertices and weight function W. The **cost** of a spanning tree is defined to be the sum of the weights of its edges; a **minimum spanning tree** is a spanning tree with cost as small as possible.

There are several algorithms for constructing minimum spanning trees for a given connected weighted graph. We are going to describe them as special cases of a general greedy method; having shown that the general method in fact succeeds in producing a minimum spanning tree we shall not need to verify separately that the special cases work.

The general method builds up a minimum spanning tree edge by edge, including appropriate low-weight edges and excluding appropriate high-weight edges. We maintain two changing subsets of E, the set of edges which are accepted, coloured blue, and those which are rejected, coloured red. Initially both sets are empty, i.e. there are no blue edges and no red edges. Thus we can certainly assert that, initially at any rate,

(∗) There is a minimum spanning tree of G which includes all the blue edges and none of the red edges.

We now carry out a sequence of colouring steps, each of which colours one edge, in such a way that (∗) holds after each step if it holds before (though the minimum spanning tree including all the blue edges may not be the same after the colouring step as it was before). Eventually, when all the edges are coloured, the blue edges actually form a minimum spanning tree; but since a tree with n vertices has $n - 1$ edges we need not complete the colouring of all the edges—we can stop as soon as $n - 1$ edges have been coloured blue.

We describe two procedures, called the *Blue Rule* and the *Red Rule*, and show that after each application of either of these Rules the property $(*)$ is maintained, i.e. if it holds before the application of the Rule then it also holds after.

Let X be a subset of the set V of vertices; we say that an edge $e = \{v, w\}$ **protrudes** (sticks out) from X if one of the ends v, w of e is in X and the other is not. Then the **Blue Rule** can be described as follows:

(1) Choose a non-empty subset X of V from which no blue edge protrudes;

(2) Among the uncoloured edges protruding from X choose one of minimum weight and colour it blue.

The **Red Rule** is

(1) Choose a simple cycle K which includes no red edge;

(2) Among the uncoloured edges of K choose one of maximum weight and colour it red.

The general greedy method consists in a non-deterministic sequence of applications of the Blue Rule and the Red Rule, i.e. applying either rule at any time in arbitrary order until $n - 1$ edges are coloured blue.

We notice that so long as at least one edge remains uncoloured at least one of the rules may be applied. (At each stage, since the blue edges are all included in a minimum spanning tree, they form a forest, which is a union of disjoint trees. Suppose there is an uncoloured edge e. If both ends of e lie in the same blue tree there is a path in that tree joining the ends of e; that path, together with e itself, constitutes a cycle K. The Red Rule can then be applied to K which has at least the uncoloured edge e. If the ends of e are in different blue trees then e is an uncoloured edge protruding from the set of vertices of one of them, T say; so the Blue Rule may be applied to T.)

Now we prove that if $(*)$ holds before an application of the Blue Rule then it also holds after the application.

Let T be a minimum spanning tree which, before the rule is applied, includes all the blue edges and none of the red edges of G.

Let X be a non-empty subset of V from which no blue edge protrudes; let e be an uncoloured edge of minimum weight protruding from X which, after the application of the Blue Rule, is coloured blue.

If e is one of the edges of the minimum spanning tree T then $(*)$ clearly holds after the application of the rule, with the same minimum spanning tree T.

So suppose e is not one of the edges of T. To fix the ideas, consider the graph below, taking X to consist of the vertices B, C, D, E and T to be the tree with edges AB, BC, BD, DE, DF; let the minimum weight uncoloured edge e protruding from X be EF.

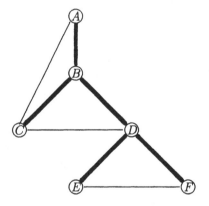

There is certainly a path in T joining the ends of e (in the graph shown this is the path E, D, F); one of the edges of this path must protrude from X—call it e' (in the graph below, e' is the edge DF). Since e' is an edge of the tree T which contains no red edge, e' is not coloured red; since no blue edge protrudes from X and e' protrudes from X, it follows that e' is not coloured blue. So e' is uncoloured. But e was chosen to be an uncoloured edge of least weight protruding from X; so $W(e') \geq W(e)$. Let T' be the tree obtained from T when we replace e' by e (so T' has edges AB, BC, BD, DE, EF). Then the cost of $T' =$ the cost of $T + W(e) - W(e') \leq$ the cost of T. Since T is a minimum spanning tree we must have the cost of $T' =$ the cost of T.

So T' is a minimum spanning tree which, after the application of the Blue Rule, includes all the blue edges and none of the red edges.

Next we prove that if (∗) holds before an application of the Red Rule then it also holds after the application.

Again let T be a minimum spanning tree which, before the rule is applied, includes all the blue edges and none of the red edges of G.

Let K be a simple cycle which includes no red edge; let e be an uncoloured edge of maximum weight included in K which, after the application of the Red Rule, is coloured red.

If e is not one of the edges of the minimum spanning tree T then (∗) clearly holds after the application of the rule, with the same minimum spanning tree T.

So suppose e is one of the edges of T. Consider again, for example, the graph above, with T as before the tree with edges AB, BC, BD, DE, DF; let K be the cycle A, C, D, B, A and suppose that the maximum weight uncoloured edge e in K is BD. When we remove the edge e from T we are left with two subtrees T_1 and T_2 (in the example T_1 has edges AB, BC and T_2 has edges DE and DF). The cycle K must include another edge which has one end in T_1 and the other in T_2; call it e' (in our example graph e' is CD). By hypothesis, T contains all the blue edges; so, since e' is not an edge of T, it follows that e' is not coloured blue. Since K includes no red edge, e' is not coloured red. Hence e' is uncoloured. But e was chosen to be an uncoloured edge of greatest weight in K; so $W(e') \leq W(e)$. Let T' be the tree formed from T_1, T_2 and the edge e' (so, in the example, T' has edges AB, BC, CD, DE, DF). Then we see that

$$
\begin{aligned}
\text{cost of } T' \;&=\; \text{cost of } T_1 + W(e') + \text{cost of } T_2 \\
&\leq\; \text{cost of } T_1 + W(e) + \text{cost of } T_2 \\
&=\; \text{cost of } T.
\end{aligned}
$$

Since T is a minimum spanning tree we must have the cost of $T' =$ the cost of T.

So T' is a minimum spanning tree which, after the application of the Red Rule, includes all the blue edges and none of the red edges.

We now describe three special applications of the general greedy method for constructing minimum spanning trees.

1. **Borůvka's algorithm.** Let G be a weighted graph with n vertices in which the weights of the edges are all distinct.

We work with a changing collection **F** of blue trees, initialised to consist of n single-vertex trees. Then, until **F** consists of a single blue tree, we repeat the following instructions:

For each tree in **F** we determine the edge of minimum weight protruding from it. Some of these minimum edges may be repeated (they may be edges of minimum weight protruding from both trees containing their end points). Let $\mathbf{F}_1$ be a subset of **F** containing enough of the trees in **F** to account for each of these minimum weight edges exactly once. Apply the Blue Rule to the sets of vertices of each of the trees in $\mathbf{F}_1$, so colouring blue the minimum weight edges. Let **F** now become the collection of trees obtained after this colouring.

The final single blue tree is the required minimum spanning tree.

To illustrate how this works, consider the graph

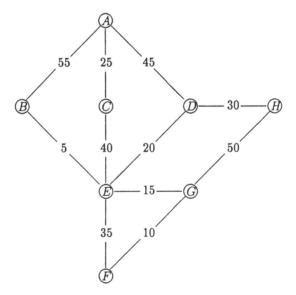

Initially **F** consists of 8 single-node trees, $(\{A\}, \emptyset), \ldots, (\{H\}, \emptyset)$.

Minimum weight edge from $(\{A\},\emptyset)$ is AC of length 25;
Minimum weight edge from $(\{B\},\emptyset)$ is BE of length 5;
Minimum weight edge from $(\{C\},\emptyset)$ is CA of length 25;
Minimum weight edge from $(\{D\},\emptyset)$ is DE of length 20;
Minimum weight edge from $(\{E\},\emptyset)$ is EB of length 5;
Minimum weight edge from $(\{F\},\emptyset)$ is FG of length 10;
Minimum weight edge from $(\{G\},\emptyset)$ is GF of length 10;
Minimum weight edge from $(\{H\},\emptyset)$ is HD of length 30;

Since $AC = CA$, $BE = EB$, $FG = GF$ each appear twice, we take $\mathbf{F_1}$ to consist of the 5 single-node trees $(\{A\},\emptyset)$, $(\{B\},\emptyset)$, $(\{D\},\emptyset)$, $(\{F\},\emptyset)$, $(\{H\},\emptyset)$ and apply the Blue Rule to their vertex sets, colouring AC, BE, DE, FG and HD blue.

$\mathbf{F}$ now consists of the three blue trees

$T_1 = (\{A,C\},\{AC\}),$
$T_2 = (\{B,E,D,H\},\{BE,ED,DH\}),$
$T_3 = (\{F,G\},\{FG\}),$

whose edges are shown as solid bold lines in the diagram:

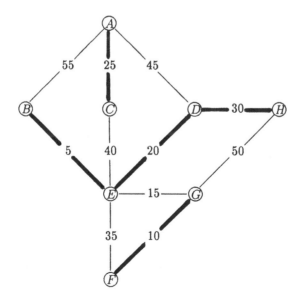

Now we see that

Minimum weight edge from T_1 is CE of length 40,
Minimum weight edge from T_2 is EG of length 15,
Minimum weight edge from T_3 is GE of length 15.

Since $EG = GE$ occurs twice we take $\mathbf{F}_1$ to consist of T_1 and T_2 and apply the Blue Rule to their vertex sets, colouring CE and EG blue.

We now have $\mathbf{F}$ consisting of a single blue tree, consisting of the bold edges in the diagram

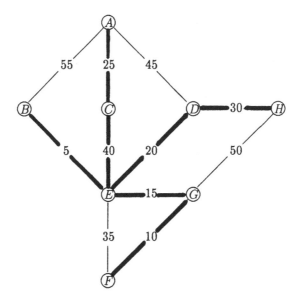

This tree, with edges AC, BE, CE, ED, EG, FG and DH is a minimum spanning tree; the total cost is 145.

2. **Kruskal's algorithm.** The first move in applying Kruskal's algorithm is to arrange the edges of the graph in non-decreasing order of weight (length); so suppose we have ordered the edges $e_1, e_2, \ldots, e_m$ so that $W(e_1) \leq W(e_2) \leq \ldots \leq W(e_m)$. As in Borůvka's algorithm we work with a changing colection $\mathbf{F}$ of blue subtrees, initialised to consist of n single-vertex trees with no edges. We then examine in turn each of the edges e_i (which are originally uncoloured). Two cases can arise:

(a) If both ends of the edge e currently under consideration are in the same blue tree T there is a path in T joining its endpoints; this path, together with e constitutes a cycle K which includes no red edge. Since e is the only uncoloured edge of K it is an uncoloured edge of maximum weight; so we may apply the Red Rule to K and colour e red.

(b) If the ends of e are in different blue trees T_1 and T_2 then no blue edge protrudes from the set V_1 of vertices of T_1 and e is an uncoloured edge of minimum weight protruding from V_1 (since all edges of weight less than e have already been coloured). So we may apply the Blue Rule to V_1 and colour e blue.

We continue until $n - 1$ edges have been coloured blue; these blue edges then make up a minimum spanning tree.

We can summarise Kruskal's algorithm as follows:

> Start with n single-vertex blue trees;
> $i := 1$;
> **Repeat**
> > if both ends of e_i are in the same blue tree
> > > **then** colour e_i red
> > > **else** colour e_i blue;
> > $i := i + 1$
> **until** there are $n - 1$ blue edges;

We illustrate the application of Kruskal's algorithm using the same graph as before. We shall use solid bold lines to represent blue edges and dotted bold lines to represent red edges.

The edges in non-decreasing order of weight are

$$BE\ (5),\ FG\ (10),\ EG\ (15),\ ED\ (20),\ AC\ (25),\ DH\ (30),$$
$$EF\ (35),\ CE\ (40),\ AD\ (45),\ GH\ (50),\ AB\ (55).$$

Initially there are 8 single-node blue trees:

$$(\{A\}, \emptyset),\ (\{B\}, \emptyset),\ \ldots,\ (\{H\}, \emptyset)$$

BE has its endpoints in two different blue trees; so colour it blue. We obtain

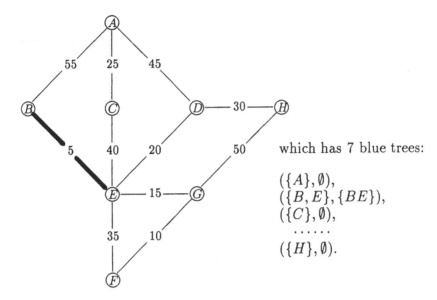

which has 7 blue trees:

$(\{A\}, \emptyset)$,
$(\{B, E\}, \{BE\})$,
$(\{C\}, \emptyset)$,
. . . . . .
$(\{H\}, \emptyset)$.

FG has its endpoints in two different blue trees; so we colour it blue and obtain

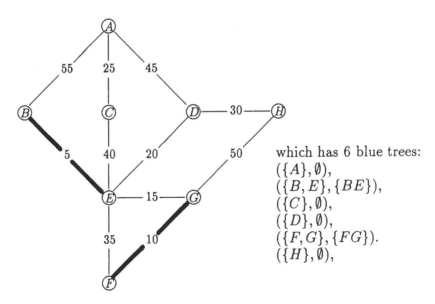

which has 6 blue trees:
$(\{A\}, \emptyset)$,
$(\{B, E\}, \{BE\})$,
$(\{C\}, \emptyset)$,
$(\{D\}, \emptyset)$,
$(\{F, G\}, \{FG\})$.
$(\{H\}, \emptyset)$,

EG has its endpoints in two different blue trees; we colour it blue, obtaining

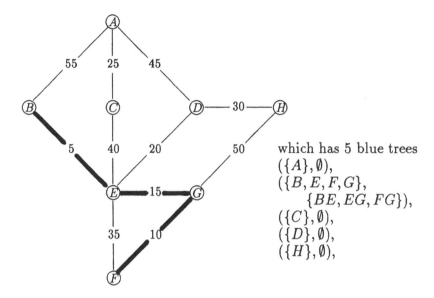

which has 5 blue trees
$(\{A\}, \emptyset)$,
$(\{B, E, F, G\}$,
   $\{BE, EG, FG\})$,
$(\{C\}, \emptyset)$,
$(\{D\}, \emptyset)$,
$(\{H\}, \emptyset)$,

ED has its endpoints in two different blue trees; we colour it blue and obtain

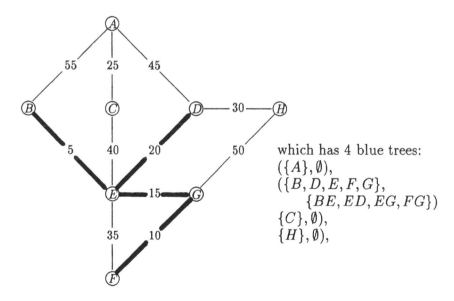

which has 4 blue trees:
$(\{A\}, \emptyset)$,
$(\{B, D, E, F, G\}$,
   $\{BE, ED, EG, FG\})$
$\{C\}, \emptyset)$,
$\{H\}, \emptyset)$,

AC has its endpoints in two different blue trees; we colour it blue, getting

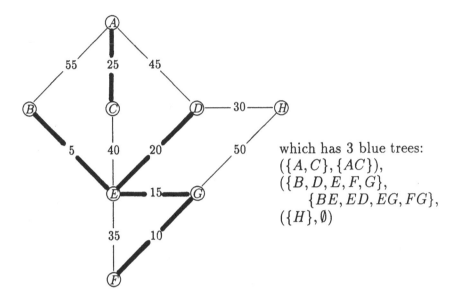

which has 3 blue trees:
$(\{A,C\},\{AC\})$,
$(\{B,D,E,F,G\}$,
　　　$\{BE,ED,EG,FG\})$,
$(\{H\},\emptyset)$

DH has its endpoints in two different blue trees; so we colour it blue and obtain

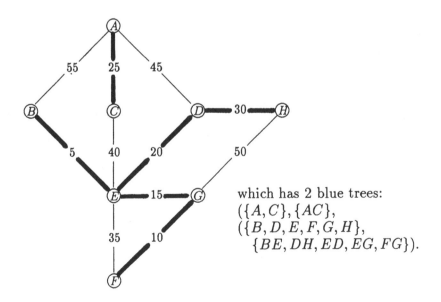

which has 2 blue trees:
$(\{A,C\},\{AC\}$,
$(\{B,D,E,F,G,H\}$,
　　　$\{BE,DH,ED,EG,FG\})$.

EF has its ends in the same blue tree; we colour it red and obtain

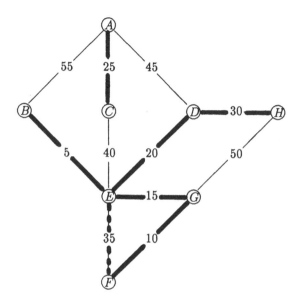

CE has its endpoints in two different blue trees; we colour it blue.
and obtain

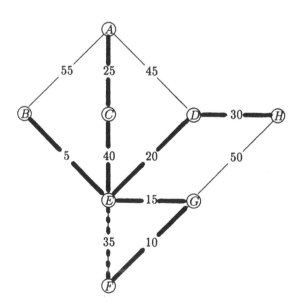

We now have a single blue tree, with edges

$$AC, BE, CE, DH, ED, EG, FG$$

which is a minimum spanning tree.

3. **Prim's algorithm** starts with an arbitrarily chosen initial vertex and proceeds to build up a minimum spanning tree one edge at a time. We start with a one-vertex blue tree T consisting of the initial vertex. Then we execute the following loop:

> **for** $i := 1$ **to** n **do begin**
> Apply the Blue Rule to the set of vertices of T;
> $T := T \cup \{$the new blue edge$\}$ **end**;

To implement Prim's algorithm we may proceed by maintaining a list of all the uncoloured edges protruding from the current version of the tree T and at each stage adjoining to T a protruding uncoloured edge of least weight. We have to be careful about the list of protruding edges. When first we think of adding an edge e to the list, e has one endpoint in T and the other, v say, not in T. At the same stage or at some later stage another protruding edge e' with the same endpoint v not in T may be a candidate for inclusion in the list; we notice that e and e' together with the path in T joining their endpoints in T form a cycle K with no red edge; we should apply the Red Rule to K.

To see how this works we examine again the same graph as before, taking A as initial vertex.

At the first stage we have $T = (\{A\}, \emptyset)$.

1. The edges protruding from T are AB (55), AC (25), AD (45). These are all uncoloured. Applying the Blue Rule to $\{A\}$ we colour AC blue and obtain

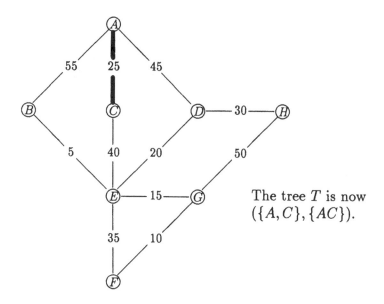

The tree T is now
$(\{A, C\}, \{AC\})$.

2. The edges protruding from T are AB (55), AD (45) as before and CE (40). These are all uncoloured and no two of them have the same endpoint. Applying the Blue Rule to $\{A, C\}$ we colour CE blue; this produces

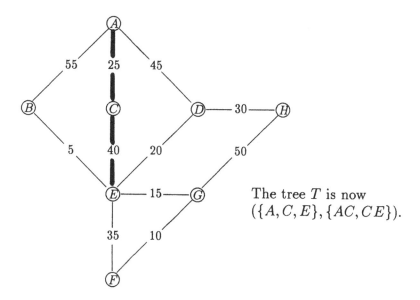

The tree T is now
$(\{A, C, E\}, \{AC, CE\})$.

3. The edges protruding from T are AB (55), AD (45) as before and EB (5), ED (20), EF (35) and EG (15). These are all uncoloured, but AB and EB have the same endpoint B outside T and AD and ED have the same endpoint D outside T. We apply the Red Rule to the cycles A, C, E, B, A and A, C, E, D, A, coloring AB and AD red. The uncoloured edges protruding from $\{A, C, E\}$ are now EB (5), ED (20), EF (35) and EG (15). Applying the Blue Rule to $\{A, C, E\}$ we colour EB blue. We have now reached the situation

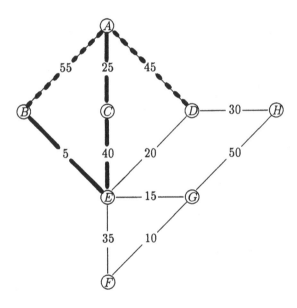

The tree T is now $\{A, B, C, E\}, \{AC, CE, EB\})$.

4. The edges protruding from T are AD, which has been coloured red, and ED (20), EF (35) and EG (15) which are still uncoloured. Applying the Blue Rule to $\{A, B, C, E\}$ we colour EG blue, obtaining

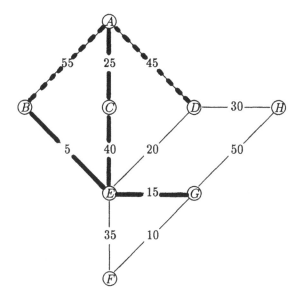

The tree T is now $(\{A, B, C, E, G\}, \{AC, CE, EB, EG\})$.

5. The protruding edges are AD, which is red, and ED (20), EF (35), GF (10) and GH (50) which are all uncoloured. Since EF and GF have the same endpoint F outside T we apply the Red Rule to the cycle E, G, F, E and colour EF red. The uncoloured edges protruding from $\{A, B, C, E, G\}$) are now ED (20), GF (10) and GH (50). Applying the Blue Rule to $\{A, B, C, E, G\}$ we colour GF blue. The resulting situation is

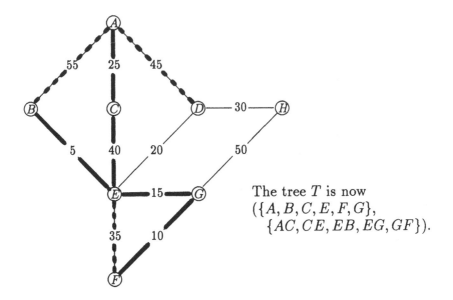

The tree T is now
($\{A, B, C, E, F, G\}$,
    $\{AC, CE, EB, EG, GF\}$).

6. The edges protruding from T are AD, which is red, ED (20) and GH (50), which are still uncoloured. Applying the Blue Rule to $\{A, B, C, E, F, G\}$ we colour ED blue and obtain

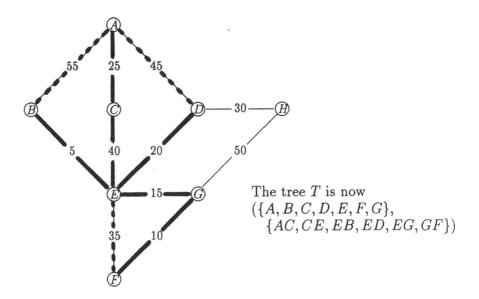

The tree T is now
($\{A, B, C, D, E, F, G\}$,
    $\{AC, CE, EB, ED, EG, GF\}$)

7. The protruding edges are GH and DH (30) which are uncoloured. They both have the same end point H outside T. We apply the Red Rule to the cycle E, D, H, G, E and colour GH red. Finally we apply the Blue Rule to $\{A, B, C, D, E, F, G\}$ and colour DH blue, obtaining finally

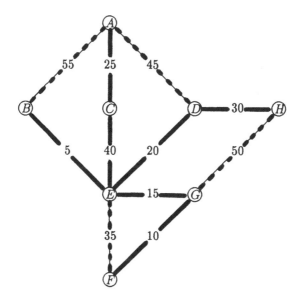

So we end up with a minimum spanning tree with edges AC, CE, EB, ED, EG, GF, DH and cost 145.

8.3 Exercises 8

1. Suppose we have a currency system having coins of (integer) values $a_1, a_2, \ldots, a_n$ where $a_1 > a_2 > \ldots > a_n \geq 1$. Consider the problem of finding a collection of coins of these denominations having total value a given integer A in such a way that the total number of coins is least. (We have to find integers $k_1, k_2, \ldots, k_n$ such that

$$k_1 a_1 + k_2 a_2 + \ldots + k_n a_n = A$$

and $k_1 + k_2 + \ldots + k_n$ is least.)

Suggest a greedy algorithm to solve this problem and show that it does not work in the case where $a_1 = 11$, $a_2 = 5$ and $a_3 = 1$ when $A = 15$.

2. Apply Dijkstra's algorithm to find the shortest paths (lists of vertices and lengths) from A to the other vertices of the digraph

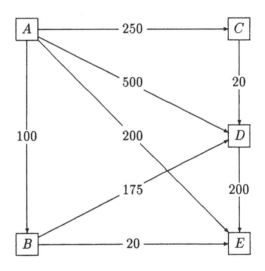

3. Discuss the complexity of Dijkstra's algorithm.

4. Use Floyd's algorithm to find the shortest paths between all ordered pairs of vertices in the digraph with adjacency matrix

$$\begin{bmatrix} 0 & 90 & 100 & 70 \\ 40 & 0 & 5 & 10 \\ 7 & \infty & 0 & 4 \\ 20 & 10 & 7 & 0 \end{bmatrix}$$

5. Discuss the complexity of Floyd's algorithm.

6. Solve the Commercial Traveller Problem for the graph with adjacency matrix

$$\begin{bmatrix} 0 & 3 & 7 & 4 & 2 \\ 3 & 0 & 3 & 4 & 6 \\ 7 & 3 & 0 & 8 & 6 \\ 4 & 4 & 8 & 0 & 5 \\ 2 & 6 & 6 & 5 & 0 \end{bmatrix}$$

7. Using the three algorithms described in this section find a minimum spanning tree for the graph

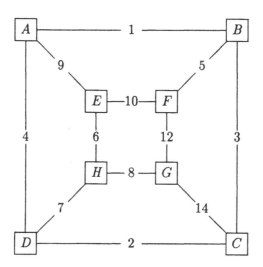

8. Given a digraph whose adjacency matrix has **boolean** entries, use the idea of dynamic programming, as in Floyd's algorithm, to determine for each ordered pair of vertices (a, b) whether there exists a path in the graph from a to b.

Chapter 9

SOME MISCELLANEOUS ALGORITHMS

9.1 Numerical multiplication algorithms

Suppose we represent the integers to be multiplied using the base b. There are two basic operations involved when we carry out the multiplication of two integers, namely addition and multiplication of single-digit numbers; each of these operations produces two single-digit results, a 'units' digit and a 'carry' digit.

Let x and y be integers which require n digits to represent them using base b.

Old-fashioned "long multiplication" which used to be taught in primary schools involves forming the product of each digit in the multiplicand (the number which is to be multiplied) by every digit in the multiplier; so there are in all n^2 single-digit multiplications involved. In addition there are n^2 single-digit additions of the form

(carry digit from previous multiplication) + (units digit of current multiplication).

Finally there are several multi-digit additions.

In several books on recreational mathematics we find a method for multiplying integers which is sometimes called **old Russian**

multiplication but is also attributed to various primitive peoples. In this method we make two columns of numbers, one under the multiplicand x and the other under the multiplier y. Then we follow the instructions

> **Repeat**
> > Double the entry in the multiplicand column;
> > Halve the entry in the multiplier column (ignoring fractions)
> **until** the entry in the multiplier column is 1;
> Add the entries in the multiplicand column which correspond to

odd entries in the multiplier column;

For example, to multiply 68 by 97 (using base 10) we have

68	97
136	48
272	24
544	12
1088	6
2176	3
4352	1

Adding 68, 2176 and 4352 corresponding to the odd entries 97, 3 and 1 we obtain the product 6596.

Any mystery there may be about how this works is dispelled at once when we carry it out using binary notation.

We turn now to a method of multiplying integers due to three Russian mathematicians, Karatusba, Ofman and Toom, which we shall describe as **new Russian multiplication**.

Again let x and y be integers which require n digits for their representation using base b and suppose that n is even, say $n = 2k$. Then we may write

$$x = x_1 b^k + x_0 \text{ and } y = y_1 b^k + y_0$$

where x_0, x_1, y_0 and y_1 are integers which can be represented using base b with at most k digits; suppose we use exactly k digits by "padding" with zeros to the left if necessary. Now the product $z = xy$ can be written as

$$z = (x_1 y_1) b^{2k} + (x_1 y_0 + x_0 y_1) b^k + (x_0 y_0)$$

which appears to require four multiplications of k-digit numbers. But consider the equation

$$x_1 y_0 + x_0 y_1 = (x_0 - x_1)(y_1 - y_0) + x_0 y_0 + x_1 y_1$$

From this we deduce that we can obtain the product $z = xy$ by means of

3 multiplications of k-digit numbers ($x_0 y_0$, $x_1 y_1$, $(x_0 - x_1)(y_1 - y_0)$);
2 subtractions of k-digit numbers ($x_0 - x_1$ and $y_1 - y_0$);
2 additions of n-digit numbers ($(x_0 - x_1)(y_1 - y_0) + x_0 y_0 + x_1 y_1$);
addition of $(x_1 y_1) b^{2k} + (x_1 y_0 + x_0 y_1) b^k + (x_0 y_0)$.

For example, if $x = 68$ and $y = 97$ (using base 10) then we have

$$x_1 = 6, \; x_0 = 8, \; y_1 = 9, \; y_0 = 7;$$
$$x_0 - x_1 = 2, \; y_1 - y_0 = 2;$$
$$(x_0 - x_1)(y_1 - y_0) + x_0 y_0 + x_1 y_1 = 2 \times 2 + 8 \times 7 + 6 \times 9 = 114.$$

Then

$$z = xy = (x_1 y_1) \times 100 + ((x_0 - x_1)(y_1 - y_0) + x_0 y_0 + x_1 y_1) \times 10 + x_0 y_0$$
$$= 54 \times 100 + 114 \times 10 + 56 = 6596 \text{ as before.}$$

We have shown how to produce the product of two n-digit numbers, where $n = 2k$ by means of

3 k-digit multiplications and
4n basic addition operations

where a "basic addition operation" is an addition or subtraction of two single-digit integers with the possibility of a "carry" or a "borrow".

We can then use the same procedure to calculate the three k-digit products. For simplicity let us assume that $n = 2^s$ (we can always achieve this by padding to the left with zeros). Then multiplication of two n-digit numbers requires

4.2^s basic addition operations
$\qquad + 3(4.2^{s-1}$ basic additions
$\qquad\qquad\qquad + 3$ multiplications of 2^{s-2}-digit numbers)

$\qquad = (4.2^s + 3.4.2^{s-1})$ basic additions
$\qquad + 3^2(4.2^{s-2}$ basic additions
$\qquad\qquad\qquad + 3$ multiplications of 2^{s-3}-digit numbers)

$\qquad = \cdots \cdots$

$\qquad = (\text{eventually}) \ (4.2^s + 3.4.2^{s-1} + 3^2.4.2^{s-2} + \ldots + 3^{s-1}.4.2)$ basic
$\qquad\qquad$ additions $+ \ 3^s$ single-digit multiplications

$\qquad = 8(3^s - 2^s)$ basic additions $+ \ 3^s$ single-digit multiplications.

So we have a method for multiplying two n-digit numbers which requires

$$3^s = 3^{\log_2 n} = n^{\log_2 3} \approx n^{1.58}$$

and at most $8\,n^{\log_2 3}$ basic additions.

9.2   Matrix multiplication algorithms

In this section we are concerned with matrices whose entries are numbers. We recall that a matrix with m rows and n columns is called an $m \times n$ matrix and that if A is such a matrix then the element in the ith row and jth column is denoted by a_{ij} $(i = 1, \ldots, m;\ j = 1, \ldots, n)$. The product AB of two matrices A and B is defined only when the number of columns of A is the same as the number of rows of B (so the row length of A is the same as the column length of B). If A is an

$m \times n$ matrix and B is an $n \times p$ matrix then their product $C = AB$ is defined to be the $m \times p$ matrix given by

$$c_{ij} = a_{i1}b_{1j} + a_{i2}b_{2j} + \ldots + a_{in}b_{nj}$$

for $i = 1, \ldots, m$; $j = 1, \ldots, p$. We notice that what we have here is "row-by-column" multiplication—the (i, j)th entry of the product is obtained by multiplying the elements of the ith row of A in turn by the corresponding elements of the jth column of B and adding up the products.

We notice in particular that if A and B are the 2×2 matrices

$$A = \begin{bmatrix} a_{11} & a_{12} \\ a_{21} & a_{22} \end{bmatrix} \quad \text{and} \quad B = \begin{bmatrix} b_{11} & b_{12} \\ b_{21} & b_{22} \end{bmatrix}$$

then their product $C = AB$ is

$$\begin{bmatrix} a_{11}b_{11} + a_{12}b_{21} & a_{11}b_{12} + a_{12}b_{22} \\ a_{21}b_{11} + a_{22}b_{21} & a_{21}b_{12} + a_{22}b_{22} \end{bmatrix}$$

We return to the general case where A and B are $m \times n$ and $n \times p$ matrices respectively. Let r, s, t be integers such that $1 \le r < m$, $1 \le s < n$ and $1 \le t < p$. The entries in the first r rows and the first s columns of A constitute an $r \times s$ matrix which we call A_{11}; clearly the (i, j)th entry of $A_{11} = [A_{11}]_{ij} = a_{ij}$ $(i = 1, \ldots, r; j = 1, \ldots, s)$. The entries in the first r rows and columns $s + 1$ to n of A make up an $r \times (n - s)$ matrix A_{12} with elements $[A_{12}]_{ij} = a_{i,s+j}$ $(i = 1, \ldots, r; j = 1, \ldots, n-s)$. In the same way we have $(m-r) \times s$ and $(m-r) \times (n-s)$ matrices A_{21} and A_{22} for which $[A_{21}]_{ij} = a_{r+i,j}$ $(i = 1, \ldots, m - r; j = 1, \ldots, s)$ and $[A_{22}]_{ij} = a_{r+i,s+j}$ $(i = 1, \ldots, m - r; j = 1, \ldots, n - s)$. We say we have *partitioned* A as

$$A = \begin{bmatrix} A_{11} & A_{12} \\ A_{21} & A_{22} \end{bmatrix}$$

Let us also partition B as

$$B = \begin{bmatrix} B_{11} & B_{12} \\ B_{21} & B_{22} \end{bmatrix}$$

where $B_{11}, B_{12}, B_{21}, B_{22}$ are respectively $s \times t$, $s \times (p-t)$, $(n-s) \times t$, $(n-s) \times (p-t)$ matrices. Now let us also partition C as

$$C = \begin{bmatrix} C_{11} & C_{12} \\ C_{21} & C_{22} \end{bmatrix}$$

where $C_{11}, C_{12}, C_{21}, C_{22}$ are respectively $r \times t$, $r \times (p-t)$, $(m-r) \times t$, $(m-r) \times (p-t)$ matrices. We claim that

$$C_{ij} = A_{i1}B_{1j} + A_{i2}B_{2j} \ (i, j = 1, 2).$$

Writing this out in full we see that what we are saying is that

$$C_{11} = A_{11}B_{11} + A_{12}B_{21}, \quad C_{12} = A_{11}B_{12} + A_{12}B_{22},$$
$$C_{21} = A_{21}B_{11} + A_{22}B_{21}, \quad C_{22} = A_{21}B_{12} + A_{22}B_{22},$$

so that the submatrices of the partitioned form of C are obtained from the submatrices of A and B by multiplying and adding in the same way as we form the product of two 2×2 numerical matrices by multiplying and adding their numerical components.

To justify this statement we compare corresponding elements of each C_{ij} and the corresponding $A_{i1}B_{1j} + A_{i2}B_{2j}$. For example, consider the (μ, ν)th entry of C_{11} (where $1 \leq \mu \leq r$, $1 \leq \nu \leq t$): this entry is

$$\begin{aligned} c_{\mu,\nu} &= a_{\mu 1}b_{1\nu} + a_{\mu 2}b_{2\nu} + \ldots + a_{\mu n}b_{n\nu} \\ &= a_{\mu 1}b_{1\nu} + \ldots + a_{\mu s}b_{s\nu} + a_{\mu,s+1}b_{s+1,\nu} + \ldots + a_{\mu n}b_{n\nu} \\ &= [A_{11}]_{\mu 1}[B_{11}]_{1\nu} + \ldots + [A_{11}]_{\mu s}[B_{11}]_{s\nu} \\ &\qquad\qquad + [A_{12}]_{\mu 1}[B_{21}]_{1\nu} + \ldots + [A_{12}]_{\mu,n-s}[B_{21}]_{n-s,\nu} \\ &= [A_{11}B_{11}]_{\mu\nu} + [A_{12}B_{21}]_{\mu\nu} \\ &= [A_{11}B_{11} + A_{12}B_{21}]_{\mu\nu} \end{aligned}$$

So $C_{11} = A_{11}B_{11} + A_{12}B_{21}$ and the other three equalities above follow by similar arguments.

We now turn away from the multiplication of general rectangular matrices to consider the multiplication of *square* matrices. One consequence of our discussion of the multiplication of partitioned matrices is that in theoretical investigations of multiplication of square matrices we may restrict ourselves to products of $N \times N$ matrices where N is a power of 2. To see this, let A and B be $n \times n$ matrices where $2^m < n < 2^{m+1}$; then we may take $N = 2^{m+1}$, $p = n$, $q = N - n$ and define

$$A_1 = \begin{bmatrix} A & O_{pq} \\ O_{qp} & O_{qq} \end{bmatrix} \quad \text{and} \quad B_1 = \begin{bmatrix} B & O_{pq} \\ O_{qp} & O_{qq} \end{bmatrix}$$

where O_{ij} denotes the $i \times j$ matrix whose elements are all zero. Then if we know how to multiply square matrices whose size is a power of 2 we form the product $A_1 B_1$ and notice that according to our description of how to multiply partitioned matrices we have

$$A_1 B_1 = \begin{bmatrix} AB & O_{pq} \\ O_{qp} & O_{qq} \end{bmatrix}$$

so we can read off the desired product AB.

Now suppose we have a method for multiplying two numerical 2×2 matrices which involves in all M numerical multiplications—if we use the method of the definition we have $M = 8$. Then we can apply this method to produce a method for multiplying two $2^k \times 2^k$ matrices which involves M multiplications of $2^{k-1} \times 2^{k-1}$ matrices.

Let $T(n)$ be the number of numerical multiplications required to multiply two numerical $n \times n$ matrices where $n = 2^k$. Then we have

$$T(n) = M\, T(\tfrac{1}{2}n) = M^2\, T(\tfrac{1}{4}n) = \ldots = M^k\, T(1) = M^k$$

since $T(1) = 1$ (because to multiply two numerical 1×1 matrices we have simply to multiply their single elements).

If we write $M^k = n^\alpha$ we have $M^k = (2^k)^\alpha$ and so, taking logarithms to base 2 of both sides we obtain $k \log_2 M = \alpha k$ and hence eventually that $\alpha = \log_2 M$.

So we have $T(n) = n^{\log_2 M}$

For the algorithm which simply applies the definition of 2×2 matrix multiplication we have $M = 8$ and so $T(n) = n^3$. This is the same number of numerical multiplications as we need if we apply the definition

directly to the given matrices, so the recursive partitioning approach
has not led to any improvement (and the overheads of successive recursive calls will undoubtedly cause a deterioration in performance). But
consider two numerical 2×2 matrices

$$A = \begin{bmatrix} a_{11} & a_{12} \\ a_{21} & a_{22} \end{bmatrix} \quad \text{and} \quad B = \begin{bmatrix} b_{11} & b_{12} \\ b_{21} & b_{22} \end{bmatrix}$$

and compute the 7 numbers $q_1, \ldots, q_7$ given by

$$q_1 = (a_{11} + a_{22}) \times (b_{11} + b_{22})$$
$$q_2 = (a_{21} + a_{22}) \times b_{11}$$
$$q_3 = a_{11} \times (b_{12} - b_{22})$$
$$q_4 = a_{22} \times (-b_{11} + b_{21})$$
$$q_5 = (a_{11} + a_{12}) \times b_{22}$$
$$q_6 = (-a_{11} + a_{21}) \times (b_{11} + b_{12})$$
$$q_7 = (a_{12} - a_{22}) \times (b_{21} + b_{22})$$

(noticing that only 7 numerical multiplications are required to carry
out this computation). Then dedicated symbol-pushing reveals that

$$q_1 + q_4 - q_5 + q_7 = a_{11}b_{11} + a_{12}b_{21} = [AB]_{11}$$
$$q_3 + q_5 = a_{11}b_{12} + a_{12}b_{22} = [AB]_{12}$$
$$q_2 + q_4 = a_{21}b_{11} + a_{22}b_{21} = [AB]_{21}$$
$$q_1 - q_2 + q_3 + q_6 = a_{21}b_{12} + a_{22}b_{22} = [AB]_{22}$$

Thus we have succeeded in evaluating the product of two numerical
2×2 matrices using 7 numerical multiplications. It follows that if we
use this technique in the recursive partitioning approach to multiplying
$n \times n$ matrices then the number of numerical multiplications required
is $n^{\log_2 7} = n^{2.81}$ which is an improvement over n^3. The definition of
$q_1, \ldots, q_7$ and the discovery of their use in computing the elements of
AB are due to Strassen and the recursive partitioning method of matrix
multiplication based on them is often called **Strassen's algorithm.**

   As in the case of other recursive algorithms we have considered—
for example Quicksort and Mergesort—there comes a point at which
the cost of the "housekeeping" operations involved in implementing the
recursion outweighs the theoretical advantage of Strassen's algorithm.

Experience suggests that it is advisable to use ordinary matrix multiplication (i.e. as in the definition) for $n \times n$ matrices with $n \leq 128$ (n a power of 2).

The attentive reader may have noticed and complain that although Strassen's method for multiplying 2×2 matrices requires only 7 multiplications it needs 18 additions in contrast to the 4 in ordinary matrix multiplication. But a detailed analysis of Strassen's algorithm for $n \times n$ matrices shows that the number of additions is $O(n^{\log_2 7})$ whereas for ordinary matrix multiplication it is $O(n^3)$.

We turn now from the problem of multiplying two square matrices to that of multiplying a sequence of several rectangular matrices each of which after the first has the same number of rows as its predecessor has columns. (Here we are thinking of using ordinary matrix multiplication, not any more elaborate algorithm such as Strassen's.)

First of all let A, B, C be respectively $p \times q$, $q \times r$, $r \times s$ matrices with numerical entries. In order to form the $p \times r$ matrix product AB we have to carry out pqr numerical multiplications (for each of the pr entries of AB we have to multiply the q entries of a row of A by the corresponding entries of a column of B). Now consider the product of the sequence of three matrices ABC. Since we have defined multiplication only for products of two matrices we have to bracket ABC either as $(AB)C$ or $A(BC)$. It is shown in every book on linear algebra and matrix theory that both these ways of bracketing lead to the same final result (this is what is meant by saying that matrix multiplication is *associative*). But, although the results are the same, the effort involved in reaching them is usually not the same for the two ways of bracketing. To form the $p \times r$ matrix AB requires pqr numerical multiplications; then to multiply this $p \times r$ matrix by the $r \times s$ matrix C requires prs numerical multiplications. So to produce $(AB)C$ requires $pqr + prs$ numerical multiplications. In a similar way we deduce that to form $A(BC)$ requires $qrs + pqs$ numerical multiplications. For example, if $p = 3$, $q = 5$, $r = 7$ and $s = 10$ the calculation of $(AB)C$ requires $3 \times 5 \times 7 + 3 \times 7 \times 10 = 315$ numerical multiplications, while that of $A(BC)$ needs $5 \times 7 \times 10 + 3 \times 5 \times 10 = 500$ numerical multiplications.

It is a fairly easy exercise in the use of mathematical induction to deduce from the fact that $(AB)C = A(BC)$ for all matrices A, B, C for which these products can be formed that for all integers $n \geq 3$ and all sequences of n matrices A_1, A_2, ..., A_n of matrices of orders $d_0 \times d_1$, $d_1 \times d_2$, ..., $d_{n-1} \times d_n$ respectively all legitimate ways of bracketing $A_1 A_2 \ldots A_n$ produce the same final result. They will not, however, all involve the same amount of work; so we find ourselves asking the question: given a sequence of matrices whose product can be formed, which way of bracketing will require the smallest number of numerical multiplications? The naïve approach—examine all ways of bracketing the product and calculate for each the number of numerical multiplications required to carry out the corresponding evaluation—is not really practicable: it can be shown that the total number of ways of bracketing a product of n matrices is $\binom{2n-2}{n-1}/n$ and that is greater than $4^{n-1}/n(2n-1)$ which grows very fast as n increases.

We notice, however, that we are in a situation where the optimality principle applies, so that we may be able to use a dynamic programming approach. For suppose we have found an optimal bracketing of $A_1 A_2 \ldots A_n$, i.e. one which involves the least possible number of numerical multiplications; this must be of the form

(some bracketing of $A_1 \ldots A_i$)(some bracketing of $A_{i+1} \ldots A_n$)

where i is some index for which $1 \leq i < n$. Then it is clear that the bracketings of $A_1 \ldots A_i$ and $A_{i+1} \ldots A_n$ which occur must themselves be optimal (otherwise we could replace them by bracketings which needed fewer numerical multiplications; but this would reduce the number required to evaluate the complete product, which is supposed to be the minimum possible).

This discussion leads us to introduce the integers m_{ij} for all indices i, j such that $1 \leq i \leq j \leq n$, where m_{ij} is defined to be the minimum number of numerical multiplications required to evaluate the product $A_i A_{i+1} \ldots A_j$. Our aim, of course, is to evaluate m_{1n}.

If $i = j$, so that the sequence $A_i A_{i+1} \ldots A_j$ consists of a single matrix A_i, we need no numerical multiplication to evaluate the "product". Hence we have

$$m_{ii} = 0 \ (i = 1, \ldots, n).$$

If $j = i+1$ the sequence $A_i A_{i+1} \ldots A_j$ consists of the product $A_i A_{i+1}$ of a $d_{i-1} \times d_i$ matrix and a $d_i \times d_{i+1}$ matrix; so the number of numerical multiplications required is $d_{i-1} d_i d_{i+1}$. Hence

$$m_{i,i+1} = d_{i-1} d_i d_{i+1} \ (i = 1, \ldots, n-1).$$

We have now to find the numbers $m_{i,i+s}$ where $s \geq 2$. The optimal bracketing of $A_i A_{i+1} \ldots A_{i+s}$ must be of the form

(optimal bracketing of $A_i \ldots A_k$)(optimal bracketing of $A_{k+1} \ldots A_{i+s}$)

for some index k such that $i \leq k < i + s$. The number of numerical multiplications required to evaluate this product is m_{ik} (to produce the $d_{i-1} \times d_k$ matrix $A_i \ldots A_k$) $+ m_{k+1,i+s}$ (to produce the $d_k \times d_{i+s}$ matrix $A_{k+1} \ldots A_{i+s}$) $+ d_{i-1} d_k d_{i+s}$ (to multiply these matrices). We don't know which choice of index k produces the optimal bracketing, so we must compute this sum for all possible k and find the minimum. Thus we have

$$m_{i,i+s} = \min_{i \leq k < i+s} \{ m_{ik} + m_{k+1,i+s} + d_{i-1} d_k d_{i+s} \}$$

for each $i = 1, \ldots, n$ and each $s = 2, \ldots, n - i$.

To see how this works in practice let A, B, C, D, E be matrices of orders 13×5, 5×89, 89×3, 3×34, 34×10 respectively. Then, in the notation we have been using we have

$$A_1 = A, A_2 = B, A_3 = C, A_4 = D, A_5 = E$$

and

$$d_0 = 13, d_1 = 5, d_2 = 89, d_3 = 3, d_4 = 34, d_5 = 10.$$

Then we have

$$m_{11} = m_{22} = m_{33} = m_{44} = m_{55} = 0,$$

$$m_{12} = d_0 d_1 d_2 = 5785,$$
$$m_{23} = d_1 d_2 d_3 = 1335,$$
$$m_{34} = d_2 d_3 d_4 = 9078,$$
$$m_{45} = d_3 d_4 d_5 = 1020,$$

$$m_{13} = \min\{m_{11} + m_{23} + d_0 d_1 d_3, m_{12} + m_{33} + d_0 d_2 d_3\}$$
$$= \min\ \{0 + 1335 + 195, 5785 + 0 + 3471\} = 1530$$
$$\text{with optimal bracketing } A_1(A_2 A_3),$$

$$m_{24} = \min\{m_{22} + m_{34} + d_1 d_2 d_4, m_{23} + m_{44} + d_1 d_3 d_4\}$$
$$= \min\ \{0 + 9078 + 15130, 1335 + 0 + 510\} = 1845$$
$$\text{with optimal bracketing } (A_2 A_3) A_4,$$

$$m_{35} = \min\{m_{33} + m_{45} + d_2 d_3 d_5, m_{34} + m_{55} + d_2 d_4 d_5\}$$
$$= \min\ \{0 + 1020 + 2670, 9078 + 0 + 30260\} = 3690$$
$$\text{with optimal bracketing } A_3(A_4 A_5),$$

$$m_{14} = \min\{m_{11} + m_{24} + d_0 d_1 d_4, m_{12} + m_{34} + d_0 d_2 d_4, m_{13} + m_{44} + d_0 d_3 d_4\}$$
$$= \min\ \{0 + 1845 + 2210, 5785 + 9078 + 39338, 1530 + 0 + 1326\} = 2856$$
$$\text{with optimal bracketing}$$
$$\text{(optimal bracketing of } A_1 A_2 A_3) A_4$$
$$= (A_1(A_2 A_3)) A_4,$$

$$m_{24} = \min\{m_{22} + m_{35} + d_1 d_2 d_5, m_{23} + m_{45} + d_1 d_3 d_5, m_{24} + m_{55} + d_1 d_4 d_5\}$$
$$= \min\ \{0 + 3690 + 4450, 1335 + 1020 + 150, 1845 + 0 + 1700\} = 2505$$
$$\text{with optimal bracketing } (A_2 A_3)(A_4 A_5).$$

Finally

$$m_{15} = \min\{m_{11} + m_{25} + d_0 d_1 d_5, m_{12} + m_{35} + d_0 d_2 d_5,$$
$$m_{13} + m_{45} + d_0 d_3 d_5, m_{14} + m_{55} + d_0 d_4 d_5\}$$
$$= \min\ \{0 + 2505 + 650, 5785 + 3690 + 11570,$$
$$1530 + 1020 + 390, 2856 + 0 + 4420\}$$
$$= 2940$$
$$\text{with optimal bracketing}$$
$$\text{(optimal bracketing of } A_1 A_2 A_3)(A_4 A_5)$$
$$= (A_1(A_2 A_3))(A_4 A_5) = (A(BC))(DE).$$

To assess the complexity of this algorithm we may count the number of arithmetic operations involved in forming the various numbers m_{ij} or the number of comparisons required to find the various minima.

First we notice that to compute the $(n-1)$ numbers $m_{i,i+1}$ $(i = 1, \ldots, n-1)$ requires 2 multiplications for each, making a total of $2(n-1)$ multiplications. Next, for each $s = 2, \ldots, n-1$ there are $n-s$ numbers $m_{i,i+s}$, namely $m_{1,1+s}$, $m_{2,2+s}$, $\ldots$, $m_{n-s,n}$. Each of these is obtained by finding the minimum of the s numbers

$$m_{ik} + m_{k+1,i+s} + d_{i-1}d_k d_{i+s} \qquad (k = i, \ldots, i+s-1)$$

which involves making $(s-1)$ comparisons. To form the s numbers requires $2s$ additions and $2s$ multiplications.

Hence the total number of additions is

$$2\{2(n-2) + 3(n-3) + \ldots + (n-1)\} = \tfrac{1}{3}(n-1)(n-2)(n+3)$$

and the total number of multiplications is

$$2(n-1) + 2\{2(n-2) + 3(n-3) + \ldots + (n-1)\} = \tfrac{1}{3}(n^3 - n).$$

Finally the total number of comparisons is

$$(n-2)(1) + (n-3)(2) + \ldots + (1)(n-2) = \tfrac{1}{6}(n-2)(n-1)n.$$

So, however we count, the algorithm has complexity $O(n^3)$.

9.3 A stable marriage algorithm

In this section we consider the situation in which there are n men and n women and each of these $2n$ people has arranged the n members of the opposite sex in strictly decreasing order of preference as marriage partners. There are $n!$ ways in which these $2n$ people can contract n non-bigamous marriages. But not all of these $n!$ marriage arrangements will be stable, where by a **stable** marriage arrangement we mean one in which we do not have a man and a woman who are not married to each other but who both prefer each other to their present partners. (If α is married to A and β is married to B but α prefers B to his wife A and B prefers α to her husband β then α and B would at least consider breaking their present marriages and marrying each other.)

Consider, for example, three men α, β, γ and three women A, B, C whose orders of preference are indicated in the tables

	1	2	3
α	A	B	C
β	B	C	A
γ	C	A	B

	1	2	3
A	β	γ	α
B	γ	α	β
C	α	β	γ

There are six possible marriage arrangements, which we list as follows, using the genealogists' standard notation $\alpha = A$ to indicate that α is married to A:

$$(1) \quad \alpha = A, \quad \beta = B, \quad \gamma = C;$$
$$(2) \quad \alpha = A, \quad \beta = C, \quad \gamma = B;$$
$$(3) \quad \alpha = B, \quad \beta = A, \quad \gamma = C;$$
$$(4) \quad \alpha = B, \quad \beta = C, \quad \gamma = A;$$
$$(5) \quad \alpha = C, \quad \beta = A, \quad \gamma = B;$$
$$(6) \quad \alpha = C, \quad \beta = B, \quad \gamma = A.$$

It is easy to check that arrangements (1), (4) and (5) are stable, while the other arrangements are unstable—in (2) A prefers γ to α and γ prefers A to B; in (3) C prefers β to γ and β prefers C to A; in (6) B prefers α to β and α prefers B to C.

The question naturally arises whether there are always stable marriage arrangements and if so how do we obtain them. The answer to the first question is that no matter what the order of preferences of the participants there is always at least one stable arrangement and the answer to the second is provided by the **Gale-Shapley algorithm** which produces one such arrangement.

In order to describe this algorithm we agree that each of the $2n$ persons involved may be either *free, (temporarily) engaged* or *married*. It is important to be clear that in the context of the Gale-Shapley algorithm engagements are not the essentially final arrangements that they mostly are in real life; it might be nearer the mark when a woman A becomes engaged to a man α to say that A has put α on her string, hoping for a better offer.

The execution of the algorithm begins with all the men and all the women free. As the execution proceeds the men may alternate between being engaged and being free; but once a woman becomes engaged she always remains engaged, though (as we suggested above) possibly to different men at different stages. As we shall see, for a man each successive engagement is to a less attractive partner, while for a woman each successive engagement is to a more attractive partner.

The procedure is as follows.

1. Each man proposes to the women on his list in decreasing order of preference until he becomes engaged (i.e. is temporarily accepted).

2. When a woman who is free receives a proposal she must accept it and become engaged, though without necessarily committing herself to marriage.

3. When a woman who is already engaged receives a proposal she compares her current fiancé with the new proposer (who must be free at the time the proposal is made). If she prefers her current partner then she refuses the offer from her new suitor, who remains free; if she prefers her new suitor then she breaks her present engagement, setting her current fiancé free, and becomes engaged to her new suitor.

4. When a man becomes free as a result of a broken engagement he proceeds to make a proposal to the next woman on his list of preferences.

The execution of the algorithm terminates when everyone is engaged; then all the engaged couples are married and we shall show that the resulting marriage arrangement is stable.

We may summarise the algorithm in pseudo-Pascal as follows:

```
Begin
    Assign each person to be free;
    while not all men engaged
            (⋆ i.e. there is at least one man m free ⋆)
        do begin
            w := first woman on m's list to whom
                                he has not yet proposed;
```

> if w is free **then** m and w become engaged
>   **else if** w prefers m to her present fiancé m'
>   **then begin** m and w become engaged ;
> m' becomes free **end**;
>   **else** w rejects m who remains free **end**
> All the couples currently engaged are married
> **End;**

We notice first of all that the execution of this algorithm is bound to terminate.

To begin with, it is clear that no man can be rejected by all the women. To see this we remark that according to the provisions of the algorithm a woman may reject a man only if she is already engaged. So, if a man is rejected by the last woman on his list all n women must be engaged; but there are only $n-1$ other men for them to be engaged to, and since no man can be engaged to more than one woman, this is impossible.

Next, since each iteration of the **while** loop involves one proposal and no man proposes to the same woman twice there can be at most n^2 iterations of the **while** loop.

We now show that the marriage arrangement produced by the algorithm is actually stable.

To see this, let m be any one of the men; suppose that when the algorithm terminates m is married to w. Now it may happen that m prefers another woman w' to his wife w. If this is the case then w' must have been higher up m's preference list than w. So m must have proposed to w' before proposing to w *and been rejected* in favour of an offer which w' found more acceptable than m's. So, although m prefers w' to his wife, nevertheless w' does not prefer m to her husband. Thus there is no instability.

To see how the algorithm works in practice consider the case of four men α, β, γ, δ and four women A, B, C, D with preference tables

	1	2	3	4
α	A	B	C	D
β	A	B	C	D
γ	B	C	A	D
δ	C	A	B	D

	1	2	3	4
A	γ	δ	α	β
B	δ	α	β	γ
C	α	β	γ	δ
D	δ	γ	α	β

The Gale-Shapley algorithm proceeds as follows:

1. α proposes to his first choice A; since A is free she accepts his proposal—α and A are engaged.

2. β proposes to his first choice, who is also A; since A is already engaged to α and since she prefers α to β she refuses β's proposal.

3. β proposes to the second woman on his list, namely B; since B is free she accepts his proposal and β and B become engaged.

4. γ proposes to his first choice B; since B is engaged to β, whom she prefers to γ, she does not accept γ's proposal.

5. γ proposes to his second choice C; since C is free she accepts—so γ and C are engaged.

6. δ proposes to his first choice C; C is engaged to γ and she prefers γ to δ; so she rejects δ's proposal.

7. δ proposes to his second choice A; A is engaged to α but she prefers δ to α; so she accepts δ's proposal—δ and A are engaged and α becomes free.

8. α proposes to his second choice B; B is engaged to β but she prefers α to β—α and B become engaged and β becomes free.

9. β proposes to his third choice C; C is engaged to γ but she prefers β to γ—β and C are engaged and γ becomes free.

10. γ proposes to his third choice A; although A is engaged to δ she prefers γ to δ—γ and A are engaged and δ is free.

11. δ proposes to his third choice B; B is engaged to α but she prefers δ to α—δ and B become engaged and α is free.

12. α proposes to his third choice C; C is engaged to β but she prefers α to β—α and C are engaged and β is free.

13. β proposes to his fourth choice D; since D is free she accepts his proposal—β and D are engaged.

All the participants are now engaged; so four marriages are celebrated:

$$\alpha = C, \ \beta = D, \ \gamma = A, \ \delta = B.$$

Some readers may complain that the Gale-Shapley algorithm is biased in favour of men, since it is the men who do the proposing; others that it is biased in favour of women, since they may make temporary engagements and later break them. It should be clear, however, that the algorithm would produce a stable marriage arrangement equally well if we reversed the rôles of the men and the women, letting the women do the proposing and the men the "stringing". If we do this in the example above it takes seven steps to produce a stable matching. In this case we reach the same matching as before, but this is not always the case—for example, in the case of the three men and three women described at the start of this section, if the men do the proposing then the stable arrangement (1) results while if the women make the proposals we end up with the stable arrangement (5).

9.4   Exercises 9

1. Using both old Russian and new Russian multiplication find the product of the binary numbers

    10111001 and 10101110.

2. Do the same for the decimal numbers

372 and 219.

3. Find the minimum number of numerical multiplications required to evaluate the product $ABCD$ where A, B, C, D are numerical matrices of size 20×10, 10×5, 5×100, 100×8 respectively.

4. Write a Pascal program fragment which will produce not only the minimum number of numerical multiplications required to evaluate a product of numerical matrices but also the bracketing which produces this minimum number.

5. Suppose we have three men α, β, γ and three women A, B, C whose orders of preference are indicated in the tables

	1	2	3
α	C	B	A
β	A	C	B
γ	C	A	B

	1	2	3
A	β	γ	α
B	β	α	γ
C	β	α	γ

Which of the following marriage arrangements are stable:

$$(1) \quad \alpha = A, \quad \beta = B, \quad \gamma = C;$$
$$(2) \quad \alpha = C, \quad \beta = A, \quad \gamma = B;$$
$$(3) \quad \alpha = C, \quad \beta = B, \quad \gamma = A?$$

6. Find a stable marriage arrangement for the four men α, β, γ and δ and four women A, B, C and D whose preferences for each other are given in the following tables:

	1	2	3	4
α	C	B	D	A
β	B	A	C	D
γ	B	D	A	C
δ	C	A	D	B

	1	2	3	4
A	α	β	δ	γ
B	γ	α	δ	β
C	γ	β	δ	α
D	β	α	γ	δ

7. By considering the four men A, B, C, D whose preferences for one another as room-mates are given by the table

	1	2	3
A	B	C	D
B	C	A	D
C	A	B	D
D	A	B	C

show that it is not always possible to arrange $2n$ people into n couples without instability.

Part III

STORING AND SEARCHING

The title of D.E. Knuth's great volume *Sorting and searching* is so familiar to all computer scientists that the title of this chapter may appear to be a misprint. But this is not so—we have said all we have space to say about sorting in Chapter 7. Nevertheless we start this chapter as we did Chapter 7 with a collection of records each of which has many fields, one of them a key field whose entries are taken from a key type which is usually, though in this chapter not necessarily, an ordered type. Thus we declare

> **Type** $K = (\star$ the key type $\star)$;
> $\qquad T = $ **Record**
> $\qquad\qquad Key : K$;
> $\qquad\qquad \ldots (\star$ other fields holding information $\star)$
> $\qquad\quad$ **end**;

The problem we are concerned with is easily stated: given the key of a particular record we want to locate the complete record so that we can retrieve the really interesting information held in the other fields of the record. It is clear that the solution to our searching problem depends on the way in which the collection of records is stored.

Of course, as we so often do in everyday life, we may impose no structure at all on the collection in which we shall be searching. In this case we can offer no systematic way of searching for a particular object. We may simply make random choices of objects and examine each choice to see whether it is in fact the one we are looking for; this has the disadvantage that we may find ourselves examining an unwanted record more than once. It is not really appropriate to think of trying to implement this random method of storing and searching in a computer. (The Pascal data type **set** may at first sight appear to correspond to random storage, but in Pascal sets are implemented, roughly speaking, as arrays.) We are led to the conclusion that we really ought to impose some kind of organisation on the collection in which we are searching, and this chapter describes various ways of doing that.

Chapter 10

STORING IN ARRAYS AND LISTS

10.1   Sequential and binary searching

Suppose we store our N records as components of a one-dimensional array introduced by the declaration

Var A : **array** $[1 .. N]$ **of** T;

Then to retrieve the record with a given key k of the key type of our records we may start at the lower end of the array (the entry which has index 1) and compare k with the key field of each component of the array in turn until either a match is found or else we reach the upper end of the array without ever finding a match (so that the required record is actually missing from our collection). This method of searching is known as **sequential search**. It can be implemented using the following Pascal procedure

Procedure array_sequential $(X : \textbf{array} [1 .. N] \textbf{ of } T; k : K)$;
Var i : **integer**;
Begin $i := 0$;
      Repeat $i := i + 1$ **until** $(X[i].Key = k)$ **or** $(i > N)$;
      if $X[i].Key = k$ **then** success at position i
                      else $(\star$ if $i > N$ $\star)$ failure
End;

If the record with key k is present in position i then i key comparisons are required to locate it; if the record with key k is absent then we require $N + 1$ comparisons to establish this fact. So the worst case complexity of sequential search in an array (counting comparisons) is $O(N)$. If we assume that we are equally likely to be searching for each of the array entries, so that the probability for each position i is $1/N$, then the expected number of comparisons to locate one of the entries of the array is

$$\tfrac{1}{N}(1 + 2 + \ldots + N) = \tfrac{1}{N}(\tfrac{1}{2}N(N + 1)) = \tfrac{1}{2}(N + 1)$$

since i comparisons are required to reach the entry in the ith place.

If the collection we are working with is liable to change through insertions or deletions then it may be more appropriate to use a linked list rather than an array to store the collection, declaring in the usual way

Type $List\_pointer = \uparrow$Node;
      $Node = $ **Record**
              $Info : T$;
              $Next : List\_pointer$
           end;
    Var $head : List\_pointer$;

Then sequential search of the list pointed to by *head* proceeds by examining the nodes of the list in turn, starting with *head*$\uparrow$ and following the *Next* pointers until either we reach a node whose *Info* field holds the record with key k or we reach the end of the list without finding such a node. To carry out sequential search in a list we use the following procedure

Procedure list_sequential (p : *List_pointer*; k : K);
Var q : *List_pointer*;
Begin $q := p$;
    while $q <>$ nil **do**
        if $q \uparrow.Info.Key = k$ **then** success **else** $q := q \uparrow.Next$;
    if $q =$ nil **then** failure
End;

The worst case complexity of sequential search in a list is clearly $O(N)$ where N is the number of records stored.

We turn now to the situation in which the keys of our records are drawn from an *ordered* type. Then, using the key field, we can sort the records by any one of the many sorting methods we learned about in Chapter 7. Let us suppose that this has been done and that our records are stored in increasing order of key in the array A. We now describe a divide-and-conquer strategy to search for the record with a given key k.

The idea is that if we look at a component $A[i]$ of the array there are these three possibilities: (1) $A[i].Key = k$; (2) $A[i].Key > k$; (3) $A[i].Key < k$. If (1) occurs then we have successfully located the record with key k in the ith position in the array. If (2) occurs then since the entries of A are sorted it follows that the record with key k must occur (if it is present at all) in the subarray of A indexed by $1 .. (i-1)$; so our search for that record can be restricted to this subarray, which is smaller than the whole array A. In the same way, if (3) occurs, then the record with key k (if it is present) must be in the subarray indexed by $(i+1) .. N$, which is again shorter than A.

The **binary search** algorithm uses this idea by choosing the component $A[i]$ to be the middle component of the array—or, to be more precise, since an array with an even number of entries doesn't have a middle component, we choose i to be $(1 + N)$ **div** 2. The same procedure is repeated, if necessary (that is if the middle component isn't the record we are searching for), by examining the middle component of the appropriate lower or upper subarray. Thus we carry out binary search by giving the command

$$\text{array\_binary\_search}(k, 1, N);$$

where we have defined

> **Procedure** array_binary_search($k : K$; *low, high* : $1 .. N$);
> **Var** *mid* : $1 .. N$;
> **Begin if** *low* > *high* **then** failure
>   **else begin**
>   *mid* := (*low* + *high*) **div** 2;
>   **if** $A[mid].Key = k$ **then** success at position *mid*
>   **else if** $k < A[mid].Key$
>   **then** array_binary_search(k, *low*, *mid* − 1)
>   **else** array_binary_search(k, *mid* + 1, *high*) **end**
> **End**;

Although this recursive procedure mirrors the underlying idea of the binary search algorithm it has the usual practical disadvantages of recursion and it may be better to rewrite the algorithm non-recursively (though perhaps a little less transparently) as follows

> **Begin**
>   *low* := 1; *high* := N;
>   **while** *low* < *high* **do begin**
>   *mid* := (*low* + *high*) **div** 2;
>   **if** $A[mid].Key = k$ **then** success at position *mid*
>   **else if** $k < A[mid].Key$ **then** *high* := *mid* − 1
>   **else** *low* := *mid* + 1 **end**;
>   **if** *low* > *high* **then** failure
> **End**;

If $2^{k-1} \leq N < 2^k$ we can see that the binary search algorithm makes at most k comparisons for a successful termination and either $k - 1$ or k comparisons in the case of failure. Since $k \approx \log_2 N$ we see that the worst case complexity of the binary search algorithm is $O(\log_2 N)$. This is much better than the $O(N)$ complexity of sequential search; but we have to take account of the work involved in sorting the array, though of course this is done once only in preparation for a large number of searches.

10.2 Hashing

Part of the process of compiling a program is the formation of a *symbol table* in which we store all the identifiers occurring in the program together with necessary information about them, such as type, location in memory and various other attributes depending on the language in which the program is written. Each time an identifier is encountered in a program we must check whether it has already appeared; if so, we retrieve from the symbol table the information associated with it; if not, we add it to the symbol table or report an error.

To implement the symbol table we might think of introducing the enumerated type *Id* consisting of all possible identifiers and storing the attributes of each identifier i which occurs in the program in the ith component of an array indexed by *Id*. This, however, is not a very good idea—the number of allowable FORTRAN identifiers has been estimated to be 1.3×10^9, so it is not really reasonable to set up an array of this size, which would make quite unreasonable demands on the space available. Most of the space set aside for such an array would inevitably remain unused, since the number of identifiers likely to occur in a given program is a very great deal less than 1.3×10^9.

A second (but still not very good) idea to implement the symbol table for a program might be to form a linked list of all the identifiers occurring in the program together with their associated information. Insertion of a new identifier at the head of such a list is quick and easy to perform; but when we come to search in such a list—to see whether an identifier has to be inserted or to retrieve information about an identifier—we have to proceed by sequential search which tends to slow down as the number of identifiers increases.

For the maintenance of symbol tables, and for many other purposes, it is convenient to use the method of storing and searching known as **hashing**. In hashing we use an array in which the array position of a record can be determined by means of simple arithmetic operations on its key field. Although we have suggested several times (in Chapters 1 and 2 and earlier in this chapter) that arrays are most suitable for the static situation in which the collection of records stored is essentially unchanging, hashing is designed so that even though it uses an array it is able to handle constantly changing collections.

As before, let K be the key type, i.e. the set of all possible keys of the records we are dealing with. We choose an array of size M, indexed by $0 .. M - 1$, where M is very much smaller than the size of K—we think of taking M to be roughly the number of records we are likely to be storing. The array is called the **hash table**; and we have to make it explicit that we have not yet said anything about the type of the entries in the hash table.

We define a mapping h from K, the set of all keys, to the index set $0 .. M - 1$ of the hash table. This mapping h is called the **hash function**. For every possible key k it returns an integer $h(k)$ such that $0 \leq h(k) \leq M - 1$. If a record has key k then we find the index $h(k)$ and say that the $h(k)$th entry in the hash table is the **home position** of the record.

The underlying rough idea of hashing is to store each record in its home position in the hash table. Unfortunately, since the size M of the hash table is very much smaller than the total number of possible keys, there must inevitably be pairs of keys k_1, k_2 such that $k_1 \neq k_2$ but $h(k_1) = h(k_2)$. Such pairs are called **collisions**. If the keys of two records form a collision then the two records have the same home position. This clearly raises a difficulty if the entries of the hash table are to be records from our collection, because we can store only one record in each component of an array.

So how do we handle collisions? We describe two ways of answering this question.

(1) **Direct chaining**. The first approach proceeds by giving up the idea that the hash table entries are of the record type T. Instead we define the entries in the hash table to be (pointers to) lists of records. Thus the ith component of the hash table is a pointer to a list consisting of all the records whose home position is i, that is for which $h(k) = i$

where k is the key of the record. We declare in the usual way

> **Type** *Pointer* = ↑Node;
>   *Node* = **Record**
>   *Info* : *T*;
>   *Next* : *Pointer*
>   **end**;

and then

> **Var** H : **array** $[0 .. M - 1]$ **of** *Pointer*;

and initialise all the entries of H to be **nil**. Then to insert a record R at the beginning or at any later stage we calculate $i = h(R.Key)$ and then perform Insert_at_head(R, $H[i]$) using the procedure defined in Section 1.4.

To search for a record in a hash table constructed in this way we proceed by finding its home position i and then searching sequentially in the list $H[i]$ ↑. This is a possible disadvantage of the direct chaining method, for, as the lists pointed to by the pointers in the hash table become long, sequential searching may become rather slow. To overcome this it is sometimes suggested that when we search for and find a record we should at once put it at the head of the list it belongs to (the thought here is that if a record is required once it is just possible that it may be required again and it will be more quickly found if it is located at the head of the list at its home position).

To delete a record we begin as usual by finding its home position i, searching sequentially in the list $H[i]$ ↑ and deleting the node holding the record by adjusting pointers in the usual way.

We have already mentioned one disadvantage of the direct chaining method of hashing, namely the time required for sequential searching in the lists pointed to by the hash table pointers. Another disadvantage is that additional space is required to hold the *Next* pointers in the nodes, though if the records themselves are large this represents only a small proportional increase in the space requirement. On the other hand there are considerable advantages in direct chaining. We have already noticed how easy it is to insert new records and to delete existing records. But the main advantage is that there is (at least in theory) no limit to the number of records which can be stored since the lists "in" the hash table may be indefinitely extended. It is not even necessary to ensure that the size M of the hash table is as large as the number of records we expect to be present—if the number is greater than M some of the lists will contain more than one node.

To estimate the complexity of direct chaining it is convenient to introduce the **load factor** $\lambda = N/M$ where N is the number of records stored and M is the size of the hash table.

If we suppose that the N records are distributed uniformly over the M lists then to make an unsuccessful search we must examine all the entries in the list corresponding to the home position of the record we are seeking, so the expected number of comparisons is the average number of entries in a list, which is just λ.

If our search for a record is successful then it occurs in the list corresponding to its home position; let us assume that the remaining $N - 1$ records are uniformly distributed over all M lists. Then the expected number of entries in the list where the record is found is $1 + (N - 1)/M$. As we saw in Section 1 of this chapter (when we discussed sequential search) the average number of comparisons required for successful sequential search in a list of length l is $\frac{1}{2}(l + 1)$. So the expected number of comparisons for a successful search in the direct chaining situation is

$$\tfrac{1}{2}(1 + (N - 1)/M + 1) = 1 + \tfrac{1}{2}(N - 1)/M \approx 1 + \tfrac{1}{2}\lambda.$$

To illustrate the working of direct chaining we set up a hash table of pointers indexed by $0..12$; we use the hash function h defined by setting $h(k) = k \bmod 13$ for each key k in K. Then to store a sequence of records with the following keys and home positions

k:	897	885	329	407	336	117
$h(k)$:	0	1	4	4	11	0

k:	115	526	586	435	138	834
$h(k)$:	11	6	1	6	8	2

we obtain the following table of lists:

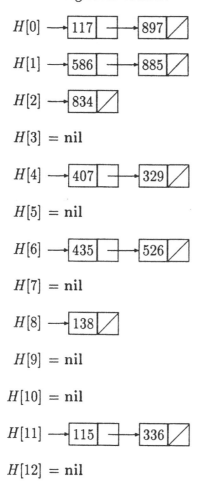

$H[0] \longrightarrow 117 \longrightarrow 897$

$H[1] \longrightarrow 586 \longrightarrow 885$

$H[2] \longrightarrow 834$

$H[3] = \text{nil}$

$H[4] \longrightarrow 407 \longrightarrow 329$

$H[5] = \text{nil}$

$H[6] \longrightarrow 435 \longrightarrow 526$

$H[7] = \text{nil}$

$H[8] \longrightarrow 138$

$H[9] = \text{nil}$

$H[10] = \text{nil}$

$H[11] \longrightarrow 115 \longrightarrow 336$

$H[12] = \text{nil}$

(Remember that incoming records are always inserted at the head of the appropriate list.)

(2) **Open addressing**. In this method of hashing the entries of the hash table are actual records; so we have to develop some strategy for handling records with different keys which have the same home position.

Initially, when all the positions in the hash table are unoccupied, the first record may clearly be inserted in its home position. For each succeeding record to be stored we calculate the home position and examine whether that home position is unoccupied. If it is, then we insert the record there; but if the home position is already occupied we must find another location to hold the new record.

The idea here is to set up what is called a **probing sequence**; this is a sequence of locations which we examine in succession until we find one which is unoccupied, whereupon we insert the new record there. There are several ways of defining probing sequences.

(*a*) The simplest approach is known as **linear probing**. Here the probing sequence to be followed if the ith position is occupied is

$$(i+1) \bmod M, (i+2) \bmod M, (i+3) \bmod M, \ldots$$

(The presence of **mod** M here indicates that when the probing sequence reaches the top end of the array it returns to the bottom end.)

To search for a record in a hash table which has been set up using the linear probing protocol we simply apply the hash function to its key to find the home position and then follow the probing sequence from the home position until the record is found or all the occupied positions in the probing sequence have been examined without finding it. We have to be careful here about what constitutes an "occupied" position—a deletion may have been made from a position in the probing sequence while there are still records stored in later positions of the sequence.

We take account of the problem we have just raised when we discuss deletion. Clearly to delete a record with a given key we calculate its home position as usual and follow the probing sequence until we find the record. We then remove it from the hash table, leaving its position unoccupied and available for use to store any new record which is following the same probing sequence (or an overlapping one from some other home position). But we must take some action to indicate that there may be some occupied positions farther along the probing sequence. One way to do this would be to put a 'deleted' mark on a location from which a record has been removed, so indicating that it is unoccupied because of a deletion and that there may still be occupied positions in the probing sequence.

We notice that in linear probing the probing sequences from different home positions tend eventually to overlap, so that a record with one of these home positions may collide with previously entered records with another home position before it is found (during searching) or an unoccupied position is found for it (during insertion). This overlapping phenomenon is known as **primary clustering**. Of course a similar situation arises for records with the same home position, which have not just overlapping but identical probing sequences; we talk here of **secondary clustering**.

It would take us too long to give a detailed discussion of the average number of comparisons involved in searching when we use open addressing; we simply record the results. As in the case of direct chaining we introduce the **load factor** $\lambda = N/M$, where N is the number of records stored and M is the size of the hash table; when we use open addressing we must have $\lambda \leq 1$. Careful analysis shows that for open addressing with linear probing the expected number of comparisons for an unsuccessful search is

$$\tfrac{1}{2}\left(1 + \frac{1}{(1 - \lambda)^2}\right)$$

while for a successful search the expected number is

$$\tfrac{1}{2}\left(1 + \frac{1}{1 - \lambda}\right)$$

We now show the working of open addressing with linear probing using the same input stream as we used to illustrate direct chaining, with the same hash function ($h(k) = k \bmod 13$) and keys and home positions

k:	897	885	329	407	336	117
$h(k)$:	0	1	4	4	11	0

k:	115	526	586	435	138	834
$h(k)$:	11	6	1	6	8	2

Then the entries in the hash table H are built up as follows:

897, 885 and 329 can be inserted in their home positions 0, 1, 4 respectively since these are unoccupied.

407 has home position 4, but this is already occupied; so we examine position 5, which is vacant, and thus we insert 407 in position 5.

336 can be inserted in its home position 11 which is vacant.

117 has home position 0, which is occupied; so is position 1. But position 2 is not yet occupied, so we insert 117 there.

115 has home position 11, which is occupied. Position 12 is still vacant, so 115 is inserted there.

526 can be inserted in its home position 6 which is free.

586's home position is 1, which is already occupied; so is the next position, 2. But position 3 is free, so we insert 586 there.

435 has home position 6, which is already occupied by 526; but position 7 is unoccupied, so we insert 435 there.

138 has home position 8, which is vacant; so 138 goes in its home position.

Finally 834 has home position 2. Positions 2, 3, 4, 5, 6, 7 and 8 are all occupied; so 834 lands eventually in position 9.

We can summarise the procedure just described by means of the following table where the records with the unbracketed keys are stored in the positions indicated, while the bracketed entries show successive attempts to find vacant positions for the records with those keys.

$H[0]$ 897 (117)
$H[1]$ 885 (117) (586)
$H[2]$ 117 (586) (834)
$H[3]$ 586 (834)
$H[4]$ 329 (407) (834)
$H[5]$ 407 (834)
$H[6]$ 526 (435) (834)
$H[7]$ 435 (834)
$H[8]$ 138 (834)
$H[9]$ 834
$H[10]$
$H[11]$ 336 (115)
$H[12]$ 115

(*b*) An alternative approach to collision handling in open addressing is **quadratic probing**. Here it is convenient to choose the hash table size to be a prime number P and to prescribe that the probing sequence to be followed if the ith position is occupied should be

$$(i + 1) \bmod P, (i + 4) \bmod P, (i + 9) \bmod P, \ldots$$

This approach still suffers from secondary clustering, since all entries with the same home position follow the same probing sequence; but primary clustering is avoided—the probing sequences from different home positions may occasionally overlap, but they will not coalesce as they do in linear probing. Quadratic probing does have the disadvantage, however, that the probing sequence will examine only half the entries in the hash table (only half the numbers $1, 2, \ldots, P - 1$ are congruent to squares $\bmod P$). We can avoid this difficulty by choosing P to be a prime number which is congruent to $3 \bmod 4$ and using the probing sequence

$$(i + 1) \bmod P, (i - 1) \bmod P, (i + 4) \bmod P, (i - 4) \bmod P,$$
$$(i + 9) \bmod P, (i - 9) \bmod P, \ldots$$

which will eventually include all the array positions.

Using $P = 13$ and the same input stream and hash function as before, the first version of quadratic probing will produce the table

$$
\begin{array}{llll}
H[0] & 897 & (117) & \\
H[1] & 885 & (117) & (586) \\
H[2] & 586 & (834) & \\
H[3] & 834 & & \\
H[4] & 329 & (407) & (117) \\
H[5] & 407 & & \\
H[6] & 526 & (435) & \\
H[7] & 435 & & \\
H[8] & 138 & & \\
H[9] & 117 & & \\
H[10] & & & \\
H[11] & 336 & (115) & \\
H[12] & 115 & &
\end{array}
$$

(c) A third approach to collision handling in open addressing which reduces clustering almost completely is **double hashing**. Here we define a second hash function h' and then for a record with key k whose home position under the first hash function h is $h(k) = i$ we follow the probing sequence

$$(i + h'(k)) \bmod M, \ (i + 2h'(k)) \bmod M, \ (i + 3h'(k)) \bmod M, \ \ldots$$

Thus secondary clustering occurs only for keys which have the same value under both hash function h and h'. Primary clustering is greatly reduced.

If we use the same input stream and hash function as before and define the second hash function h' by $h'(k) = 1 + (k \bmod 11)$ then we have

k:	897	885	329	407	336	117
$h(k)$:	0	1	4	4	11	0
$h'(k)$:	7	6	11	1	7	8

$$
\begin{array}{ccccccc}
k: & 115 & 526 & 586 & 435 & 138 & 834 \\
h(k): & 11 & 6 & 1 & 6 & 8 & 2 \\
h'(k): & 6 & 10 & 4 & 7 & 7 & 10
\end{array}
$$

and we produce the table

$$
\begin{array}{llll}
H[0] & 897 & (117) & (435) \\
H[1] & 885 & (586) & \\
H[2] & 138 & (834) & \\
H[3] & & & \\
H[4] & 329 & (407) & (115) \\
H[5] & 407 & (586) & \\
H[6] & 526 & (435) & \\
H[7] & 435 & & \\
H[8] & 117 & (138) & \\
H[9] & 586 & & \\
H[10] & 115 & & \\
H[11] & 336 & (115) & \\
H[12] & 834 & &
\end{array}
$$

We have not yet discussed the question of how we choose a hash function. It is clear that since the purpose of hashing is to provide quick access to records we should use a hash function which is easy to compute; furthermore, although we cannot expect to avoid collisions entirely, we would certainly like to avoid the situation where only a few of the entries in the hash table occur as home positions for records in our collection—it would be preferable to have a hash function whose values were uniformly spread over the index set of the hash table. Various approaches have been suggested for the definition of suitable functions.

The first idea is to transform the keys of our records into integers. (This can be done in many ways; for example, when we are forming a symbol table we might form a number from an identifier by adding up the ordinal numbers of its constituent characters.) Then we choose for the size M of the hash table, indexed by $0 .. M - 1$, a large prime number (in practice it is suggested that a number with all its prime factors greater than about 20 would be acceptable) and define the hash function h by setting $h(k) = (k \bmod M)$ for all keys k.

Alternatively we may choose the hash table size to be a power of 2, say $M = 2^m$. Then the elements of the index set $0 .. M - 1$ can all be expressed using m binary digits. Here again we transform the keys of our records into integers, expressing them this time in binary notation. Then various hash functions may be defined by constructing m-bit sequences from the binary representations of the keys. For example, we may simply choose the m most significant bits; or we may cut the binary form of each key into m-bit sections, add these and take the m least significant bits of the sum; again it is sometimes recommended that we square the binary form of the key and extract m bits from the middle of the binary representation of the square.

10.3   Exercises 10

1. Illustrate the working of binary search by looking for the records with *Key* fields 30 and 14 in the array A indexed by $1 .. 16$ given by

Index	1	2	3	4	5	6	7	8
Entry	5	7	8	10	13	15	18	20

Index	9	10	11	12	13	14	15	16
Entry	22	24	25	26	27	30	32	38

2. If you want to test a program you have written to implement binary search for an array with N records in increasing order of *Key* field, how many test runs would convince you that your program is correct?

3. Can you suggest how we might devise a "ternary" search algorithm which would split the array in which we are searching into three parts rather than two as in binary search?

4. Show how to insert a stream of records with *Key* fields as follows

   534 702 105 523 959 699 821 883 842 686 658 4 20 382 570 344

   in a hash table H of size 19 (indexed by $0..18$), using the hash function h given by $h(k) = (k \bmod 19)$ and
   (a) linear probing;

(*b*) quadratic probing (both versions);

(*c*) double hashing, using the secondary hash function h' given by $h'(k) = 1 + (k \bmod 17)$.

In each case find the average number of comparisons required to search for a record which is present in the hash table.

5. Show the result of using the direct chaining method to store the same input stream, using a hash table of size 13 (indexed by $0 .. 12$) and the hash function h_1 given by $h_1(k) = (k \bmod 13)$.

Chapter 11

STORING IN BINARY TREES

11.1 Storing in binary search trees

We recall from Chapter 3 that a **binary search tree** is a binary tree whose nodes hold records in such a way that for every node in the tree the key field of its information field (assumed of ordered type) is greater than that of every node in its left subtree and less than that of every node in its right subtree. Although we did not discuss the problem in Chapter 3 it is clear how to search for an item stored in a binary search tree—we compare its key with the key of the information field of the element stored at the root node (the "root key"); if they are the same then our search has been successful; if not, then we search recursively in the left or right subtree of the root according as the key of the item we are searching for is less than or greater than the root key.

Using the declarations of Chapter 3 we search in a binary search tree using the procedure

Procedure tree_binary_search $(k : K; p : Tree\_pointer)$;
Begin if $p = $ **nil then** failure
    else if $p \uparrow.Info.Key = k$ **then** success
        else if $p \uparrow.Info.Key > k$
            then tree_binary_search$(k, p \uparrow.Left)$
                else tree_binary_search$(k, p \uparrow.Right)$
End;

or non-recursively by introducing a **boolean** variable *done* and proceeding as follows:

Begin Repeat
    if $p = $ **nil then begin** failure; *done* := **true end**
    else if $p \uparrow.Info.Key = k$ **then begin** success;
                                  done := **true end**
        else begin
                done := **false**;
                if $k < p \uparrow.Info.Key$
                        then $p := p \uparrow.Left$
                            else $p := p \uparrow.Right$ **end**
    until *done*
End;

To determine the complexity of tree_binary_search we begin by noticing that the maximum number of key comparisons which will be required is one more than the height of the tree in whose nodes the items are stored. The height of a binary search tree containing a collection of items will depend not only on the number of items but on the order in which they were inserted in the tree. For example, if a collection of items with keys 1, 2, ..., 7 is inserted in increasing or decreasing order of key then the resulting tree reduces to a list and so has height 6; but if the keys appear in the order 4, 2, 6, 1, 3, 5, 7 then the tree which is produced is

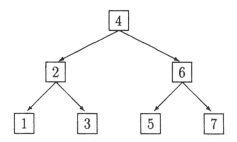

which has height 2.

In general the height h of a binary search tree with N nodes satisfies

$$\lfloor \log_2 N \rfloor \le h \le N - 1$$

where $\lfloor x \rfloor$ denotes the largest integer less than or equal to the real number x.

Thus in the worst case the maximum number of key comparisons required to find one of N items stored in a binary search tree is N, while in the most favourable case the maximum number is $1 + \lfloor \log_2 N \rfloor$. It can be shown that if all $N!$ possible arrangements of the keys in the input stream are equally likely then the average number of comparisons over all items and all $N!$ binary search trees is approximately $2 \ln N$, where ln denotes the natural logarithm, and this is approximately $1.386 \log_2 N$.

Speaking very roughly we can say that if we want to reduce the height of a binary search tree (and so the maximum number of comparisons required in searching) we should try to balance the left and right subtrees. This idea of balancing can be formalised in two ways, sometimes described as weight-balancing and height-balancing.

Using the first approach we introduce **perfectly balanced trees**: a binary tree is said to be perfectly balanced if for the root node and every other node of the tree the number of nodes in its left subtree and the number of nodes in its right subtree differ by at most 1. If we know the number of items we are dealing with, N say, it is easy to devise a recursive procedure to construct a perfectly balanced tree to store them: we store the first item in the root node, then use the next N **div** 2 items to form a perfectly balanced tree, which is taken to be the left subtree of the root, and then finally we use the remaining $N - N$ **div** $2 - 1$ items to form a perfectly balanced tree and take it to be the right subtree of the root. The trouble with this simple idea is that, although the resulting tree is perfectly balanced, there is no guarantee that it will be a binary *search* tree. Even if it were a search tree we would still have to face the problem of maintaining both the search tree property and perfect balance every time we carry out insertion or deletion of an item.

11.2   Storing in AVL-trees

Since the maximum number of comparisons required to search for an item is so closely related to the height of the tree in which our collection is stored, it seems natural in the context of storing and searching to consider height-balance rather than weight-balance. So we introduce the so-called AVL-trees, first described by the Russian mathematicians Adel'son-Vel'skii and Landis. An **AVL-tree** is a binary search tree in which for every node the heights of the left and right subtrees differ by at most 1. Thus, for example,

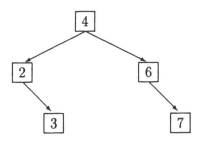

is an AVL-tree, while

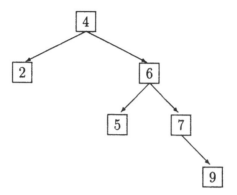

is not, since the height of the left subtree of the root is 1 while that of its right subtree is 3.

We consider now the operation of inserting a new item in an AVL-tree. Since an AVL-tree is a binary search tree we begin by carrying out ordinary binary search tree insertion as described in Chapter 3. It may happen that after this operation has been carried out the resulting binary search tree is still an AVL-tree. For example, if we insert 1 or 9 in the AVL-tree

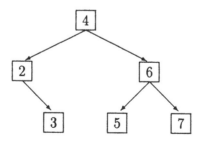

we produce the trees

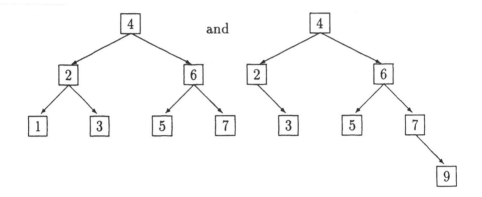

and

which are both AVL-trees. But if we insert 1, 3, 5 or 7 in the AVL-tree

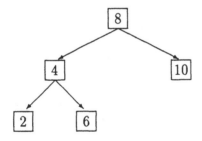

we destroy the AVL property; for example, inserting 3 produces the tree

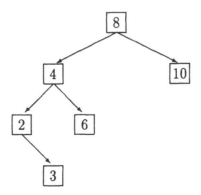

which is not an AVL-tree since the height of the left subtree of the root is 3 while that of its right subtree is 1.

In order to discuss the action to be taken when binary search tree insertion in an AVL-tree destroys the AVL property it is convenient to attach to each node of the tree an additional field

$$Balance : -1 .. 1$$

with the understanding that the *Balance* field of a node has the value

Height of the left subtree of the node − Height of its right subtree.

When we insert a new item in a binary search tree we start at the root and follow a sequence of nodes until eventually we create a new left or right child for the last node in the sequence and use it to hold the new item; we call this sequence of nodes the **search path** for the new item—it is, after all, the path we would take if we were searching for the new item.

Now we specialise to the case of an AVL-tree. If it happens that for every node on the search path of a new item we have *Balance* = 0 then insertion of the new item will change the *Balance* field of each of these nodes, but only to −1 or 1, so that the tree retains the AVL property. This is illustrated by the insertion of an item with *Key* 3 in the AVL-tree

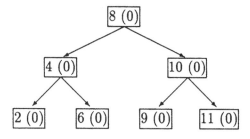

(where the numbers in parentheses are the *Balance* fields of the nodes). After insertion we have

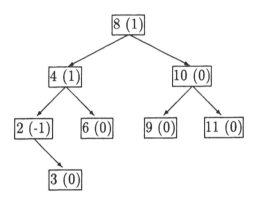

Next suppose that at least one node on the search path has nonzero *Balance*; let *A* be the node on the search path with nonzero balance which is closest to the new node which would be required for ordinary binary search tree insertion. We call *A* the **pivot node**. Consider, for example, the AVL-tree

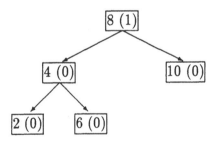

To insert an item with *Key* field 5 we follow the search path 8, 4, 6 and to insert an item with *Key* field 9 the search path is 8, 10; in both cases the node *A* holding the item with *Key* 8 is the pivot node.

Since the *Balance* field of *A* is nonzero its subtrees are of unequal height—let us call them the higher and the lower subtree. It is clear that if the insertion under consideration is to be in the lower of the two subtrees of *A* then the *Balance* field of *A* will become 0 and the augmented tree will satisfy the AVL property without any further adjustment. This is what happens when we insert 9 in the above tree.

We have next to consider what happens when the insertion should be made in the higher of the two subtrees of A. Here straightforward binary search tree insertion would change the *Balance* of A to 2 or -2 and so destroy the AVL property. We now show how to reorganise the entries in the subtree with root A together with the new item so as to form an AVL-tree. This will clearly make the whole augmented tree into an AVL-tree.

Suppose first that the higher subtree of A is the left subtree, so that the *Balance* field of A is 1. Let the root node of this subtree be B; according to the definition of the pivot node A the *Balance* field of B is 0. Before the insertion of the new item the subtree with root A can be represented schematically as

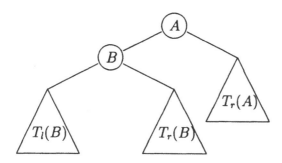

where $T_r(A)$ is the right subtree of A and $T_l(B)$ and $T_r(B)$ are the left and right subtrees respectively of B. Since A has *Balance* $= 1$ and B has *Balance* $= 0$, the three subtrees $T_r(A)$, $T_l(B)$ and $T_r(B)$ all have the same height.

Now there are two cases to consider:

(1) which we denote by *LL*: the new item should be inserted in the left subtree $T_l(B)$ of B. Straightforward insertion would produce a new left subtree $T_l'(B)$ of height 1 greater than $T_l(B)$, so the subtree with root A becomes

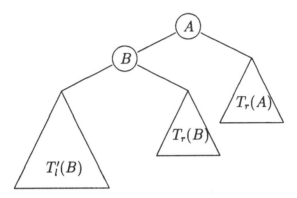

in which A has *Balance* $= 2$, which is not allowed.

In this case we form the tree represented schematically by

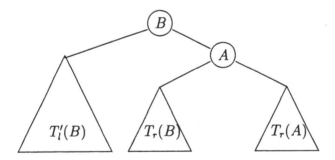

which has the AVL property; the nodes A and B both have *Balance* $= 0$.

The *LL* adjustment (often called an *LL*-**rotation**) may be described as follows: The left child B of the pivot node A takes the position of the pivot node, carrying with it its left subtree; the pivot node becomes the right child of B, carrying with it its right subtree and acquiring the right subtree of B as its left subtree.

Consider for example the insertion of a record with *Key* field 2 in
the AVL-tree

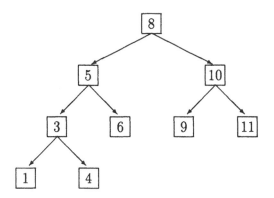

The search path for 2 is 8, 5, 3, 1; the pivot node is $A = 5$ and
its left child is $B = 3$. Straightforward binary search tree insertion
produces the non-AVL tree

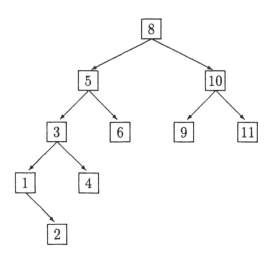

Since 2 was inserted in the left subtree of B we are in the situation LL; so we readjust the tree according to the description above, obtaining

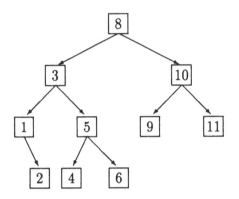

(2) The second case we have to consider is denoted by LR: in this case the new item should be inserted in the right subtree $T_r(B)$ of B.

There are here three possibilities to consider, but they are all dealt with in a similar way.

(a) It may happen that the node B has no children, i.e. $T_l(B)$ and $T_r(B)$ (and so also $T_r(A)$) are all **nil**. In this situation we must introduce a new node as right child C for B and store the new item in C. This produces the subtree

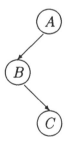

rooted at A, in which A has *Balance* = 2, which is not allowed and B has *Balance* = 1. To restore the AVL property we replace this subtree by

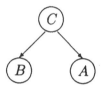

This is the situation we find ourselves in when we have to insert a new record with *Key* field 7 in the AVL-tree

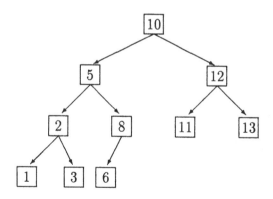

The search path is 10, 5, 8, 6; the pivot node A is the node containing 8; B is the node containing 6. If we introduce a new node containing 7 as right child for B we obtain

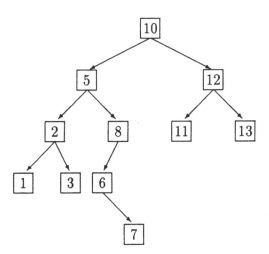

This is not an AVL-tree, so we must rebalance according to the general discussion above, obtaining

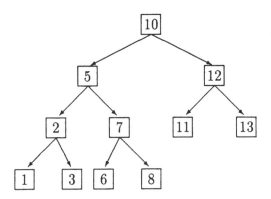

(*b*) It may happen that the right subtree of B (in which the new item is to be inserted) is not **nil** but has root node which we denote by C and left and right subtrees $T_l(C)$ and $T_r(C)$ (possibly **nil**). We illustrate schematically by

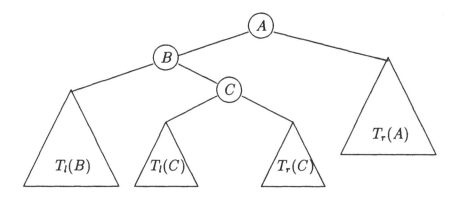

Here B and C have *Balance* $= 0$ since A is the last node on the search path with non-zero *Balance*. So $T_l(C)$ and $T_r(C)$ have the same height, h say, and it follows that $T_l(B)$ and $T_r(A)$ have height $h + 1$.

Suppose the new item is to be inserted in $T_l(C)$. Ordinary binary search tree insertion would produce a new left subtree $T_l'(C)$ of height 1 greater than $T_l(C)$. This would alter the *Balance* of A to 2, which is illegal. We restore the AVL property by replacing the inadmissible

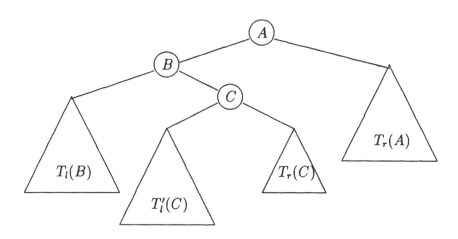

by

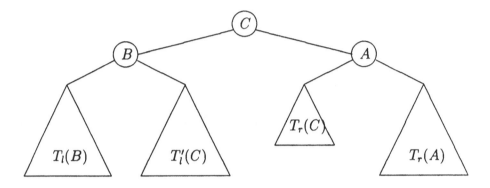

in which B and C have *Balance* $= 0$ and A has *Balance* $= -1$.

(c) Suppose the situation is as in (b) but that this time the new item is to be inserted in the right subtree $T_r(C)$ of C. Ordinary insertion would produce the non-AVL tree

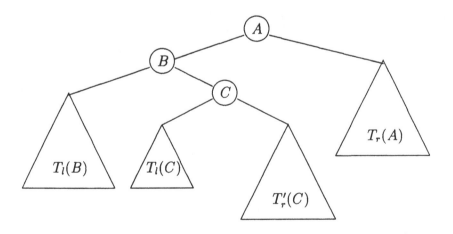

where $T'_r(C)$ is the tree of height $h + 1$ obtained by inserting the new item in $T_r(C)$. In this case the AVL property is restored by replacing the above non-AVL tree by

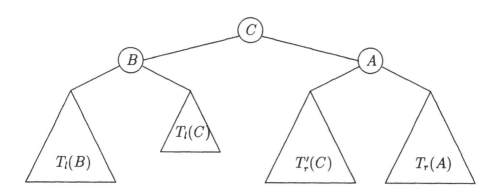

in which A and C have *Balance* $= 0$ and B has *Balance* $= 1$.

The three versions of the LR adjustment (often called LR-**rotations**) can all be described in the same general way. As above, let A be the pivot node, B its left child, and let C be the right child of B. Then C takes the position of the pivot node A; B becomes its left child and A its right child. B retains its left subtree and acquires the left subtree of C as its right subtree. A retains its right subtree and acquires the right subtree of C as its left subtree.

We illustrate (c) by examining the insertion of a record with *Key* $= 7$ in the AVL-tree

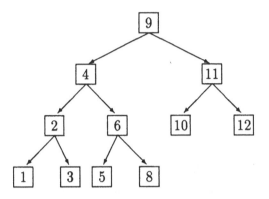

The search path is 9, 4, 6, 8; the pivot node A is the node containing 9; B is the node containing 4; the record with $Key = 7$ is to be inserted in the right subtree of B, so we are in case $LR(c)$. Straightforward insertion produces the non-AVL tree

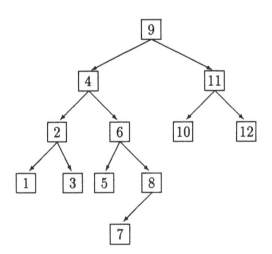

and the rebalancing described above produces the AVL-tree

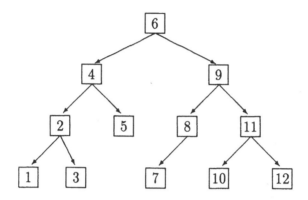

So far we have been dealing only with the situation where the pivot node for a particular insertion has *Balance* $= 1$ and the new item has to be inserted in the left subtree of the pivot node. There were two cases to consider, one, which we called *LL*, where the new item must be inserted in the left subtree of the left child of the pivot and the other, which we called *LR* where the insertion must be made in the right subtree of this left child.

We turn now to the situation where the pivot node has *Balance* $= -1$, so that the right subtree of the pivot node is the higher, and we have to insert a new item in this higher right subtree. Again there are two cases to consider, which are symmetric in the obvious sense to *LL* and *LR*:

(1) *RR-rotation*. Here the new item must be inserted in the right subtree of the right child B of the pivot node A. In this case B takes the place of A, carrying with it its right subtree; A becomes the left child of B, carrying with it its left subtree and acquiring the left subtree of B as its right subtree.

(2) *RL-rotation*. Here the new item is to be inserted in the left subtree of B, the right child of the pivot A. If C is the left child of B after ordinary binary search tree insertion then C takes the place of A; B becomes its right child and A becomes its left child. B retains

its right subtree and acquires C's right subtree as its left subtree; A retains its left subtree and acquires C's left subtree as its right subtree.

It has been shown by examination of a large body of empirical evidence that just over half the insertions in an AVL-tree require no rebalancing, and that of those which do require rebalancing roughly half are of types LL or RR and roughly half of type LR or RL.

Since the number of key comparisons required to search for a record in a binary search tree is at most 1 greater than the height of the tree, we now investigate what can be said about the height of an AVL-tree when we know the number of nodes, i.e. the number of records stored in the tree.

It is clear that if we have a binary search tree of height h then the number of its nodes is between $h + 1$ and $2^{h+1} - 1$ inclusive. So if N is the number of records stored in an AVL-tree of height h we have

$$N \le 2^{h+1} - 1$$

and so

$$h \ge \log_2(N + 1) - 1.$$

Now let N_h be the least number of records which can be stored in a binary search tree of height h without violating the AVL property. Clearly $N_0 = 1$ and $N_1 = 2$. If $h \ge 2$ then an AVL-tree of height h with as few entries as possible must consist of a root node whose subtrees are AVL-trees of heights $h - 1$ and $h - 2$ each with as few entries as possible. Thus for $h \ge 2$ we have

$$N_h = 1 + N_{h-1} + N_{h-2}.$$

Recall the definition of the Fibonacci numbers:

$$F_0 = 0, \ F_1 = 1 \text{ and, for all integers } k \ge 2, \ F_k = F_{k-1} + F_{k-2}.$$

It is easy to establish using mathematical induction that for all integers $h \ge 0$ we have $N_h = F_{h+3} - 1$. So if we have N records stored in an AVL-tree of height h we must have

$$N \geq N_h = F_{h+3} - 1.$$

It is known that for all integers $k \geq 0$ we have the inequality

$$F_k > \frac{1}{\sqrt{5}} \varphi^k - 1$$

where $\varphi = \frac{1}{2}(1 + \sqrt{5})$. Hence we have

$$N > \frac{1}{\sqrt{5}} \varphi^{h+3} - 2.$$

Taking logarithms to base 2 we have

$$\log_2(N + 2) > (h + 3) \log_2 \varphi - \log_2(\sqrt{5})$$

from which we deduce eventually that

$$h < 1.4404 \log_2(N + 2) - 1.328.$$

Thus if N items are stored in an AVL-tree then the height h of the tree is restricted by the inequalities

$$\log_2(N + 1) - 1 \leq h < 1.4404 \log_2(N + 2) - 1.328.$$

In fact it has been found as a result of extensive experimentation that if all $N!$ arrangements of an input stream of N records are equally likely then the average height of all $N!$ AVL-trees is approximately $\log_2 N + 0.25$. It can also be shown that for an AVL-tree with N entries the operations of searching for a record, inserting a new record and deleting an existing record are all $O(\log_2 N)$ operations.

11.3   Exercises 11

1. Starting with the AVL-tree

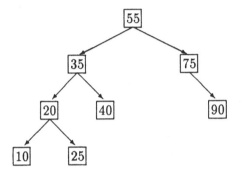

   insert in order records with keys 15, 22, 37, 39, maintaining the AVL property after each insertion.

2. Starting with the same AVL-tree

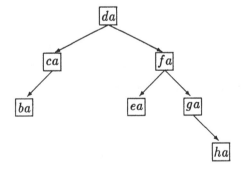

   in each case, construct the AVL-trees which result from inserting (a) hf, then ia; (b) hf, df, then bf.

3. Build up an AVL-tree from the input stream

$$D, E, G, B, A, C, F.$$

Chapter 12

STORING IN MULTIWAY TREES

12.1 Multiway search trees

Suppose, as usual, that we have a collection of records each of which has, among many others, a field *Key* of some ordered type. In thinking of a way to generalise the binary search tree structure, whose usefulness has been described in the previous Chapter, we might be tempted to introduce a structure made up of nodes each having a fixed number n of children (which are again structures of the same type or possibly empty) and containing $n - 1$ records—binary trees correspond to the case $n = 2$. It turns out that it is better not to be quite so restrictive, but rather to require only that each node have at most n children and contain one fewer record than it has children.

So we make the following definition. Let n be an integer greater than or equal to 2. Then a **multiway search tree of order** n is either **nil** or else consists of a distinguished node, called its **root**, which contains m records (where $1 \leq m < n$) arranged in increasing order of *Key* field and has associated with it $m + 1$ multiway search trees of order n, called its **subtrees**, in such a way that if the subtrees of the root are $S_1, S_2, \ldots, S_{m+1}$ and $k_1, k_2, \ldots, k_m$ are the *Key* fields (in increasing order) of the records stored in the root then

(1) for every record X in the root of S_1 we have $X.Key \leq k_1$;

(2) if $1 < i < m + 1$ then for every record X in the root of S_i we have $k_{i-1} < X.Key \leq k_i$;

(3) for every record X in the root of S_{m+1} we have $X.Key > k_m$.

To implement multiway search trees in Pascal it is convenient to extend the type T of the records to be stored by adding a "null" or "absent" record to T; we call the augmented type T'. This extension allows us to pretend that every node contains $n - 1$ records, where n is the order of the multiway search tree—namely, we add to the right of the m actual records held in the node $n - m - 1$ of the "null" records. In the same way we may pretend that each node has n subtrees, simply by introducing **nil** subtrees to make up the number. Then we make the declarations

```
Const order = n;
Type Multiway_tree_pointer = ↑Node;
        Node = Record
                    Element : array [1 .. order −1] of T';
                    Child : array [1.. order] of Multiway_tree_pointer;
                    Number : 1 .. order −1
              end;
```

where we use the *Number* field to hold the number of actual (non-"null") records held in the node. For some purposes it is necessary to add another field *Parent* of type *Multiway_tree_pointer*: its name makes its meaning clear.

In order to discuss the operation of searching in a multiway search tree it is useful to introduce a function

Function place $(k : K; B : Node) : 1 .. \; order;$

with the property that

if (1) $k \leq B.Element[1].Key$ then place$(k, B) = 1$;

· if (i) $B.Element[i - 1].Key < k \leq B.Element[i].Key$ (where $1 < i < order$) then place$(k, B) = i$;

if (n) $B.Element[order -1].Key < k$ then place$(k, B) = order$.

The details of the definition of this function are left to the reader. If the order is not very large it may be as well just to use a sequential search type of approach; but since the keys of the elements in the node B are in increasing order a modified binary search approach would also be appropriate.

Suppose now that we are searching for a record with key k_1 in the multiway search tree whose root is $p \uparrow$, i.e. is the node pointed to by the *Multiway_tree_pointer* p. Let $i = \text{place}(k_1, p \uparrow)$.

If $1 \leq i \leq order - 1$ and $k_1 = p \uparrow .Element[i].Key$ then we report success and our search is terminated—the record we are looking for is the ith record in the node $p \uparrow$. Otherwise k_1 will satisfy the inequality numbered (i) with $\leq$ replaced by $<$ (notice that here i may be equal to the order n); in this case we follow the pointer $p \uparrow .Child[i]$ and repeat the process recursively.

When we carry out a search in a multiway search tree we really want to know two things—(1) the node which holds the record we are looking for and (2) its position in that node. Since a Pascal function cannot return more than one result we write a function which returns a pointer to the node (1) and we set a global variable *position* to hold the position (2). Thus we declare

Var *position* : $0 .. order - 1$;

(we allow 0 as a possible value for *position* to deal with the case where the record we are looking for is not present) and then write the recursive

Function search $(k : K; q : Multiway\_tree\_pointer) : Multi-way\_tree\_pointer;$
 Var $t : Multiway\_tree\_pointer;$
  $i : 1 .. order;$
 Begin $t := q;$
   if $t = \text{nil}$ then **begin** search $:= \text{nil}; position := 0$ **end**
    else begin
      $i := \text{place}(k, t \uparrow);$
      if $k = t \uparrow .Element[i].Key$
        then begin search $:= t; position := i$ **end**
        else search $:= \text{search}(k, t \uparrow .Child[i])$ **end**
 End;

This can, as usual, be transformed into a non-recursive version, as follows:

Function search1 $(k\ :\ K;\ q\ :\ Multiway\_tree\_pointer)\ :\ Multiway\_tree\_pointer;$
    Var $t\ :\ Multiway\_tree\_pointer;$
        $i\ :\ 1\ ..\ order;$
        found : **boolean**;
    Begin $t := q;$
        found := **false**;
        while $(t <> $ nil$)$ **and** (**not** *found*) **do begin**
            $i := $ place$(k, t \uparrow);$
            if $k = t \uparrow .Element[i].Key$ **then** *found* := **true**
                else $t := t \uparrow .Child[i]$ **end**;
        if *found* **then begin** search1 := t; *position* := i **end**
            else begin search1 := **nil**; *position* := 0 **end**
    End;

Perhaps the most frequent use of multiway search trees is in situations where we have to deal with vast collections of data, too large to be stored in the internal memory of our computer. In such situations we shall think of the nodes of our search trees as residing in external memory—on disk, say—and pointed to by variables of type *Ext_pointer* whose values are the addresses in external memory of the locations holding the nodes they point to. In order to work with the contents of a node we must read its contents into internal memory. We handle this by declaring a variable *block* of type *Node* and defining a procedure diskread with an *Ext_pointer* parameter such that the command diskread(p) reads the contents of the node $p \uparrow$ on disk into the *Node* variable *block*. Then searching can be carried out by using the following function:

> **Function** ext_search $(k : K; q : Ext\_pointer) : Ext\_pointer;$
> **Var** $t : Ext\_pointer;$
> $i : 1 .. order;$
> $found :$ **boolean**;
> **Begin** $t := q;$
> $found :=$ **false**;
>   **while** $(t <>$ nil$)$ **and** (**not** $found$) **do begin**
>   diskread$(t);$
> $i :=$ place$(k, block);$
>   **if** $k = block.Element[i].Key$ **then** $found :=$ **true**
>   **else** $t := block.Child[i]$ **end**;
>   **if** $found$ **then begin** ext_search $:= t;$ $position := i$ **end**
>   **else begin** ext_search $:=$ nil; $position := 0$ **end**
> **End**;

Each execution of the **while** loop of the procedure ext_search involves accessing a node in external memory and transferring its contents to internal memory: only then can the search proceed. The access-and-transfer operation tends to be more time-consuming than the work done after the transfer is made; so the whole process will become more efficient if the number of disk accesses can be reduced. The desire to do this raises a general question about the storage of information items—should we store complete items or just their keys along with the addresses of the locations where the corresponding complete items are stored? The maximum size of a node—the amount of information which can be transferred in one disk access—is usually determined for us by the computer we are using; but since complete records typically take 5 to 40 times as much space as their keys we can store in a node many more key-and-address pairs than complete records. Of course once such a pair is found another disk access will be necessary to retrieve all the interesting information fields of the corresponding record.

We turn now to the operation of insertion in a multiway search tree. By an obvious modification of the search procedure we find the node of the tree in which the new item would be stored if it were present and also the position it would occupy among the items stored in that node (we recall that the items in a node are arranged in increasing order of *Key* field). We should decide what action to take if the item we are trying to insert is already present. If it is not already present then the node we reach by means of the search procedure will be a leaf, i.e. all its subtrees are **nil**.

If this leaf is not full, i.e. if it contains fewer than the maximum permitted number of actual records (*order* -1), then we insert the new record in its proper position, so that the *Key* fields are still in increasing order, and the insertion process terminates. If the leaf reached is full then we must introduce a new node, with the new record as its only entry, and make it the appropriate child of the full leaf node—if $k_1 < k_2 < \ldots < k_{n-1}$ are the keys in the leaf node and $k_{i-1} < k < k_i$ where k is the key of the new record then the *Child*[i] pointer from the leaf node points to the new node.

As in the case of binary search trees this insertion procedure may produce very unbalanced trees, in which searching for some entries may require a large number of node accesses. Furthermore, since when leaves are created they contain only one item, and new leaves may be created before previously created leaves are full, space may be wasted in setting aside space for new nodes which are nearly empty and time wasted in transferring nearly empty nodes from disk. On the other hand new nodes are not created until their parents are full; the nodes nearest the root tend to be full, so many keys will be found on short paths.

12.2   B-trees

At the end of the last Section we mentioned some disadvantages of general multiway search trees caused by using the natural method of inserting new items—the tree may become unbalanced and there may be many nearly empty nodes. In an attempt to avoid these difficulties we introduce a special type of multiway search tree as follows: a **B-tree of order** n is a multiway search tree of order n such that

(1) the root node may contain between 1 and $n - 1$ records;
(2) each non-root node must contain between $(n - 1)$ **div** 2 and

$n - 1$ records;
(3) all the leaves are at the same level.

Searching in a B-tree is carried out according to the procedures which we described in the last Section for searching in general multiway search trees; but the procedure described there for insertion in general multiway search trees would destroy the B-tree property since it involves creating 1-element leaf nodes which (at least for $n > 4$) would contradict condition (2). To illustrate the insertion procedure which is used in order to maintain the B-tree property consider the following examples where the order n is 5 and so n **div** 2 is 2. (In real life situations the order of the B-trees in use is likely to be very much larger, perhaps around 100.)

Suppose we start with a B-tree consisting of a root node which contains 3 records:

(We show only the *Key* fields of the entries; the order relation for the two-letter keys is dictionary order.)

There is still room in the root node to insert a record whose *Key* is *da* (we shall just talk of "inserting *da*"); but once this insertion is made we have the node full:

If we want to insert *fa* we cannot put it in the root node which is now full, nor can we introduce a 1-element leaf, which would not be permissible in a B-tree of order 5. Instead we carry out the following "node-splitting" operation:

(1) we split the given node into two nodes L and R;
(2) we put the records with the smallest two keys (among the

original four and the new record) into the left node L;

(3) we put the records with the largest two keys among the five into the right node R;

(4) we create a new root node;

(5) we put the record with the middle key into the new root node (where we are allowed to have only a single entry) and introduce pointers to the left and right of this record pointing to L and R respectively.

We obtain

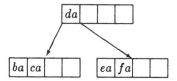

To insert cf we notice that cf precedes da in dictionary order; so it must be inserted in the subtree of the root node to the left of da, which consists of the leaf containing ba and ca. Similarly ec and ee come later in the dictionary than da and so they must be inserted in the subtree to the right of da, which consists of the leaf containing ea and fa. Hence, inserting cf, ec and ee (in any order) we obtain eventually

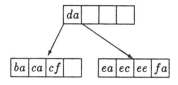

Suppose now that we want to insert eb. Since eb is later than da in dictionary order it should go to the right of da. But all we have to the right of da is a full node. So we split the node containing ea, ec, ee and fa into two, sending ea and eb to the left of the two new nodes, ee and fa to the right and promoting ec to the root node, with pointers to its left and right pointing to the new nodes. Thus we have

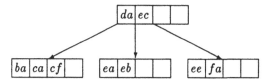

To insert *di* we notice that *di* occurs in the dictionary between *da* and *ec*, so it must go in the subtree pointed to by the arrow between *da* and *ec*, which consists of a leaf node which is not yet full. So *di* is inserted in its dictionary-order place in this leaf. In the same way we insert *dc* and *fg* to obtain

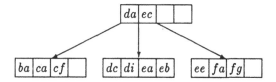

If at this stage we have to insert any entry between *da* and *ec* the middle leaf must split; thus if *de* is inserted we obtain

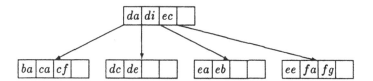

In the same way, if we insert *fi*, *ga*, *fc* and *fe* we reach eventually

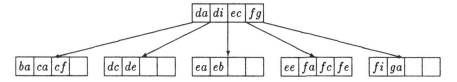

Next suppose we want to insert a record with *Key* field between *ec* and *fg*. Such an item ought to go in the fourth leaf—but this is already full. So we split it in the usual way and promote an item to the parent,

which is the root node. But the root node is also full, so it must be
split and an item passed up to a newly created root node containing
just this single item. So, for example, if we insert *eg* we split the fourth
leaf into a node containing *ee* and *eg* and one containing *fc* and *fe*;
and we pass *fa* up to the root node. This is then split into a node
containing *da* and *di* and one containing *fa* and *fg*. The new root
node contains only *ec*. So the B-tree we have constructed is

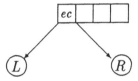

where the left subtree *L* of *ec* is

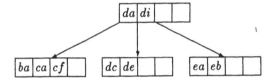

and its right subtree *R* is

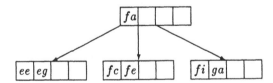

To sum up what we have learned from building this B-tree, we have
the following instructions:

To insert a new item in a **nil** B-tree we create a new node with the
new item as its only entry. To insert a new item in a non-**nil** B-tree
we begin by finding the leaf node *N* which would contain the item if it
were present (by following a search path in the usual multiway search
tree fashion). Then

(1) if N is not already full (i.e. contains fewer than $n - 1$ items, where n is the order of the B-tree), introduce the new item into N so as to keep the entries of N in sorted order of *Key* fields;

(2) if N is full (i.e. contains $n - 1$ items),

(*a*) arrange the new item and the $n - 1$ pre-existing items of N in increasing order of *Key* field, say

$$X_1, X_2, \ldots, X_n \text{ where } X_1.Key < X_2.Key < \ldots < X_n.Key;$$

(*b*) split the node N into a left-hand node L containing X_1, $\ldots$, X_q, where $q = (n - 1)$ **div** 2 and a right-hand node R containing $X_{q+2}, \ldots, X_n$;

(*c*) if N has a parent node P which is not full, insert X_{q+1} in P using (1) and let the pointers to the left and right of X_{q+1} point to L and R respectively;

if N has a parent node P which is full, apply (2) recursively;

if N has no parent node, create a new node with the promoted item X_{q+1} as its only item and its two pointers pointing to L and R.

We repeat that insertion in a B-tree always begins by trying to add an element to a leaf node. The B-tree resists increasing its height by examining all the nodes on the search path from root node to this leaf to see if any of them has room for an extra element. Only if all these nodes are full do we have to create a new root and increase the height of the B-tree by 1.

Suppose we have a B-tree of order n; let $q = (n - 1)$ **div** 2. Consider the following table:

Level	Minimum Number of nodes	Maximum Number of nodes	Minimum Number of items	Maximum Number of items
0	1	1	1	$n-1$
1	2	n	$2q$	$n(n-1)$
2	$2(q+1)$	n^2	$2q(q+1)$	$n^2(n+1)$
3	$2(q+1)^2$	n^3	$2q(q+1)^2$	$n^3(n-1)$
$\vdots$				
h	$2(q+1)^{h-1}$	n^h	$2q(q+1)^{h-1}$	$n^h(n-1)$

whose entries can be deduced directly from the definition of B-trees.

Thus the minimum number of items in a B-tree of order n and height h $(h \geq 2)$ is

$$1 + 2q + 2q(q+1) + 2q(q+1)^2 + \ldots + 2q(q+1)^{h-1}$$

$$= 1 + 2q(1 + (q+1) + (q+1)^2 + \ldots + (q+1)^{h-1})$$

$$= 1 + 2q\frac{(q+1)^h - 1}{(q+1) - 1}$$

$$= 1 + 2((q+1)^n - 1) = 2(q+1)^h - 1$$

So if a B-tree of order n and height h contains N items we must have

$$N \geq 2(q+1)^h - 1,$$

where $q = (n-1)$ **div** 2, from which we deduce that

$$h \leq \log_{q+1}(\tfrac{1}{2}(N+1))$$

and so the maximum number of nodes which have to be examined in order to locate an item, which is 1 more than the height, is at most

$$1 + \log_{q+1}(\tfrac{1}{2}(N+1)).$$

The maximum number of items in a B-tree of height h is

$$(n-1) + n(n-1) + n^2(n-1) + \ldots + n^h(n-1)$$
$$= (n-1)(1 + n + n^2 + \ldots + n^h)$$
$$= (n-1)\frac{n^{h+1} - 1}{n - 1} = n^{h+1} - 1$$

Thus, for example, in B-trees of order 100 ($n = 100$, $q = (n-1)\mathbf{div}2 = 49$) and heights 1, 2, 3 we can store up to 9999, 999999, 99999999 items respectively.

We have next to consider the problem of how to delete an item from a B-tree without destroying the B-tree property. First of all we persuade ourselves that we may confine our attention to the problem of deleting an item from a leaf of the B-tree. Suppose we have an item X somewhere in a B-tree. Consider the right pointer of X, i.e. if X is $p \uparrow .Element[i]$ for some node $p \uparrow$ ($1 \le i \le n-1$), we look at $p \uparrow .Child[i+1]$. All the items in the subtree pointed to by this pointer have *Key* field greater than $X.Key$. The item in this subtree with least *Key* field is the first entry in the leftmost leaf of the subtree. If we delete this element from the B-tree (maintaining the B-tree property) and then replace X by this element we are left with a B-tree with X deleted.

For example, suppose we want to delete the record with *Key* 32 from the B-tree of order 5

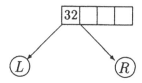

where the left subtree L of 32 is

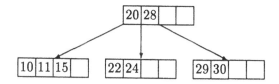

and its right subtree R is

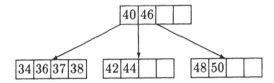

We look at the leftmost leaf in R; this is the node

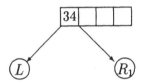

We remove the record with lowest *Key* field in this node, 34, and use it to replace the record with *Key* field 32 in the root node, which we want to delete. This produces

We have seen by the preceding discussion and example that the problem of deleting an entry from a B-tree reduces to the question: How do we delete an entry from a leaf node N?

If N is also the root node then, since the minimum number of entries in the root node of a B-tree is 1, we may simply remove elements from N without destroying the B-tree property until there is only one left; and when the last element in the root node is deleted we are left with

where L is as before and the new right subtree R_1 is

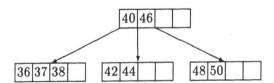

a **nil** B-tree.

Suppose now that N is a leaf node but not the root.

(1) If N has more than $q = (n-1)$ **div** 2 entries we simply remove the item to be deleted and readjust the numbering of the elements in the node; after this removal N still has at least q entries, the minimum allowable for a non-root node in a B-tree. We carried out this operation in removing 34 from

34	36	37	38

to form

36	37	38	

(2) If N has exactly q entries then removal of one of them would leave N with fewer than the minimum number of entries allowed in a non-root node of a B-tree.

Two possibilities can occur. To describe them it is useful to introduce a modest amount of terminology which is almost self-explanatory. Suppose N is the node pointed to by the ith *Child* pointer of its *Parent* node P. If $1 < i \leq n$ then the node pointed to by $P.Child[i-1]$ is called the **left sibling** of N and if $1 \leq i < n$ then that pointed to by $P.Child[i+1]$ is called the **right sibling** of N.

(*a*) It may happen that N has either a left or right sibling (or both) with more than q entries. Let S be such a sibling. (If we were writing a program to implement this we would have to say which sibling to choose if both had more than q entries.) Suppose S is the left sibling of N. Then consider the sequence

> entries of S,
> > "separating" element $P.Element[i-1]$ in P,
> > > remaining entries of N after deletion.

This sequence is in increasing order of *Key* field. Suppose the number of entries in this sequence is k: certainly $k \geq (q+1) + 1 + (q-1) = 2q + 1$, from which we deduce easily that k **div** $2 \geq q$ and hence also

$k - 1 - (k \mathbf{\ div\ } 2) \geq q$. We relocate the k entries of the sequence, putting the first $k \mathbf{\ div\ } 2$ entries in S and the last $k - 1 - (k \mathbf{\ div\ } 2)$ entries in N; the remaining element of the sequence is promoted to the parent node P and becomes the new separating element. It is clear how to amend this procedure if S is the right sibling of N.

For example, if we remove the records with *Key* fields 22 and 42 from the B-tree

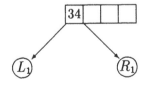

where the left subtree L of 34 is

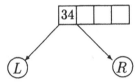

and its right subtree R is

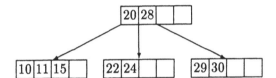

we obtain

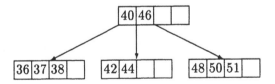

where the new left subtree L_1 of 34 is

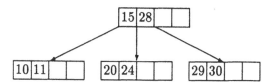

and its new right subtree R_1 is

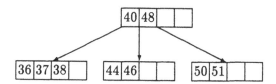

(b) On the other hand it may happen that no sibling of N has more than q entries.

In this case let S be one of the siblings of N (again, if we were writing a program to implement this we would have to say which sibling to choose). Form a new node N' containing $2q$ entries—q from the chosen sibling S, the $q-1$ entries remaining in N after the deletion and the separating element in the parent node P. But this is not the end of the story: we have to examine the effect on the parent node P.

(1) If P still has at least q entries after the separating element is "demoted" to N' then all that remains to do is to move down one place the entries to the right of the separating element and readjust the numbering of the subtree pointers.

For example, to remove the record with *Key* field 44 from the B-tree of order 5

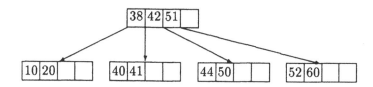

then, using the left sibling of the node N containing the record we want to delete, we form a new node

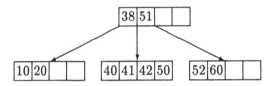

and attach it to the readjusted parent node as shown:

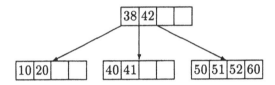

If we had used the right sibling of N we would have produced

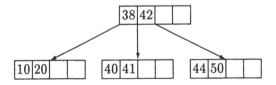

(2) If P is the root node and at least one element remains after the demotion of the separating element then, since the root node of a B-tree may have as few as one entry, the B-tree condition is not violated and we need only move down entries and readjust the numbering of the subtrees as in (1). For example, removal of the entry with *Key* field 41 from the B-tree of order 5

produces

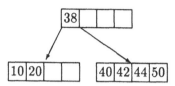

If before the deletion P has 1 element and 2 subtrees each with q entries, then when an element is removed from one of the children a new node is formed using the $2q$ remaining entries arranged in increasing order of *Key* field, and this new node becomes the root. Thus on removing the record with *Key* field 40 from the B-tree of order 5

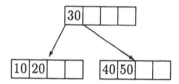

we are left with the single node

$$\boxed{10|20|30|50}$$

(3) If P is not the root node and has fewer than q entries after the demotion of the separating element then we examine the siblings of P to see whether one of them has more than q entries—if so, then we proceed as in (a) above; if not, then we proceed as in (b).

The reader is invited to check that if we remove the record with *Key* field fi from the B-tree of order 5 we constructed earlier, namely

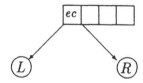

where L is

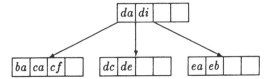

and R is

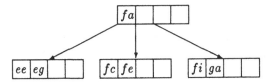

then we end up with the B-tree

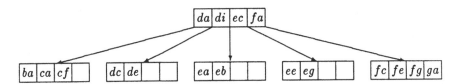

The idea behind the requirement that every non-root node in a B-tree be at least half full was to ensure that the work in reading a node from disk should result in the transfer of a reasonable number of records for processing; it also reduced the number of nodes and the amount of allocated but unused space which might be required in a general multiway search tree. We can move a bit further in the same direction by requiring that each non-root node be at least (roughly) two-thirds full. Thus we introduce the notion of a **B*-tree of order** n. This is a structure similar to a multiway search tree of order n; its root node, however, may hold more elements than any node in such a search tree. Formally

(1) the root node may contain between 1 and $2((2n - 2) \textbf{ div } 3)$ records;

(2) each non-root node must contain between $(2n - 2) \textbf{ div } 3$ and

$n - 1$ records;

(3) all the leaves are at the same level.

For example, for a B*-tree of order 7 the root node may contain between 1 and 8 records and each non-root node must contain between 4 and 6 records.

To understand why the maximum number of entries in the root node is not the same as the maximum number for the non-root nodes, we have to think about what happens when the root node becomes full and we try to insert an additional entry. Following the example of the B-tree situation we would split the contents of the root and the new entry into a single element for the root and entries for two new nodes which will be children of the root. Thus the maximum number of elements in the root node must be twice the minimum number in the non-root nodes.

We look briefly at the operation of insertion in a B*-tree, taking for our examples $n = 7$ and starting with the root node

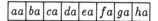

which is full. If we want to insert *ia* then we split the root node and obtain

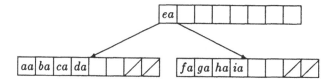

(We have used diagonal lines in the non-root nodes to indicate that they may not hold more than 6 entries; this would be dealt with in a Pascal program by use of the *Number* field of the *Node* variables involved.)

Insertion of records with *Key* fields *ja* and *ka* produce the B*-tree

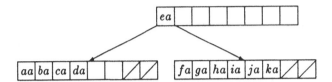

The right leaf is now full, but its left sibling still has room for two further entries. Following the example of B-tree insertion we see that adding records with *Key* fields *la* and *na* produces successively

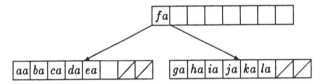

and

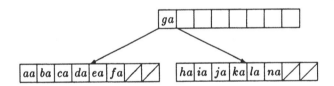

When we come to the situation where we want to insert a new record in a full leaf node N where there is no free space in a sibling then we examine the $(n-1)$ elements of N, the $(n-1)$ elements of a chosen sibling S, the separator of N and S in the parent node P and the new element—there are $2n$ elements there altogether. Using these we form 3 leaf nodes and 2 separating elements in P. The three nodes must all satisfy the B*-tree property about the minimum number of entries in a non-root node; we can achieve this by giving them $(2n-2)$ **div** 3, $(2n-1)$ **div** 3 and $2n$ **div** 3 elements. (The reader is invited to check that these add up to $2n-2$ elements—to do this, consider separately the cases where n **mod** 3 is 0, 1 or 2.)

In the case where $n = 7$ we have $(2n-2)$ **div** $3 = (2n-1)$ **div** $3 =$

$2n$ **div** $3 = 4$. Thus, if we insert in the above B*-tree of order 7 a new record with *Key* field *pa* we end up with

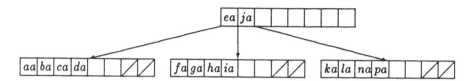

In Section 12.1 we suggested that storage space may be saved by storing only key-and-address pairs in our search trees rather than complete records. Even more space might be saved if we were to store keys only, though of course there must eventually be some means of accessing a complete record from its key. In a B-tree it is easy to access sequentially all the records whose key-and-address pairs are stored in a single node; but sequential access beyond a single node would require a more complicated procedure involving following *Parent* pointers. B$^+$-trees constitute an attempt to deal with the two points we have mentioned, space saving and sequential access.

B$^+$-trees of order n resemble B-trees of order n in that their root nodes may contain between 1 and $n - 1$ entries while their non-root nodes must contain between $(n - 1)$ **div** 2 and $n - 1$ entries. But

(1) the non-leaf nodes of a B$^+$-tree contain only keys of records;

(2) the leaf nodes of a B^+-tree, which are all at the same level, contain key-and-address pairs for *all* the records being stored (or possibly complete records);

(3) there is a pointer from each leaf node (except the last) to the next.

Notice that the keys in the non-leaf nodes are there solely to help construct search paths to the actual records. Thus, in order to locate a record with a given key, we must continue the standard multiway search procedure until we reach a leaf node, for it is only the leaf nodes that contain the associated information or address. Since the key of a record stored (or pointed to) in a leaf node may also occur in a non-leaf node we must establish a convention to decide whether we move to the left or the right when we come across in a non-leaf node the key of the record we are searching for. In the example shown below the convention followed is to go to the left.

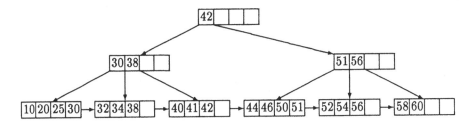

Insertion in a B$^+$-tree is similar to that in a B-tree except that when a node is split the middle key is retained in the left "half-node" as well as being promoted to the parent node.

Notice that when we delete a record from a leaf node it is unnecessary to remove its key from any non-leaf node in which it occurs: it can still function perfectly satisfactorily as a separator.

12.3 Tries

In all the searching algorithms we have studied so far the objects in the *Key* field of our records have been indivisible: they have been members of an ordered type K and the only operation we have carried out on them is comparison. But if the keys were words, for example, we could subdivide them into their constituent letters and think of searching for them letter by letter, starting with the first.

The data structure used to put this idea into practice is called a *trie*. (Although the word was invented by taking the middle four letters of the word "retrieve" it is usually pronounced "try".)

Formally we define a **trie of order** n to be either empty or else an ordered sequence of n tries of order n.

Thinking of our keys as words of a certain limited length made up of the 26 lower case letters we might declare

> **Const** *maxlength* = ... ;
> **Type** *Letter* = 'a' .. 'z';
>   *Letter_and_space* = (⋆ 'a' .. 'z' and space character ⋆);
>   *K* = **array** [1 .. *maxlength*] **of** *Letter*;
>   *Trie_pointer* = ↑*Node*;
>   *Node* = **Record**
>   *Branch* : **array** [*Letter*] **of** *Trie_pointer*;
>   *Info* : *T*
>   **end**;
> **Function** length (*w* : *K*) : 0 .. *maxlength*;

(We think of a key word of length l being stored in the first l components of an array of type K, with the remaining components being filled with space characters. Clearly length(w) is to be the number of letters in the key word w.)

To access the information associated with the key word w we initialise a *Trie_pointer* variable p to point to the root of the trie and an **integer** variable i to 1. Then we execute the loop

> **while** $i <=$ length(w) **do begin**
> $p := p \uparrow .Branch[w[i]]$;
> $i := i + 1$ **end**;

The information required (or its address) is then in the *Info* field of the node pointed to by the final version of p.

In the following example we have restricted the type *Letter* to 'a'..'c'; the key words are the words in the Oxford English Dictionary which are formed using these letters. We have represented the *Info* fields of the nodes by integers, which we think of as the addresses of the locations storing the definitions of the corresponding key words (we set this field to be 0 if there is no correponding record). To save space we have not labelled the branches from the nodes of the trie but have represented the tails of the 'a', 'b' and 'c' pointers from each node by three dots, the first for *Branch*['a'], the second for *Branch*['b'] and the

third for *Branch*['c']. Dots from which no arrows emerge are supposed
to represent **nil** pointers.

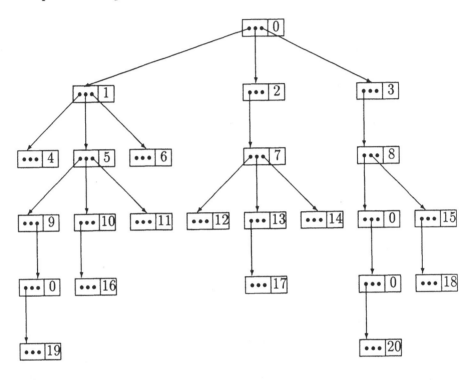

To search in this trie for the record with key word 'caaba' we start
at the root node and follow in turn the 'c', the 'a', the 'a', the 'b' and
then the 'a' pointers, arriving finally at the bottom right leaf node in
the picture, with *Info* field 18. Looking in location 18 we find

   18. *caaba* : The sacred edifice at Mecca, which contains the 'black
          stone', and is the 'Holy of Holies' of Islam.

   To insert new entries in a trie we trace our way down the trie step
by step using the pointers corresponding to the successive letters of the
key word. If at any stage the pointer corresponding to the next letter
of the key word is **nil** we introduce a new node and replace the nil
pointer by a pointer to this node.

To delete a record we follow the path indicated by the letters of its key word until we reach the node containing (or pointing to) the record. If this node is not a leaf then we amend the *Info* field to indicate that there is no corresponding record (in our example we would set the *Info* field to 0). If the node corresponding to the deleted record is a leaf then we move to its parent and make the pointer to it from its parent **nil**. If all the other pointers from the parent are **nil** then we can dispose of the parent and possibly also ancestors of previous generations. Thus to delete the record with key word 'caaba' from our sample trie we would remove the corresponding node and also its parent and grandparent. If we are to be deleting records from a trie then we ought to include a *Parent* field in the definition of *Node*. Clearly also, in programming the deletion operation it would be a good idea as we move down the trie to stack the nodes we have visited so that we can dispose of them in turn if their pointers are all **nil**.

Suppose the key "words" were all possible 4-letter sequences: there are $26^4 = 156,976$ of these. In a trie of order 26 any one of these words can be located in at most 4 steps. Search in a binary search tree would require (on average) $\log_2(26^4) \approx 10.8$ comparisons, though of course the number would be reduced by using B-trees of higher order.

12.4 Exercises 12

1. Build up a multiway search tree of order 5 using the following input stream (of keys):

$$25, 17, 31, 42, 21, 19, 26, 33, 47, 44, 45, 43, 8, 9.$$

2. Build up a multiway search tree of order 5 using the following input stream (of keys):

$$20, 19, 18, 17, 16, 15, 14, 13, 12, 11, 10, 9, 8, 7, 6, 5, 4, 3, 2, 1.$$

3. Construct a B-tree of order 5 using an input stream of records with two-letter keys

   ca ea ba da bf df ah cg bi cc af eg bd ec ch ai dc di ce ef cf.

4. Show how to insert a record with key *ff* in the B-tree of order 5

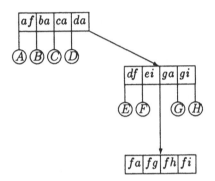

   where $A, \ldots, H$ are subtrees whose detailed structure need not concern you.

5. Using the same input stream as in Exercise 3, but stopping at the record with key *dc* construct a B$^+$-tree of order 5.

6. Using the same input stream as in Exercise 3 construct a B*-tree of order 7.

7. Show the sequence of B-trees formed as we delete from the B-tree of order 5 constructed in Exercise 1 the records with keys

   cf, ef, ce, di, dc, ai, ch, eg, bd, ec, af, cc, bi, cg, ah, df, bf.

8. Show the sequence of B$^+$-trees formed as we delete from the B$^+$-tree of order 5 constructed in Exercise 3 the records with keys

   dc, ai, ch, eg, bd, ec, af, cc, bi, cg, ah, df, bf.

9. Build a trie with the aid of which you can retrieve the information associated with the following keywords formed using the letters 'a', 'r', 's', 't':

> *a, art, arts, as, astart, at, ras, rast, rat, rats, sat, star,*
> *stars, start, ta, tar, tars, tart, tartar, tat, tatt, tsar.*

10. Show how to delete the record with key *hd* from the B-tree of order 5
    below.

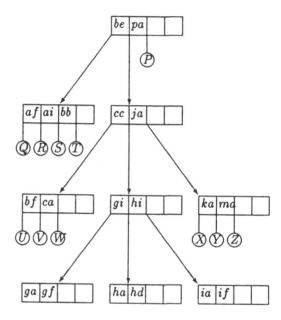

where $P, \ldots, Z$ are subtrees whose detailed structure need not concern
you.

Part IV

SOLUTIONS

Chapter 13

SOLUTIONS TO EXERCISES 1

1. (a) $addr(i) = 991 + 4i$;

   (b) $addr(i, j) = 749 + 56i + 8j$;

   (c) $addr(i, j) = 3687 + 8i + 5j$;

   (d) $addr(i_1, i_2, i_3) = 300 + 50i_1 + 10i_2 + i_3$.

2. **Procedure** update $(i, j : 1 .. N; x : \textbf{real})$;
   Begin if $i <= j$ **then** $A1[(i * (i - 1)) \textbf{ div } 2 + j] := x$
           else update(j, i, x) **End**;

3. **Function** extract $(i, j : 1 .. N) : \textbf{real}$;
   Begin if $i = j$ **then** extract $:= 0$
       else if $i < j$ **then** extract $:= S1[((i - 1) * (i - 2)) \textbf{ div } 2 + j]$
         else extract $:= -$extract(j, i) **End** ;

   Procedure update $(i, j : 1 .. N; x : \textbf{real})$;
   Begin if $(i = j)$ **and** $(x <> 0)$ **then** Writeln('illegal update')
       else if $i < j$ **then** $S1[((i - 1) * (i - 2)) \textbf{ div } 2 + j] := x$
         else update$(j, i, -x)$ **End**;

4. a_{11}, for which $i = j = 1$, is stored in $T1[1]$ and $2 * i + j - 2 = 1$.
   a_{12}, for which $i = 1, j = 2$, is stored in $T1[2]$ and $2 * i + j - 2 = 2$.
   If $i > 1$ then to store the subdiagonal, diagonal and superdiagonal elements in the first $i - 1$ rows we require $2 + 3(i - 2) = 3i - 4$ entries

in $T1$. The elements in the i-th row to be stored are $a_{i,i-1}$, a_{ii} and (if $i < N$) $a_{i,i+1}$ and these are stored in position

$$3i - 4 + 1 = 2i + (i - 1) - 2$$
$$3i - 4 + 2 = 2i + i - 2$$

and (if $i < N$)

$$3i - 4 + 3 = 2i + (i + 1) - 2.$$

Thus each a_{ij} with $|i - j| \leq 1$ is stored in $T1[2 * i + j - 2]$.

Function extract $(i, j : 1 .. N)$: **real**;
Begin if abs$(i - j) > 1$ **then** extract := 0
       else extract := $T1[2 * i + j - 2]$ **End**;

Procedure update $(i, j : 1 .. N; x :$ **real**$)$;
Begin if $($abs$(i - j) > 1)$ **and** $(x <> 0)$
       then Writeln('illegal update')
       else $T1[2 * i + j - 2] := x$ **End**;

5. Each object in the **record** type T consists of an integer and an array of 20 characters and hence requires

$$L_T = L_{\text{integer}} + 20\, L_{\text{char}}$$

bytes to store it, where L_{integer} and L_{char} are the component lengths of the types **integer** and **char** respectively.

If b is the base address then the addresses of the first bytes of

$$a.List[1],\ a.List[2],\ a.List[3] \text{ and } a.List[4]$$

are respectively

$$b,\ b + L_T,\ b + 2\, L_T \text{ and } b + 3\, L_T.$$

We store $a.List[4]$ by storing successively its

$$Key,\ Info[1],\ Info[2],\ \ldots,\ Info[15]$$

fields. So the address of the first byte of $a.List[4].Info[13]$ is

$$b + 3\, L_T + L_{\text{integer}} + 12\, L_{\text{char}}$$

and similarly the address of the first byte of $a.Season$ is $b + 15\, L_T$.

6. (a) We introduce the auxiliary *List_pointer* variable p, initialised to l, and an **integer** variable *count*, initialised to 0. If p $(= l)$ is nil we take no action, so *count* remains 0; otherwise we enter a **while** loop on each execution of which we increase *count* by 1 and replace p by $p \uparrow$.*Next*, stopping when we reach the end of the list, i.e. when the current value of p is **nil**. The value returned by the function is the final value of the variable *count*. So we write

```
Function length (l : List_pointer) : integer;
Var p : List_pointer;
        count : integer;
Begin p := l; count := 0;
        while p <> nil do begin
                                count := count + 1;
                                p := p ↑ .Next end;
        length := count
End;
```

(b) First we decide what action to take if l is **nil**. It would not be wrong to do nothing but perhaps it would be better to output a message that the list is empty. If l is not **nil** we initialise an auxiliary *List_pointer* variable p to l and enter a **Repeat** loop which writes out the *Info* field of $p \uparrow$ and then replaces p by $p \uparrow$.*Next*, stopping when p is **nil**. Thus we write

```
Procedure print (l : List_pointer);
Var p : List_pointer;
Begin if l = nil then Writeln('The list is empty')
            else begin
                    p := l;
                    Repeat Write(p ↑ .Info);
                            p := p ↑ .Next
                    until p = nil end
End;
```

(c) If either of the lists headed by $p \uparrow$ or $q \uparrow$ is **nil** then the concatenation is the other list. Otherwise we must proceed node by node down the list headed by $p \uparrow$ until we reach the last node, whose *Next* field will be **nil**; we alter this **nil** *List_pointer* to q. The Pascal version is

```
Function concatenate (p, q : List_pointer) : List_pointer;
Var r, s : List_pointer;
Begin if p = nil then concatenate := q
    else if q = nil then concatenate := p
      else begin
            r := p; s := p;
            while s ↑.Next <> nil do s := s ↑ .Next;
            s ↑ .Next := q;
            concatenate := r end
End;
```

(d) We remark first that we cannot remove the last entry from a **nil** list and that if we remove the last entry from a one-element list we are left with the **nil** list. To deal with lists having more than one element we introduce two auxiliary *List_pointer* variables p and q initialised to point to the first and second nodes in the list respectively. Then we move down the list, repeatedly replacing p and q by their successors until q points to the last node (signalled by $q \uparrow .Next =$ **nil**) and then setting $p \uparrow .Next$ to be **nil**. The Pascal version of this is as follows:

```
Procedure dock (Var l : List_pointer);
Var p, q : List_pointer;
Begin if l = nil then writeln ('You cannot dock an empty
list')
            else if l ↑ .Next = nil then l := nil
                else begin
                      p := l; q := l ↑ .Next;
                      while q ↑ .Next <> nil do begin
                                        p := q;
                                        q := q ↑ .Next end;
                      p ↑ .Next := nil end
End;
```

(e) We have to go down the list node by node until either we find x
for the first time, in which case we return a pointer to the node
where x occurs as *Info* field, or else we come to the end of the list
without finding x, in which case we return **nil**. We introduce an
auxiliary *List_pointer* variable as usual to help us move down the
list and a **boolean** variable *found*, initially set to **false**, which
will enable us to stop going further down the list once we have
found x. The Pascal version is:

> **Function** search $(x : T; l : List\_pointer) : List\_pointer$;
> **Var** $p : List\_pointer$;
>   *found* : **boolean**;
> **Begin** $p := l$; *found* := **false**;
>   **while** $(p <> \textbf{nil})$ **and** (**not** *found*) **do**
>   **if** $p \uparrow .Info = x$ **then** *found* := **true**
>   **else** $p := p \uparrow .Next$;
>   **if** *found* **then** search := p **else** search := **nil**
> **End**;

(f) We notice first that if $l = \textbf{nil}$ or $l \uparrow .Next = \textbf{nil}$ (i.e. if the
list headed by $l \uparrow$ has either no node or only one node) then
reverse(l) = l. If there are two nodes or more in the list to be
reversed then (1) the *Next* field of the head node must be set to
nil (because it is to be the last node of the reversed list); (2) the
Next field of the second node must be set to point to the first
node; (3) then (if there is a third node) we must move down the
list, setting the *Next* field of the third node to point back to the
second and so on; (4) eventually, when we reach the end of the
list, reverse(l) must be set to point to the last node. To carry
this out in Pascal we write:

> **Function** reverse $(l : List\_pointer) : List\_pointer$;
> **Var** $p, q, r : List\_pointer$;
> **Begin if** $l = \textbf{nil}$ **then** reverse := l
>   **else if** $l \uparrow .Next = \textbf{nil}$ **then** reverse := l
>   **else begin**
> $p := l$; $p \uparrow .Next := \textbf{nil}$;
> $q := l \uparrow .Next$;
>   **while** $q \uparrow .Next <> \textbf{nil}$ **do begin**

$$r := q \uparrow .Next;$$
$$q \uparrow .Next := p;$$
$$p := q; \; q := r \; \textbf{end};$$
$$q \uparrow .Next := p;$$
$$reverse := q \; \textbf{end}$$

End;

(g) If l is **nil** no action is required. If the element x which is to be removed occurs in the *Info* field of the head node $l \uparrow$ then we replace l by its successor $l \uparrow .Next$ and apply the procedure remove recursively. Otherwise we introduce two auxiliary *List_pointer* variables p and q pointing to the head node and its successor if it has one. If the head node has no successor (i.e. $q =$ **nil**) no action is taken. Otherwise we check whether $q \uparrow .Info = x$; if it is the node $q \uparrow$ must be deleted—this is done by altering the *Next* field of $p \uparrow$; if not, p is altered to point to $q \uparrow$; and in both cases q is altered to point to its successor. The process is repeated until the updated value of q is **nil**. The Pascal version is:

```
Procedure remove (x : T; Var l : List_pointer);
Var p, q : List_pointer;
Begin if l <> nil then begin
         if l ↑ .Info = x then begin
                 l := l ↑ .Next;
                 remove(x, l) end
         else begin
                 p := l; q := l ↑ .Next;
                 while q <> nil do begin
                         if q ↑ .Info = x
                         then p ↑ .Next := q ↑ .Next
                         else p := q;
                         q := q ↑ .Next end end end
End;
```

(h) Clearly if $m = n$ no action is required. Otherwise we move auxiliary pointers p and q down the list until they point to the m-th and n-th nodes and then apply the usual programming device to swap their *Info* fields. To avoid counting down from the head of the list twice to find the m-th and n-th nodes we might begin by

finding the larger and smaller of m and n, counting down to the smaller and then counting on to the larger.
The Pascal version is as follows:

```
Procedure interchange (m, n ; 1 ..  maxint; Var l :
List_pointer);
    Var i : integer; x : T;
          p, q : List_pointer;
    Procedure min_max (m, n : integer;
                          Var min, max : integer);
    Begin
      if m <= n then begin min := m; max := n end
              else begin min := n; max := m end
    End;
Begin if m <> n then begin
                  min_max (m, n, min, max);
                  p := l;
                  for i := 1 to min − 1 do p := p ↑ .Next;
                  q := p;
                  for i := 1 to max − min do q := q ↑ .Next;
                  x := p ↑ .Info;
                  p ↑ .Info := q ↑ .Info;
                  q ↑ .Info := x end
    End;
```

7. If the list f represents a constant polynomial (that is if we have $f \uparrow .Exponent = 0$) then derivative(f) must represent the zero polynomial; otherwise derivative(f) is a pointer to a node whose *Coefficient* field is $(f \uparrow .Coefficient)*(f \uparrow .Exponent)$, whose *Exponent* field is $(f \uparrow .Exponent - 1)$ and whose *Next* field is the pointer derivative($f \uparrow .Next$). Thus we define:

```
Function derivative (p : Polynomial_pointer) :
                          Polynomial_pointer;
Var q : Polynomial_pointer;
Begin if p ↑.Exponent = 0 then begin
                  new (q);
                  q ↑.Coefficient := 0;
                  q ↑.Exponent := 0;
```

$$q \uparrow .Next := \textbf{nil end}$$
```
    else begin
        new (q);
        q ↑.Coefficient := (p ↑.Coefficient) * (p ↑.Exponent);
        q ↑.Exponent := (p ↑.Exponent) −1;
        q ↑.Next := derivative(p ↑.Next) end;
    derivative := q
End;
```

8. Declare

```
Type Pointer = ↑ Node;
     Node = Record
                Info : T;
                Pred, Succ : Pointer
            end;
Var head : Pointer;
```

Suppose we wish to insert an information item in a new node after a given node pointed to by a pointer p. Then we must create the new node, using **new** as usual, and set its *Info* field to the given information item. Its *Pred* field must contain a pointer to the node pointed to by p and its *Succ* field a pointer to the successor of the node pointed to by p. The *Succ* field of $p \uparrow$ must be altered to hold a pointer to the new node and so must the *Pred* field of the original successor of $p \uparrow$ (unless $p \uparrow .Succ$ is **nil**). In Pascal this becomes

```
Procedure insert_after (a : T; p : Pointer);
Var q, r : Pointer;
Begin if p <> nil then begin
            new (q);
            with q ↑ do begin
                q ↑ .Info := a;
                q ↑ .Succ := p ↑ .Succ;
                q ↑ .Pred := p end;
            r := p ↑.Succ;
            if r <> nil then r ↑.Pred := q;
            p ↑ .Succ := q end
End ;
```

As in the case of (singly) linked lists we have to deal separately with insertion at the head of a doubly linked list. We proceed by creating a new head node, setting its *Info* field to be the given information item, its *Pred* field to be **nil** and its *Succ* field to be a pointer to the old head node; the *Pred* field of the old head node must be altered from **nil** to be a pointer to the new head node. Thus we have

```
Procedure insert_at_head (a : T; Var head : Pointer);
Var q : Pointer;
Begin new(q);
        with q ↑ do begin
                        Info := a;
                        Pred := nil ;
                        Succ := head end;
            head↑.Pred := q;
            head := q
    End;
```

To delete the node after a given node pointed to by a pointer p we do nothing (except possibly output a warning message) if either p or $p \uparrow.Next$ is **nil** . Otherwise we adjust the *Succ* field of p and the *Pred* field of $(p \uparrow.Succ) \uparrow.Succ$ (unless it is **nil**). So we have

```
Procedure delete_after (p : Pointer);
Var q, r : Pointer;
Begin if (p <> nil ) and (p ↑.Next <>nil ) then begin
                        q := p ↑.Succ;
                        r := q ↑.Succ;
                        p ↑.Succ := r;
                        if r <>nil then r ↑.Pred := p;
                        Dispose(q) end
    End;
```

Finally, to handle deletion of the head node we use:

Procedure delete_at_head (**Var** *head* : *Pointer*);
Var *q, r* : *Pointer*;
Begin *q* := *head*;
    r := *q* ↑.*Succ*;
    r ↑.*Pred* := nil ;
    head := *r*;
    Dispose(*q*)
End;

9. Starting at the head of the list pointed to by s we follow the *Next* pointers until either we reach a node with *Row* field i and *Column* field j or else reach the end of the list without finding such a node. In the first case the function value is the *Entry* field of the "(i, j)" node; in the second case the function returns 0. Thus we define

Function extract (*s* : *Matrix_pointer*; *i* : *Row_index*;
                     j : *Column_index*) : *Number*
Var *q* : *Matrix_pointer*;
    found : **boolean**;
    Begin *q* := *s*;
        found := **false**;
        while (q <> **nil**) **and** (*found* = **false**) **do begin**
                if (q ↑.*Row* = i) **and** (q ↑.*Column* = j)
                    then begin
                            extract := *q* ↑.*Entry*;
                            found := **true end**
                else *q* := *q* ↑.*Next* **end**;
        if not *found* **then** extract := 0
    End;

To update the (i, j)-th entry we proceed down the list until either we reach a node with *Row* field i and *Column* field j or else a node with *Row* field k and *Column* field l where either $k > i$ or else $k = i$ and $l > j$. In the first case we alter the *Entry* field of the "(i, j)" node to x if x is nonzero or delete it if x is zero. In the second case we do nothing if x is zero; but if x is nonzero we insert before the "(k, l)" node a new node with *Row* field i, *Column* field j and *Entry* field x.

Chapter 14

SOLUTIONS TO
EXERCISES 2

1. (a) The sequence of commands

    push('A',X); push('B',X); out(X); push('C',X); push('D',X);
    out(X); out(X); push('E',X); push('F',X); out(X); out(X);
    out(X);

    produces the output $BDCFEA$.

    (b) If 'D' is to be the first character in the output stream we must
    have pushed 'A', 'B', 'C', 'D' successively onto the stack; when
    we pop the stack to obtain 'D' the head of the stack is 'C' and we
    cannot extract 'B' before 'C'. So $BDACEF$ cannot be obtained
    by any arrangement of push and out operations.

    (c) The sequence of commands

    push('A',X); out(X); push('B',X); out(X); push('C',X);
    out(X);
    push('D',X); out(X); push('E',X); out(X); push('F',X);
    out(X);

    produces the output $ABCDEF$.

    (d) If 'E' is to be the first character in the output stream we must
    have pushed 'A', 'B', 'C', 'D', 'E' onto the stack in that order.
    Then we pop to obtain 'E'; after we have done this the head of
    the stack is 'D', which must be popped before we can extract

'B'. So $EBFCDA$ cannot be obtained by any arrangement of push and out operations.

(e) The sequence of commands

push('A',X); push('B',X); push('C',X); push('D',X);
push('E',X); push('F',X); out(X); out(X); out(X);
out(X); out(X); out(X);

produces the output $FEDCBA$.

2. (a)   **Function** stack_top $(s : P) : T$;
Var $a : T$;
Begin pop(a,s); push(a, s);
     stack_top := a
End;

(b)   **Function** second $(s : P) : T$;
Var $a, b : T$;
Begin pop(a, s); pop(b, s); push(b, s); push(a, s);
     second := b
End;

(c)   **Procedure** two_off (**Var** $s : P$; $a : T$);
Begin pop (a, s); pop(a, s) **End**;

(d)   **Procedure** bottom (**Var** $s : P$;**Var** $a : T$);
Begin **if** empty(s) **then** Writeln ('The stack is empty')
            else **while** **not** empty(s) **do** pop(a, s)
End;

(e)   **Function** last $(s : P) : T$;
Var $a : T$; $s1 : P$;
Begin **if** empty(s) **then** Writeln ('The stack is empty')
       else **begin**
         while **not** empty (s) **do** **begin**
           pop(a, s); push(a, $s1$) **end**;
      last := a;
      while **not** empty(s) **do** **begin**
          pop(a, $s1$); push(a, s) **end**
End;

3. Read the incoming string character by character, pushing each character in turn onto the stack until the character 'A' appears. Ignore

'A', i.e, do not push it onto the stack. Now continue to read the incoming stream one character at a time and as each character is read compare it with the character obtained by popping the stack. If at any stage the character read and the character popped are different then the input string is not of the required form xAx^*. If the input string terminates before the stack is empty or if the stack becomes empty before the input string terminates then again the input is not of the required form.

4. We work with a stack whose elements are opening brackets of various types.
   The input string is read character by character. Input characters other than brackets pass by the stack; opening brackets are pushed onto the stack. When the input character is a closing bracket then
   1. if the stack is empty there is no matching opening bracket, so the input string is invalid;
   2. if the stack is nonempty we compare the types of the incoming closing bracket and the opening bracket at the top of the stack:
   (a) if the types are different then the input string is invalid;
   (b) if the types are the same we pop the stack and continue reading the input string.
   When we come to the last closing bracket in the input string and 2(b) applies we examine the stack;
   1. if the stack is nonempty then the input string is invalid, for it contains more opening brackets than closing brackets;
   2. if the stack is empty then the input string is valid.

5. (a) Postfix form is $abc * /$.

   (b) Postfix form is $ab/c*$.

   (c) Postfix form is $abc \wedge \wedge$

   (d) Postfix form is $ab \wedge c\wedge$.

   (e) Postfix form is $ab - c-$.

   (f) Postfix form is $abc - -$.

   (g) Postfix form is $a5 \wedge 4a3 \wedge * + 3a2 \wedge * - 7+$

   (h) Postfix form is $ab + cd - *$.

   (i) Postfix form is $Sabn \wedge +\wedge$

6. We write our stacks horizontally with head to the left:

(a)   Input   Stack

$$
\begin{array}{cl}
3 & 3 \\
4 & 4\ 3 \\
+ & 7 \qquad \text{(Pop 4, pop 3, form } 3 + 4 = 7, \text{ push 7)} \\
5 & 5\ 7 \\
* & 35 \qquad \text{(Pop 5, pop 7, form } 7 * 5 = 35, \text{ push 35)}
\end{array}
$$

Thus the value of the expression is 35.

(b)   Input   Stack

$$
\begin{array}{cl}
3 & 3 \\
4 & 4\ 3 \\
5 & 5\ 4\ 3 \\
+ & 9\ 3 \qquad \text{(Pop 5, pop 4, form } 4 + 5 = 9, \text{ push 9)} \\
* & 27 \qquad \text{(Pop 9, pop 3, form } 3 * 9 = 27, \text{ push 27)}
\end{array}
$$

Thus the value of the expression is 27.

(c)   Input   Stack

$$
\begin{array}{cl}
3 & 3 \\
4 & 4\ 3 \\
\wedge & 81 \qquad \text{(Pop 4, pop 3, form } 3{\wedge}4 = 81, \text{ push 81)} \\
5 & 5\ 81 \\
3 & 3\ 5\ 81 \\
+ & 8\ 81 \qquad \text{(Pop 3, pop 5, form } 5 + 3 = 8, \text{ push 8)} \\
* & 648 \qquad \text{(Pop 8, pop 81, form } 81 * 8 = 648, \text{ push 648)}
\end{array}
$$

Thus the value of the expression is 648.

7. We write the queue Q with its front to the right and its rear to the left. Then after operation (1) Q consists of A alone, which is both front and rear; after operation (2) Q is B A; after (3) Q is C B A; after (4) Q is C B and *first* = A; after (5) Q is D C B; after (6) Q is E D C B; after (7) Q is E D C and *first* = B; after (8) Q is E D and *first* = C; after (9) Q is F E D; after (10) Q is F E and *first* = D.

8. (a)   **Procedure** front_to_rear $(q : Q)$;
     Var $a : T$;
     Begin while not empty(q) **do begin**
            serve(q, a); write(a) **end**
     End;

(b)   **Procedure** rear_to_front $(q : Q)$;
     Var $a : T$; $s : P$; ($\star$ P is the type representing stacks $\star$)
     Begin while not empty(q) **do begin**
            serve(q, a); push(a, s) **end**;
         while not empty(s) **do begin**
            pop(s, a); write(a) **end**
     End;

9. (a) Make the declarations

     Const N = maxsize;
     Type $T = Element\_type$;
        $Deque$ = **Record**
                $Deque\_array$: **array** $[1 .. N]$ **of** T;
                $Front, Rear : 0 .. N$
          end ;

Then we define **Function** full $(D : Deque)$: **boolean** and **Function** empty $(D : Deque)$: **boolean** exactly as for queues. To add an element at the rear of a deque we use **Procedure** insert_at_rear $(a : T$; **Var** $D : Deque)$ identical with the *enqueue* operation for queues. To remove an element from the front of a deque we use **Procedure** remove_from_front (**Var** $D : Deque$; $a : T$) identical with the *serve* procedure for queues. To add an element to the front of a deque we define

     Procedure insert_at_front $(a : T$; **Var** $D : Deque)$;
     Begin if full(D) **then** ... ($\star$ take appropriate action $\star$)
            else with D **do begin**
                if $Front = 0$ **then** $Front := N - 1$
                   else $Front := Front - 1$ **end**
                $Deque\_array[Front + 1] := a$ **end**
     End;

To remove an element from the rear we use:

Procedure remove_from_rear (**Var** D : *Deque*; **Var** a : T);
  Begin if full(D) **then** ... ($\star$ take appropriate action $\star$)
        else with D **do begin**
                a := *Deque_array*[*Rear*];
                if $Rear = 1$ **then** $Rear := N$
                    else $Rear := Rear - 1$ **end**
End;

(b) Make the declarations:

Type T = *Element_type*;
    Deque_pointer = $\uparrow$ *Node*;
    Node = **Record**
           Info : T;
           Next : *Deque_pointer*
        end;
    Deque = **Record**
           Front, Rear : *Deque_pointer*
        end;

Functions full and empty and procedures insert_at_rear and remove_from_front are defined as for the pointer representation of queues.
To add an element at the front we define:

Procedure insert_at_front (**Var** D : *Deque*; a : T);
Var p : *Deque_pointer*;
Begin new (p); $p \uparrow$.*Info* := a; $p \uparrow$.*Next* := D.*Front*;
    if D.*Front* = **nil then** D.*Rear* := p;
    D.*Front* := p
End;

To remove an element from the rear we use

Procedure remove_from_rear (**Var** D : *Deque*;
                            Var a : T);

Var p : *Deque_pointer*;
Begin if empty(D) **then** ... ($\star$ take appropriate action $\star$)
    else with D **do begin**

$a := Rear\uparrow.Info;$
if $Front = Rear$ then begin
      $Front :=$ nil; $Rear :=$ nil end;
  else begin
    $p := Front;$
    Repeat $p := p\uparrow.Next$
      until $p\uparrow.Next =$ nil;
  $Rear := p$ end end End;

Chapter 15

SOLUTIONS TO EXERCISES 3

1. The 14 trees with 4 nodes are

and the mirror images of these in the vertical through the root.

2. For every natural number n each node at level n in a binary tree has n ancestors.

   Proof by induction: (1) There is only one node at level 0, namely the root, and it has 0 ancestors.

   (2) Suppose we have shown for some natural number k that every node at level k in a binary tree has k ancestors. Let N be any node at level $(k + 1)$. Then

   number of ancestors of N = 1 (i.e. its parent) +
   (number of ancestors of its parent) = $1 + k$

   This establishes the induction.

3. (a) **Function** number_of_nodes(t : *Tree_pointer*) : **integer**;
       Begin if t = **nil then** number_of_nodes := 0
                        else number_of_nodes := number_of_nodes($t \uparrow.Left$)
                                + number_of_nodes($t \uparrow.Right$)
       End ;

   (b) **Function** height(t : *Tree_pointer*) : **integer**;
           Function max(m, n : **integer**) : **integer**;
           Begin if $m \geq n$ **then** max := m **else** max := n **End**;
       Begin if t = **nil then** height := -1
               else height := 1 + max(height($t \uparrow.Left$), height($t \uparrow.Right$))
       End ;

   (c) **Function** count(t : *Tree_pointer*) : **integer**;
       Begin if t = **nil then** count := 0
               else count := ($t \uparrow.Info$) + count($t \uparrow.Left$) + count($t \uparrow.Right$)
       End ;

4. **Function** strictly_binary (t : *Tree_pointer*) : **boolean**;
       Function leaf (t : *Tree_pointer*) : **boolean**;
       Begin leaf := ($t \uparrow.Left$ = **nil**) **and** ($t \uparrow.Right$ = **nil**) **End**;
       Function two_kids (t : *Tree_pointer*) : **boolean**;
       Begin two_kids := ($t \uparrow.Left$ <> **nil**) **and** ($t \uparrow.Right$ <> **nil**)
       End;
   Begin if t = **nil then** strictly_binary := **true**
               else if leaf(t) **then** strictly_binary := **true**
                   else if two_kids(t) **then**
                       strictly_binary := strictly_binary($t \uparrow.Left$)
                                       and strictly_binary($t \uparrow.Right$)
                       else strictly_binary := **false**
   End;

5. Preorder: $A\ P\ Q\ M\ E\ N\ D\ R\ T\ B\ C$
   Inorder: $Q\ M\ P\ N\ E\ D\ A\ R\ B\ T\ C$
   Postorder: $M\ Q\ N\ D\ E\ P\ B\ C\ T\ R\ A$

6. Since the preorder traversal starts with A it follows that the root node contains A.
   The inorder traversal then shows that
       (1) the inorder traversal of the left subtree is $D\ C\ E\ B$ and
       (2) the inorder traversal of the right subtree is $U\ Z\ T\ X\ Y$.
   The preorder traversal of the left subtree comes immediately after the

root in the preorder traversal of the whole tree and must consist of the same nodes as the inorder traversal—so we see that the preorder traversal of the left subtree must be $B\ C\ D\ E$.

Thus the left subtree has root B.

Examining the inorder traversal $D\ C\ E\ B$ we see that the inorder traversal of the left subtree of (the tree with root) B is $D\ C\ E$ and hence the right subtree of B is **nil**.

The preorder traversal of the left subtree of B must be $C\ D\ E$, so its root is C. It follows easily that the left subtree of B is

and arguing in a similar way for the right subtree we find eventually that the required tree is

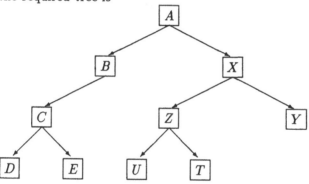

7. (a) The binary tree representation of $a/(b*c)$ is:

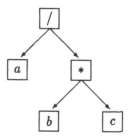

The Polish (prefix) form is $/\ a\ *\ b\ c$.

The reverse Polish (postfix) form is $a\ b\ c\ *\ /$.

(b) The binary tree representation of $a^5 + 4a^3 - 3a^2 + 7 = ((a^5 + 4a^3) - 3a^2) + 7 = (((a \uparrow 5) + (4 * (a \uparrow 3))) - (3 * (a \uparrow 2)) + 7)$ is:

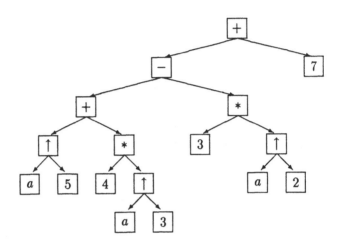

The Polish form is $+ - + \uparrow a\,5 * 4 \uparrow a\,3 * 3 \uparrow a\,2\,7$. The reverse Polish form is $a\,5 \uparrow 4\,a\,3 \uparrow * + 3\,a\,2 \uparrow * - 7 +$.

(c) The binary tree representation of $(a + b) * (c - d)$ is:

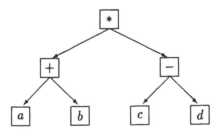

The Polish form is $* + a\,b - c\,d$.
The reverse Polish form is $a\,b + c\,d - *$.

(d) The binary tree representation of $S^{a+b^n} = S \uparrow (a + (b \uparrow n))$ is:

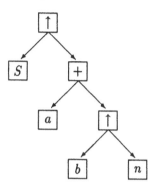

The Polish form is $\uparrow\ S\ +\ a\ \uparrow\ b\ n$.
The reverse Polish form is $S\ a\ b\ n\ \uparrow\ +\ \uparrow$.

8. (a)   (b)

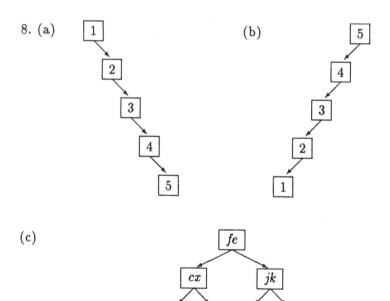

(c)

9.

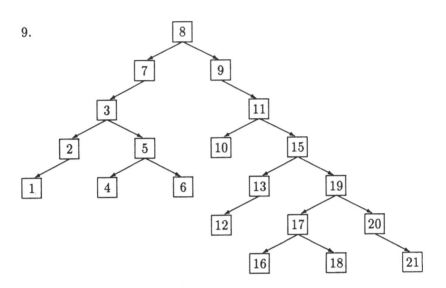

When 2 is deleted the tree becomes:

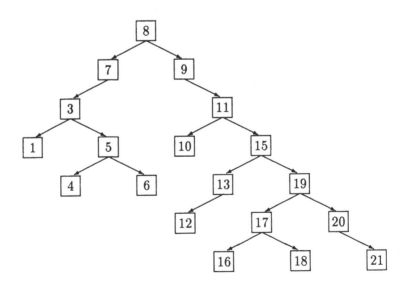

When 10 is deleted the tree becomes:

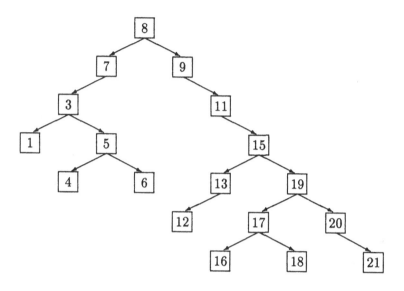

When 19 is deleted the tree becomes:

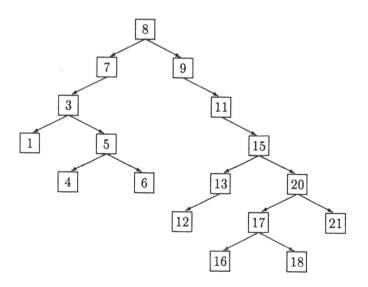

When 8 is deleted the tree becomes:

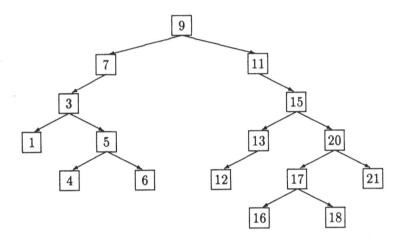

When 20 is deleted the tree becomes:

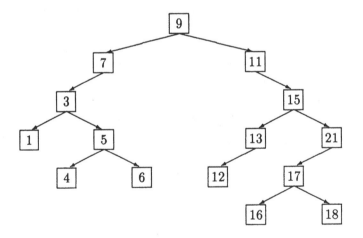

Chapter 16

SOLUTIONS TO EXERCISES 4

1. The array representation is

| 93 | 84 | 73 | 69 | 74 | 38 | 52 | 13 | 51 | 12 | 48 | 20 | | | |

2. We begin by inserting 75 in the first unoccupied position in the array:

| 93 | 84 | 73 | 69 | 74 | 38 | 52 | 13 | 51 | 12 | 48 | 20 | 75 | | |

Since 75 is greater than its parent 38 we interchange 75 and 38, obtaining

| 93 | 84 | 73 | 69 | 74 | 75 | 52 | 13 | 51 | 12 | 48 | 20 | 38 | | |

Now 75 is greater than its new parent 73; so we interchange 75 and 73, obtaining

| 93 | 84 | 75 | 69 | 74 | 73 | 52 | 13 | 51 | 12 | 48 | 20 | 38 | | |

which is the array representation of a heap.

337

3. We begin by removing the entry in the first position and replacing it by the entry in the last position, obtaining:

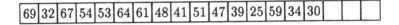

For the first version of the trickle procedure we begin by finding the maximum of $A[1] = 32$, $A[2] = 69$ and $A[3] = 67$ (involving two comparisons); interchange 32 and 69 to obtain

| 69 | 32 | 67 | 54 | 53 | 64 | 61 | 48 | 41 | 51 | 47 | 39 | 25 | 59 | 34 | 30 | | | |

Now find the maximum of $A[2] = 32$, $A[4] = 54$ and $A[5] = 53$ (again involving two comparisons); interchange 32 and 54, obtaining

| 69 | 54 | 67 | 32 | 53 | 64 | 61 | 48 | 41 | 51 | 47 | 39 | 25 | 59 | 34 | 30 | | | |

Next find the maximum of $A[4] = 32$, $A[8] = 48$ and $A[9] = 41$ (using two more comparisons); interchange 32 and 48 to obtain

| 69 | 54 | 67 | 48 | 53 | 64 | 61 | 32 | 41 | 51 | 47 | 39 | 25 | 59 | 34 | 30 | | | |

Finally find the larger of $A[8] = 32$ and $A[16] = 30$; since $32 > 30$ the most recently obtained array represents a heap.

For the second version of trickle we begin by comparing $A[2] = 69$ and $A[3] = 67$; we interchange 32 with the larger, 69, obtaining

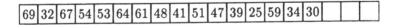

Now compare $A[4] = 54$ and $A[5] = 53$; interchange 32 with the larger, 54, to obtain

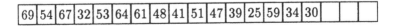

Now compare $A[8] = 48$ and $A[9] = 41$; interchange 32 with the larger,

48, so obtaining

| 69 | 54 | 67 | 48 | 53 | 64 | 61 | 32 | 41 | 51 | 47 | 39 | 25 | 59 | 34 | 30 | | | |

$A[8]$ has only one child, $A[16] = 30$; we interchange 32 and its child:

| 69 | 54 | 67 | 48 | 53 | 64 | 61 | 30 | 41 | 51 | 47 | 39 | 25 | 59 | 34 | 32 | | | |

Now compare $A[16] = 32$ with its parent $A[8] = 30$; since $30 < 32$ we interchange these entries, getting

| 69 | 54 | 67 | 48 | 53 | 64 | 61 | 32 | 41 | 51 | 47 | 39 | 25 | 59 | 34 | 30 | | | |

Compare $A[8] = 32$ with its parent $A[4] = 48$. Since $48 > 32$ the most recently obtained array represents a heap.

The first method involves 7 comparisons, the second only 5.

4. The execution of trickle(4, A) on the array

$$A = \boxed{43 \mid 12 \mid 94 \mid 17 \mid 55 \mid 19 \mid 68 \mid 73}$$

produces

| 43 | 12 | 94 | 73 | 55 | 19 | 68 | 17 |

(since $A[8] = 73 > A[4] = 17$). Since $A[3] = 94$ is greater than both its children $A[6] = 19$ and $A[7] = 68$, trickle(3,A) leaves this array unchanged. When we apply trickle(2,A) we see that $A[2] = 12$ is less than both its children $A[4] = 73$ and $A[5] = 55$; so we interchange 12 and 73, obtaining

| 43 | 73 | 94 | 12 | 55 | 19 | 68 | 17 |

Since the new $A[4] = 12$ is less than its child $A[8] = 17$ these must be interchanged. So the final result of trickle(2,A) is

| 43 | 73 | 94 | 17 | 55 | 19 | 68 | 12 |

Finally trickle(1,A) first interchanges $A[1] = 43$ with its larger child $A[3] = 94$ and then the new $A[3] = 43$ with its larger child $A[7] = 68$. The required heap is then

| 94 | 73 | 68 | 17 | 55 | 19 | 43 | 12 |

For the array

$$B = \boxed{10 \mid 12 \mid 20 \mid 34 \mid 45 \mid 76 \mid 87 \mid 98}$$

execution of trickle(4,B) produces

| 10 | 12 | 20 | 98 | 45 | 76 | 87 | 34 |

Then trickle(3,B) gives

| 10 | 12 | 87 | 98 | 45 | 76 | 20 | 34 |

Next trickle(2,B) gives first

| 10 | 98 | 87 | 12 | 45 | 76 | 20 | 34 |

and then

| 10 | 98 | 87 | 34 | 45 | 76 | 20 | 12 |

Finally, trickle(1,B) gives first

| 98 | 10 | 87 | 34 | 45 | 76 | 20 | 12 |

and eventually

| 98 | 45 | 87 | 34 | 10 | 76 | 20 | 12 |

which represents a heap.

Chapter 17

SOLUTIONS TO EXERCISES 5

1. (a) The adjacency matrix for the given graph is

$$
\begin{bmatrix}
0 & 1 & 1 & 1 & 0 & 0 & 0 & 0 & 0 \\
1 & 0 & 0 & 0 & 1 & 0 & 0 & 0 & 0 \\
1 & 0 & 0 & 0 & 1 & 0 & 0 & 0 & 0 \\
1 & 0 & 0 & 0 & 0 & 1 & 0 & 0 & 0 \\
0 & 1 & 1 & 0 & 0 & 0 & 1 & 1 & 0 \\
0 & 0 & 0 & 1 & 0 & 0 & 0 & 1 & 0 \\
0 & 0 & 0 & 0 & 1 & 0 & 0 & 0 & 1 \\
0 & 0 & 0 & 0 & 1 & 1 & 0 & 0 & 1 \\
0 & 0 & 0 & 0 & 0 & 0 & 1 & 1 & 0
\end{bmatrix}
$$

When the graph is changed to a digraph in the way described the adjacency matrix becomes

$$
\begin{bmatrix}
0 & 1 & 1 & 1 & 0 & 0 & 0 & 0 & 0 \\
0 & 0 & 0 & 0 & 1 & 0 & 0 & 0 & 0 \\
0 & 0 & 0 & 0 & 1 & 0 & 0 & 0 & 0 \\
0 & 0 & 0 & 0 & 0 & 1 & 0 & 0 & 0 \\
0 & 0 & 0 & 0 & 0 & 0 & 1 & 1 & 0 \\
0 & 0 & 0 & 0 & 0 & 0 & 0 & 1 & 0 \\
0 & 0 & 0 & 0 & 0 & 0 & 0 & 0 & 1 \\
0 & 0 & 0 & 0 & 0 & 0 & 0 & 0 & 1 \\
0 & 0 & 0 & 0 & 0 & 0 & 0 & 0 & 0
\end{bmatrix}
$$

(*b*) The adjacency lists for the given graph are

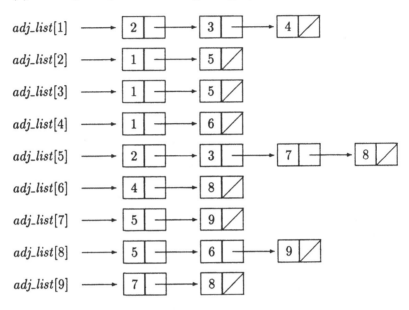

When the graph is changed to a digraph as described, the adjacency lists become

adj_list[9] = **nil**

2. (*a*) For the depth first traversal we write the stack S horizontally with head to the left. For the graph in Exercise 1 we have initially $visited[i]$ = **false** for $i = 1, \ldots, 9$. Then dft_from(1) proceeds as follows:

(1) S consists of 1 alone; pop produces 1; since $visited[1] = $ **false** we process v_1, set $visited[1]$ to **true** and push the unvisited neighbours of 1.

(2) S is now 2 3 4; pop produces 2; since $visited[2] = $ **false** we process v_2, set $visited[2]$ to **true** and push the unvisited neighbour of 2.

(3) S is now 5 3 4; pop produces 5; since $visited[5] = $ **false** we process v_5, set $visited[5]$ to **true** and push the unvisited neighbours of 5.

(4) S is now 3 7 8 3 4; pop produces 3; since $visited[3] = $ **false** we process v_3 and set $visited[3]$ to **true** ; we would push the unvisited neighbours of 3 if it had any, but it doesn't.

(5) S is now 7 8 3 4; pop produces 7; since $visited[7] = $ **false** we process v_7, set $visited[7]$ to **true** and push the unvisited neighbour of 7.

(6) S is now 9 8 3 4; pop produces 9; since $visited[9] = $ **false** we process v_9, set $visited[9]$ to **true** and push the unvisited neighbour of 9.

(7) S is now 8 8 3 4; pop produces 8; since $visited[8] = $ **false** we process v_8, set $visited[8]$ to **true** and push the unvisited neighbour of 8.

(8) S is now 6 8 3 4; pop produces 6; since $visited[6] = $ **false** we process v_6, set $visited[6]$ to **true** and push the unvisited neighbour of 6.

(9) S is now 4 8 3 4; pop produces 4; since $visited[4] = $ **false** we process v_4, set $visited[4]$ to **true** ; 4 has no unvisited neighbour.

(10) The remaining entries in the stack have all been visited, so as we pop them in turn we take no further action.

Thus the depth first traversal from 1 visits the vertices in the order

1 2 5 3 7 9 8 6 4

and since this exhausts all the vertices of the graph we have completed its depth first traversal.

For the digraph in Exercise 2 we have

(1) S is 1; pop 1; process v_1; push 2, 3, 6.

(2) S is 6 3 2; pop 6; process v_6; push 4.

(3) S is 4 3 2; pop 4; process v_4; 4 has no neighbours, visited or unvisited.

(4) S is 3 2; pop 3; process v_3; 3 has no unvisited neighbours.

(5) S is 2; pop 2; process v_2; push 5.

(6) S is 5; pop 5; process v_5; 5 has no unvisited neighbours.

Thus dft_from(1) visits the vertices

$$1\ 6\ 4\ 3\ 2\ 5$$

in that order.

Since 2, 3, 4, 5 and 6 have been visited dft_from(2), ..., dft_from(6) take no action. Finally dft_from(7) processes v_7. So depth first traversal of the digraph visits the vertices in the order

$$1\ 6\ 4\ 3\ 2\ 5\ 7$$

(*b*) For the breadth first traversal we write the queue Q horizontally with front to the right and rear to the left. For the graph in Exercise 1 we have initially *visited*[*i*] = **false** for $i = 1, ..., 9$. Then bft_from(1) proceeds as follows:

(1) *visited*[1] := **true** ; serve produces *first* = 1; process v_1; enqueue unvisited neighbours of 1 and mark them 'visited'.

(2) Q is now 4 3 2; serve produces *first* = 2; process v_2; enqueue the unvisited neighbour of 2 and mark it 'visited'.

(3) Q is now 5 4 3; serve produces *first* = 3; process v_3; 3 has no unvisited neighbour.

(4) Q is now 5 4; serve produces *first* = 4; process v_4; enqueue the unvisited neighbour of 4 and mark it 'visited'.

(5) Q is now 6 5; serve produces *first* = 5; process v_5; enqueue the unvisited neighbours of 5 and mark them 'visited'.

(6) Q is now 8 7 6; serve produces *first* = 6; process v_6; 6 has no unvisited neighbour.

(7) Q is now 8 7; serve produces *first* = 7; process v_7; enqueue the unvisited neighbour of 7 and mark it 'visited'.

(8) Q is now 9 8; serve produces *first* = 8; process v_8; 8 has no unvisited neighbour.

(9) Q is now 9; serve produces *first* = 9; process v_9; 9 has no unvisited neighbour.

Thus the breadth first traversal from 1 visits the vertices in the order

$$1\ 2\ 3\ 4\ 5\ 6\ 7\ 8\ 9$$

and since this exhausts all the vertices of the graph we have completed its breadth first traversal.

For the digraph in Exercise 2 we have

(1) Q is 1; process v_1; enqueue 2, 3 and 6.

(2) Q is 6 3 2; process v_2; enqueue 5.

(3) Q is 5 6 3; process v_3; enqueue 4.

(4) Q is 4 5 6; process v_6; 6 has no unvisited neighbour.

(5) Q is 4 5; process v_5; 5 has no unvisited neighbour.

(6) Q is 4; process v_4; 4 has no unvisited neighbour.

Q is now empty. Thus bft_from(1) visits the vertices

$$1\ 2\ 3\ 6\ 5\ 4$$

in that order.

Since 2, 3, 4, 5 and 6 have been visited bft_from(2), ... , bft_from(6) take no action. Finally bft_from(7) processes v_7. So breadth first traversal of the digraph visits the vertices in the order

$$1\ 2\ 3\ 6\ 5\ 4\ 7$$

Chapter 18

SOLUTIONS TO EXERCISES 6

1. Since $p < q$ we have $\lim(n^p/n^q) = \lim n^{p-q} = 0$; so n^p is $O(n^q)$.

   If n^q were $O(n^p)$ there would be a positive real number K and an integer n_0 such that $n^q \leq K n^p$ and so $n^{q-p} \leq K$ for all integers $n \geq n_0$. But this is not possible: since $q > p$ we have $\lim n^{q-p} = \infty$ and so n^{q-p} is eventually greater than any positive real number we choose, in particular greater than K.

   So n^q is not $O(n^p)$.

2. For all positive integer n we have

$$f(n)/n^k = 4n^{3-k} - 3n^{2-k} + 2n^{1-k} - n^{-k}.$$

   If $k = 3$ we have $\lim(f(n)/n^k) = 4$.

   If $k > 3$ we have $\lim(f(n)/n^k) = 0$.

   If $k < 3$ we have $\lim(f(n)/n^k) = \infty$.

   Thus $f(n)$ is $O(n^k)$ for all $k \geq 3$ and $\Omega(n^k)$ for all $k \leq 3$. It follows that $f(n)$ is $\Theta(n^k)$ only for $k = 3$.

3. (1) If f is $O(g)$ then there is a positive real number K and an integer n_0 such that $f(n) \leq K g(n)$ for all integers $n \geq n_0$. It follows that $g(n) \geq (1/K)f(n)$ for all integers $n \geq n_0$ and so g is $\Omega(f)$.

(2) If f is $\Theta(g)$ then f is $O(g)$ and f is $\Omega(g)$. It follows from (1) that g is $\Omega(f)$ and a similar argument shows that since f is $\Omega(g)$ we have that g is $O(f)$. So g is $\Theta(f)$.

4. Taking the multiplication of two numbers as our basic operation we see that the total number of basic operations carried out is n^3. So we estimate the complexity as $O(n^3)$.

5. Let W be the worst case complexity of the algorithm.

    Then for $n > 1$ we have

$$W(n) = 2W(n-1) = 2^2 W(n-2) = \ldots = 2^{n-1} W(1)$$

    So $W(n)$ is $O(2^{n-1} = O(2^n)$.

    If we rewrite the **else** clause as

$$F := 2 * F(n-1)$$

    we reduce the complexity to $O(n)$.

6. In the worst case the complete loop will be executed n times (this is the case in which the condition C is never satisfied).

    So the worst case complexity is

$$n* \{(\text{worst case complexity of } \ldots \text{ before test for } C)$$
$$+ (\text{worst case complexity of evaluating } C)$$
$$+ (\text{worst case complexity of } \ldots \text{ after test for } C)\}.$$

7. Worst case complexity $=$ Worst case complexity of evaluating C
$$+ (\text{the larger of the worst case complexity of } S_1$$
$$\text{and the worst case complexity of } S_2).$$

Chapter 19

SOLUTIONS TO EXERCISES 7

1. (a) We show the state of the array before each comparison-and-possible-exchange step; the entries in bold type are those which have to be compared.

$i = 2$:

$j = 8$	*dog*	*egg*	*rum*	*gin*	*and*	*rye*	**nog**	**for**
$j = 7$	*dog*	*egg*	*rum*	*gin*	*and*	**rye**	**for**	*nog*
$j = 6$	*dog*	*egg*	*rum*	*gin*	**and**	**for**	*rye*	*nog*
$j = 5$	*dog*	*egg*	*rum*	**gin**	**and**	*for*	*rye*	*nog*
$j = 4$	*dog*	*egg*	**rum**	**and**	*gin*	*for*	*rye*	*nog*
$j = 3$	*dog*	**egg**	**and**	*rum*	*gin*	*for*	*rye*	*nog*
$j = 2$	**dog**	**and**	*egg*	*rum*	*gin*	*for*	*rye*	*nog*

$i = 3$:

$j = 8$	*and*	*dog*	*egg*	*rum*	*gin*	*for*	**rye**	**nog**
$j = 7$	*and*	*dog*	*egg*	*rum*	*gin*	**for**	**nog**	*rye*
$j = 6$	*and*	*dog*	*egg*	*rum*	**gin**	**for**	*nog*	*rye*
$j = 5$	*and*	*dog*	*egg*	**rum**	**for**	*gin*	*nog*	*rye*
$j = 4$	*and*	*dog*	**egg**	**for**	*rum*	*gin*	*nog*	*rye*
$j = 3$	*and*	**dog**	**egg**	*for*	*rum*	*gin*	*nog*	*rye*

$i = 4$:

$j = 8$	*and*	*dog*	*egg*	*for*	*rum*	*gin*	**nog**	**rye**
$j = 7$	*and*	*dog*	*egg*	*for*	*rum*	**gin**	**nog**	*rye*
$j = 6$	*and*	*dog*	*egg*	*for*	**rum**	**gin**	*nog*	*rye*
$j = 5$	*and*	*dog*	*egg*	**for**	**gin**	*rum*	*nog*	*rye*
$j = 4$	*and*	*dog*	**egg**	**for**	*gin*	*rum*	*nog*	*rye*

$i = 5$:

$j = 8$	*and*	*dog*	*egg*	*for*	*gin*	*rum*	**nog**	**rye**
$j = 7$	*and*	*dog*	*egg*	*for*	*gin*	**rum**	**nog**	*rye*
$j = 6$	*and*	*dog*	*egg*	*for*	**gin**	**nog**	*rum*	*rye*
$j = 5$	*and*	*dog*	*egg*	**for**	**gin**	*nog*	*rum*	*rye*

$i = 6$:

$j = 8$	*and*	*dog*	*egg*	*for*	*gin*	*nog*	**rum**	**rye**
$j = 7$	*and*	*dog*	*egg*	*for*	*gin*	**nog**	**rum**	*rye*
$j = 6$	*and*	*dog*	*egg*	*for*	**gin**	**nog**	*rum*	*rye*

$i = 7$:

| $j = 8$ | *and* | *dog* | *egg* | *for* | *gin* | *nog* | **rum** | **rye** |
| $j = 7$ | *and* | *dog* | *egg* | *for* | *gin* | **nog** | **rum** | *rye* |

$i = 8$:

| $j = 8$ | *and* | *dog* | *egg* | *for* | *gin* | *nog* | **rum** | **rye** |

The final sorted version is then

and dog egg for gin nog rum rye

(b) For each stage ($i = 2, \ldots, 8$) we show the successive states of the array as the element shown in bold type is repositioned.

| $i = 2$ | *dog* | **egg** | *rum* | *gin* | *and* | *rye* | *nog* | *for* |

| $i = 3$ | *dog* | *egg* | **rum** | *gin* | *and* | *rye* | *nog* | *for* |

| $i = 4$ | *dog* | *egg* | *rum* | **gin** | *and* | *rye* | *nog* | *for* |
| | *dog* | *egg* | **gin** | *rum* | *and* | *rye* | *nog* | *for* |

$i = 5$	*dog*	*egg*	*gin*	*rum*	**and**	*rye*	*nog*	*for*
	dog	*egg*	*gin*	**and**	*rum*	*rye*	*nog*	*for*
	dog	*egg*	**and**	*gin*	*rum*	*rye*	*nog*	*for*
	dog	**and**	*egg*	*gin*	*rum*	*rye*	*nog*	*for*
	and	*dog*	*egg*	*gin*	*rum*	*rye*	*nog*	*for*

$i = 6$	*and*	*dog*	*egg*	*gin*	*rum*	**rye**	*nog*	*for*

$i = 7$	*and*	*dog*	*egg*	*gin*	*rum*	*rye*	**nog**	*for*
	and	*dog*	*egg*	*gin*	*rum*	**nog**	*rye*	*for*
	and	*dog*	*egg*	*gin*	**nog**	*rum*	*rye*	*for*

$i = 8$	*and*	*dog*	*egg*	*gin*	*nog*	*rum*	*rye*	**for**
	and	*dog*	*egg*	*gin*	*nog*	*rum*	**for**	*rye*
	and	*dog*	*egg*	*gin*	*nog*	**for**	*rum*	*rye*
	and	*dog*	*egg*	*gin*	**for**	*nog*	*rum*	*rye*
	and	*dog*	*egg*	**for**	*gin*	*nog*	*rum*	*rye*

Thus the sorted version is, as before,

$$\textit{and dog egg for gin nog rum rye}$$

(c) For each stage ($i = 2, \ldots, 7$) we show the minimum entry of the subarray indexed by $i \mathinner{..} 8$ and the result of interchanging it with the i-th entry:

$i = 1$	*dog*	*egg*	*rum*	*gin*	**and**	*rye*	*nog*	*for*
	and	*egg*	*rum*	*gin*	*dog*	*rye*	*nog*	*for*

$i = 2$	*and*	*egg*	*rum*	*gin*	**dog**	*rye*	*nog*	*for*
	and	**dog**	*rum*	*gin*	*egg*	*rye*	*nog*	*for*

$i = 3$	*and*	*dog*	*rum*	*gin*	**egg**	*rye*	*nog*	*for*
	and	*dog*	**egg**	*gin*	*rum*	*rye*	*nog*	*for*

$i = 4$	*and*	*dog*	*egg*	*gin*	*rum*	*rye*	*nog*	**for**
	and	*dog*	*egg*	**for**	*rum*	*rye*	*nog*	*gin*

$i = 5$	*and*	*dog*	*egg*	*for*	*rum*	*rye*	*nog*	**gin**
	and	*dog*	*egg*	*for*	**gin**	*rye*	*nog*	*rum*

$i = 6$	*and*	*dog*	*egg*	*for*	*gin*	*rye*	**nog**	*rum*
	and	*dog*	*egg*	*for*	*gin*	**nog**	*rye*	*rum*

$$i = 7 \quad and \quad dog \quad egg \quad for \quad gin \quad nog \quad rye \quad \mathbf{rum}$$
$$and \quad dog \quad egg \quad for \quad gin \quad nog \quad \mathbf{rum} \quad rye$$

So the sorted version is, once again,

and dog egg for gin nog rum rye

2. (a) For Quicksort we shall always choose as pivot to partition a sub-array the larger of the first two entries which are distinct. So we begin by choosing 66 as pivot. Starting with the left pointer at 66 and moving right till we reach an entry greater than or equal to the pivot, and with the right pointer at 16, moving left till we reach an entry less than the pivot, we stop at the situation

66 36 79 45 13 62 **16** 76

and swap 66 and 16, obtaining

16 36 79 45 13 62 **66** 76.

Moving the pointers as before we reach the situation

16 36 **79** 45 13 **62** 66 76.

We swap 79 and 62, getting

16 36 **62** 45 13 **79** 66 76.

Moving again, the left pointer stops at 79, the right at 13—so the pointers have crossed over and we have reached the partition

16 36 62 45 **13** | **79** 66 76

We proceed similarly with the two subarrays.

(b) We begin by making the given array A into a heap-array by executing the loop

for $i := 4$ **downto** 1 **do** trickle(i, A)

$i = 4$ 66   36   79   **45**   13   62   16   76
          66   36   79   76   13   62   16   **45**

$i = 3$ 66   36   **79**   76   13   62   16   45

$i = 2$ 66   **36**   79   76   13   62   16   45
          66   76   79   **36**   13   62   16   45
          66   76   79   45   13   62   16   **36**

$i = 1$ **66**   76   79   45   13   62   16   36
          79   76   **66**   45   13   62   16   36

Now for $i = 8, \ldots, 2$ we interchange the entries in positions 1 and i and make the subarray $A[1..i-1]$ into a heap-array by trickling down the new first entry:

$i = 8$ **36**   76   66   45   13   62   16   79
          76   **36**   66   45   13   62   16   79
          76   45   66   **36**   13   62   16   79

$i = 7$ **16**   45   66   36   13   62   76   79
          66   45   **16**   36   13   62   76   79
          66   45   62   36   13   **16**   76   79

$i = 6$ **16**   45   62   36   13   66   76   79
          62   45   **16**   36   13   66   76   79

$i = 5$ **13**   45   16   36   62   66   76   79
          45   **13**   16   36   62   66   76   79
          45   36   16   **13**   62   66   76   79

$i = 4$ **13**   36   16   45   62   66   76   79
          36   **13**   16   45   62   66   76   79

$i = 3$ **16**   13   36   45   62   66   76   79

$i = 2$ **13**   16   36   45   62   66   76   79

So the sorted version is

13 16 36 45 62 66 76 79

3. We prove the result by mathematical induction.

The basis for the inductive proof is given by the observation that the inorder traversal of a binary search tree with 1 node produces its output (which just consists of a single record) in increasing order of key.

Suppose now that for some natural number k we have shown that the inorder traversal of every binary search tree with fewer than k nodes produces its output in increasing order of key; notice that we have certainly done this for $k = 2$. Let T be a binary search tree with exactly k nodes. The left and right subtrees L and R of T each have fewer than k nodes; so, by the inductive hypothesis, their inorder traversals produce their output in increasing order of key. The inorder traversal of T consists of the inorder traversal of L followed by the item stored at the root followed by the inorder traversal of R. Since every record stored in L has key less than the key of the record stored at the root and every record stored in R has key greater than the key of the record stored at the root, and since the inorder traversals of L and R are in increasing order, it follows that the inorder traversal of T produces its output in increasing order of key.

This completes the inductive step, so the result is established.

For the given array the binary search tree produced is

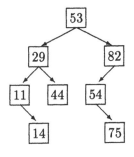

and the inorder traversal gives the sorted output

11 14 29 44 53 54 75 82.

If the given array is already sorted (or is in the reverse of sorted order) the number of comparisons required to construct the corresponding binary search tree (which reduces to a single list) is

$$1 + 2 + \ldots + (N - 1) = \tfrac{1}{2}N(N - 1).$$

4. We try to define a recursive function

$$\textbf{Function } \text{order } (i, j : \textbf{Index}; q : \textbf{Integer}) : T;$$

such that order(i, j, q) is the entry in the subarray indexed by $i .. j$ which is q-th in order of key. Then to find the entry of the complete array, indexed by $1 .. N$, which is k-th in order of key we evaluate order$(1, N, k)$.

To see how to define the function order we notice first that for the expression order(i, j, q) to make sense we must have $0 < q \leq j - i + 1$ (the number of elements in the subarray indexed by $i .. j$); next, if $i = j$, in which case q must be 1, order$(i, i, 1)$ should be $A[i]$.

Suppose now that $i < j$ and $0 < q \leq j - i + 1$. We proceed as in Quicksort by choosing a pivot p for the subarray $A[i .. j]$ and partitioning the subarray using the procedure call partition(i, j, p, r). This produces a left subarray $L = A[i .. r - 1]$, all of whose entries have keys less than those of the entries in the right subarray $R = A[r .. j]$. If $q \leq r - i$, the number of elements in L, then order$(i, j, q) = $ order$(i, r - 1, q)$; otherwise the q-th element of $A[i .. j]$ in order of key is the $(q - (r - i))$-th element of R in order of key and so order$(i, j, q) = $ order$(r, j, q - r + i)$.

5. We decompose the array into 16 subarrays, each with one element and merge successive pairs to form 8 runs each with 2 elements:

$$22\ 66 \mid 6\ 36 \mid 26\ 79 \mid 45\ 75 \mid 13\ 31 \mid 27\ 62 \mid 33\ 76 \mid 16\ 47$$

We now merge successive pairs of these 2-element runs to form 4 runs each with 4 elements:

$$6\ 22\ 36\ 66 \mid 26\ 45\ 75\ 79 \mid 13\ 27\ 31\ 62 \mid 16\ 33\ 47\ 76$$

Again merging successive pairs of runs we produce 2 8-element runs:

6 22 26 36 45 66 75 79 | 13 16 27 31 33 47 62 76

The final merging of these runs produces the sorted version

6 13 16 22 26 27 31 33 36 45 47 62 66 75 76 79.

6. As in two-pass radix sort we introduce a queue Q to hold the input stream of records to be sorted and Qu, an **array** $[0 .. 9]$ of queues.

We take the records from Q in turn and add each to the element of Qu indexed by the least significant (units) digit of the key of the record. We concatenate $Qu[0]$, ..., $Qu[9]$ into a single input stream, again called Q. Then we take the records from Q and add each to the element of Qu indexed by the next-to-least (tens) digit of its key. Again we concatenate $Qu[0]$, ..., $Qu[9]$ into Q and taking the records from Q in turn we add each to the element of Qu indexed by the most significant (hundreds) digit of the key. When finally $Qu[0]$, ..., $Qu[9]$ are concatenated the resulting queue is ordered from head to tail.

After the first pass of three-pass radix sort for the given input stream we have

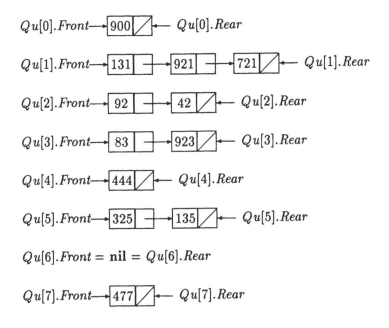

$Qu[8].Front$ ──▸ 508 ─┼─ ▸ 8 ─┼─ ▸ 698 ╱ ◂── $Qu[8].Rear$

$Qu[9].Front = \mathbf{nil} = Qu[9].Rear$

Concatenating these queues we obtain the input stream for the second pass:

900 131 921 721 92 42 83 923 444 325 135 477 508 8 698.

After the second pass we have

$Qu[0].Front$ ──▸ 900 ─┼─ ▸ 508 ─┼─ ▸ 8 ╱ ◂── $Qu[0].Rear$

$Qu[1].Front = \mathbf{nil} = Qu[1].Rear$

$Qu[2].Front$ ──▸ 921 ─┼─ ▸ 721 ─┼─ ▸ 923 ─┼─ ▸ 325 ╱ ◂── $Qu[2].Rear$

$Qu[3].Front$ ──▸ 131 ─┼─ ▸ 135 ╱ ◂── $Qu[2].Rear$

$Qu[4].Front$ ──▸ 42 ─┼─ ▸ 444 ╱ ◂── $Qu[4].Rear$

$Qu[5].Front = \mathbf{nil} = Qu[5].Rear$

$Qu[6].Front = \mathbf{nil} = Qu[6].Rear$

$Qu[7].Front$ ──▸ 477 ╱ ◂── $Qu[7].Rear$

$Qu[8].Front$ ──▸ 83 ╱ ◂── $Qu[8].Rear$

$Qu[9].Front$ ──▸ 92 ─┼─ ▸ 698 ╱ ◂── $Qu[9].Rear$

Concatenating again we obtain the input stream for the third pass:

900 508 8 921 721 923 325 131 135 42 444 477 83 92 698.

Then the third pass produces

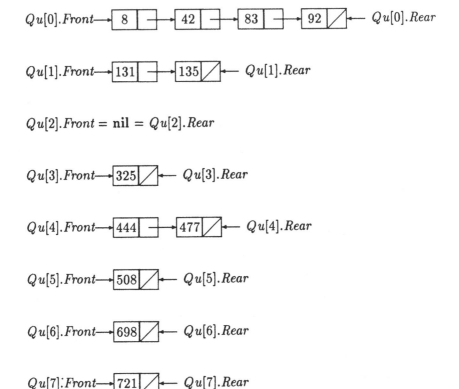

Concatenating the queues for the last time we obtain the sorted output

8 42 83 92 131 135 325 444 477 508 698 721 900 921 923.

7. The data should be processed in three stages.

The first stage should produce an output stream in which the *Day* fields are in non-decreasing order. This might be done by setting up 31 queues and enqueuing each item in the queue corresponding to its *Day* field; or else, if this is thought to be too extravagant of space, we could use a two-pass radix sort, first with 10 queues corresponding to the units digit and second with 4 queues indexed by 0..3 corresponding to the tens digit.

The second stage should produce an output stream in which both *Day* and *Month* fields are in non-decreasing order. This could be achieved by setting 12 queues and enqueuing each item in the output stream from the first stage in the queue corresponding to its *Month* field.

Finally in the third stage we produce the required ordered output. If the number of different *Year* fields occurring in our collection is small we might do this by setting up one queue for each possible year; but if the spread of *Year* fields is large it might be better to carry out the third stage in several passes, perhaps as many as 4.

We would clearly have to think further if some of the dates were B.C.

8.
```
        Function mark (F : Text) : Text;
        Var G : Text;
             m, n : Integer;
        Begin Reset(F); Rewrite(G);
             If not eof(F) then begin
                        Readln(F, m); Writeln(G, m) end;
             Repeat
                   If not eof(F) then Readln(F, n);
                   If m ≤ n then begin
                              Writeln(G, n); m := n end
                        else begin
                              Writeln(G, ' '); Writeln(G, n);
                              m := n end
             until eof(F);1
             mark := G
        End;
```

9. We introduce four files $F1$, $F2$, $F3$, $F4$.

Then we read successive groups of 5 integers from F, sort them, and write the resulting runs alternately to $F1$ and $F2$. This produces the arrangement:

$F1$: 22 31 36 66 97 | 19 26 45 46 75 | 33 72 76
$F2$: 6 15 32 44 79 | 8 13 17 62 88

Now we read 5-member runs from $F1$ and $F2$, merge them, and write the resulting 10-member runs to $F3$ and $F4$ alternately, obtaining

$F3$: 6 15 22 31 32 36 44 66 79 97 | 33 72 76
$F4$: 8 13 17 19 26 45 46 62 75 88

We read 10-member runs from $F3$ and $F4$, merging them and writing the resulting runs alternately to $F1$ and $F2$ so that we have

$F1$: 6 8 13 15 17 19 22 26 31 32 36 44 45 46 62 66 75 79
        88 97
$F2$: 33 72 76

Finally we merge the single runs on $F1$ and $F2$ to obtain

$F3$: 6 8 13 15 17 19 22 26 31 32 33 36 44 45 46 62 66 72
        75 76 79 88 97
$F4$: empty

10. We read successive runs from the input file and write them alternately to $F1$ and $F2$, obtaining

$F1$: 66 | 22 97 | 15 | 44 | 19 45 46 75 | 76
$F2$: 31 | 36 | 6 32 79 | 26 | 8 13 17 62 88 | 33 72

Then, merging and distributing in the usual way we obtain successively

$F3$: 31 66 | 6 15 32 79 | 8 13 17 19 45 46 62 75 88
$F4$: 22 36 97 | 26 44 | 33 72 76

$F1$: 22 31 36 66 97 | 8 13 17 19 33 45 46 62 72 75 76 88
$F2$: 6 15 26 32 44 79

$F3$: 6 15 22 26 31 32 36 44 66 79 97
$F4$: 8 13 17 19 33 45 46 62 72 75 76 88

$F1$: 6 8 13 15 17 19 22 26 31 32 33 36 44 45 46 62 66 72
     75 76 79 88 98
$F2$: empty

11. As in the Balanced Mergesort described in Section 7.3 we would repeatedly read in from the input file as many records as can be held
in internal memory along with an internal sorting program, use the
program to form a run, and write away the merged run, using F_1,
$F_2 \ldots$, F_M in cyclic order (i.e. after we have written a run to F_i we
write the next one to F_{i+1} if $i = 1, 2, \ldots, M - 1$ or F_1 if $i = M$). Then
we repeatedly merge the leading runs on $F_1, \ldots, F_M$ into longer runs,
which we write in cyclic order to $F_{M+1}, \ldots, F_N$. We then interchange
the roles of $F_1, \ldots, F_M$ and $F_{M+1}, \ldots, F_N$ and continue in this way
until there is only one run.

To merge M runs we must repeatedly find the minimum of the keys
of the leading entries of the M runs and transfer to the merged run
the record which has this minimum key.

Chapter 20

SOLUTIONS TO
EXERCISES 8

1. The natural greedy strategy would be as follows:

   Take k_1 to be the largest integer k such that $ka_1 \leq A$; thus we take $k_1 = A$ **div** a_1;

   Take k_2 to be the largest integer k such that $ka_2 \leq A - k_1 a_1$; thus $k_2 = (A - k_1 a_1)$ **div** a_2,

   and proceed in this way.

   If we apply this method in the case where we have coins of value $11, 5$ and 1 then to change 15 we would offer one coin of value 11, none of value 5 and 4 of value 1, a total of 5 coins in all; but 3 coins of value 5 would be a better solution!

2. Initially $S = \{A\}$ and we have

$$d[B] = 100,\ d[C] = 250,\ d[D] = 500,\ d[E] = 200,$$
$$p[B] = A,\ p[C] = A,\ p[D] = A,\ p[E] = A.$$

The minimum entry in the array d is $d[B] = 100$, so we adjoin B to S; then for $X = C, D, E$ we alter $d[X]$ to $\min\{d[X], d[B] + \text{length}(BX)\}$. This produces

$$d[C] = \min\{250, 100 + \infty\} = 250;\ p[C] = A;$$
$$d[D] = \min\{500, 100 + 175\} = 275;\ p[D] = B;$$
$$d[E] = \min\{200, 100 + 20\} = 120,\ p[E] = B.$$

The minimum entry in d is $d[E] = 120$, so we adjoin E to S; then for $X = C, D$ we change $d[X]$ to $\min\{d[X], d[E] + \text{length}(EX)\}$. This gives

$$d[C] = \min\{250, 120 + \infty\} = 250; \; p[C] = A;$$
$$d[D] = \min\{275, 120 + \infty\} = 275; \; p[D] = B.$$

The minimum entry in d is $d[C] = 250$, so we adjoin C to S; then we alter $d[D]$ to $\min\{d[D], d[C] + \text{length}(CD)\}$. So we have

$$d[D] = \min\{275, 250 + 20\} = 270; \; p[D] = C.$$

Thus the shortest paths are

$$AB(100), AC(250), ACD(270), ABE(120).$$

3. Consider the main loop of Dijkstra's algorithm which we can rewrite as follows:

> **for** $i := 1$ **to** $n - 1$ **do begin**
>   Choose a vertex v not in S for which $d[v]$ is least;
>   Adjoin v to S;
>   For each vertex w not in S do
>   **if** $d[w] > d[v] + W((v, w))$ **then** $d[w] := d[v] + W((v, w))$
> **end**

At the beginning of the i-th iteration of the loop there are $n - i$ vertices not in S. So $n - i - 1$ comparisons are required to find the vertex v not in S for which $d[v]$ is least; and $n - i - 1$ comparisons are required to determine whether the entries $d[w]$ corresponding to the remaining vertices w have to be updated. Thus the total number of comparisons is

$$2((n - 1) + (n - 2) + \ldots + 3 + 2 + 1) = (n - 1)(n - 2).$$

Hence, counting comparisons, Dijkstra's algorithm is $\Theta(n^2)$.

4. The initial versions of the matrices D and P are

$$\begin{bmatrix} 0 & 90 & 100 & 70 \\ 40 & 0 & 5 & 10 \\ 7 & \infty & 0 & 4 \\ 20 & 10 & 7 & 0 \end{bmatrix} \quad \text{and} \quad \begin{bmatrix} 0 & 0 & 0 & 0 \\ 0 & 0 & 0 & 0 \\ 0 & 0 & 0 & 0 \\ 0 & 0 & 0 & 0 \end{bmatrix}$$

respectively.

We now make the assignments

$$D[i,j] := \min\{D[i,j], D[i,1] + D[1,j]\}$$

and

$$P[i,j] := 1 \text{ if } D[i,j] \text{ has been reduced.}$$

Thus we have

$D[2,3] := \min\{D[2,3], D[2,1] + D[1,3]\} = \min\{5, 40 + 100\} = 5$
$D[2,4] := \min\{D[2,4], D[2,1] + D[1,4]\} = \min\{10, 40 + 70\} = 10$
$D[3,2] := \min\{D[3,2], D[3,1] + D[1,2]\} = \min\{\infty, 7 + 90\} = 97$
  and $P[3,2] := 1$
$D[3,4] := \min\{D[3,4], D[3,1] + D[1,4]\} = \min\{4, 7 + 70\} = 4$
$D[4,2] := \min\{D[4,2], D[4,1] + D[1,2]\} = \min\{10, 20 + 90\} = 10$
$D[4,3] := \min\{D[4,3], D[4,1] + D[1,3]\} = \min\{7, 20 + 100\} = 7$

So we have

$$D = \begin{bmatrix} 0 & 90 & 100 & 70 \\ 40 & 0 & 5 & 10 \\ 7 & 97 & 0 & 4 \\ 20 & 10 & 7 & 0 \end{bmatrix} \text{ and } P = \begin{bmatrix} 0 & 0 & 0 & 0 \\ 0 & 0 & 0 & 0 \\ 0 & 1 & 0 & 0 \\ 0 & 0 & 0 & 0 \end{bmatrix}$$

We now make the assignments

$$D[i,j] := \min\{D[i,j], D[i,2] + D[2,j]\}$$

and

$$P[i,j] := 2 \text{ if } D[i,j] \text{ has been reduced.}$$

Thus we have

$D[1,3] := \min\{D[1,3], D[1,2] + D[2,3]\} = \min\{100, 90 + 5\} = 95$
  and $P[1,3] := 2$
$D[1,4] := \min\{D[1,4], D[1,2] + D[2,4]\} = \min\{70, 90 + 10\} = 70$
$D[3,1] := \min\{D[3,1], D[3,2] + D[2,1]\} = \min\{7, 97 + 40\} = 7$
$D[3,4] := \min\{D[3,4], D[3,2] + D[2,4]\} = \min\{4, 97 + 10\} = 4$
$D[4,1] := \min\{D[4,1], D[4,2] + D[2,1]\} = \min\{20, 10 + 40\} = 20$
$D[4,3] := \min\{D[4,3], D[4,2] + D[2,3]\} = \min\{7, 10 + 5\} = 7$

So we have

$$D = \begin{bmatrix} 0 & 90 & 95 & 70 \\ 40 & 0 & 5 & 10 \\ 7 & 97 & 0 & 4 \\ 20 & 10 & 7 & 0 \end{bmatrix} \text{ and } P = \begin{bmatrix} 0 & 0 & 2 & 0 \\ 0 & 0 & 0 & 0 \\ 0 & 1 & 0 & 0 \\ 0 & 0 & 0 & 0 \end{bmatrix}$$

We now make the assignments

$$D[i,j] := \min\{D[i,j], D[i,3] + D[3,j]\}$$

and

$$P[i,j] := 3 \text{ if } D[i,j] \text{ has been reduced.}$$

Thus we have
$D[1,2] := \min\{D[1,2], D[1,3] + D[3,2]\} = \min\ \{90, 95 + 97\} = 90$
$D[1,4] := \min\{D[1,4], D[1,3] + D[3,4]\} = \min\ \{70, 95 + 4\} = 70$
$D[2,1] := \min\{D[2,1], D[2,3] + D[3,1]\} = \min\ \{40, 5 + 7\} = 12$
    and $P[2,1] := 3$
$D[2,4] := \min\{D[2,4], D[2,3] + D[3,4]\} = \min\ \{10, 5 + 4\} = 9$
    and $P[2,4] := 3$
$D[4,1] := \min\{D[4,1], D[4,3] + D[3,1]\} = \min\ \{20, 7 + 7\} = 14$
    and $P[4,1] := 3$
$D[4,2] := \min\{D[4,2], D[4,3] + D[3,2]\} = \min\ \{10, 7 + 97\} = 10$

So we have

$$D = \begin{bmatrix} 0 & 90 & 95 & 70 \\ 12 & 0 & 5 & 9 \\ 7 & 97 & 0 & 4 \\ 14 & 10 & 7 & 0 \end{bmatrix} \text{ and } P = \begin{bmatrix} 0 & 0 & 2 & 0 \\ 3 & 0 & 0 & 3 \\ 0 & 1 & 0 & 0 \\ 3 & 0 & 0 & 0 \end{bmatrix}$$

We now make the assignments

$$D[i,j] := \min\{D[i,j], D[i,4] + D[4,j]\}$$

and

$$P[i,j] := 4 \text{ if } D[i,j] \text{ has been reduced.}$$

Thus we have

$D[1,2] := \min\{D[1,2], D[1,4] + D[4,2]\} = \min\ \{90, 70 + 10\} = 80$
  and $P[1,2] := 4$
$D[1,3] := \min\{D[1,3], D[1,4] + D[4,3]\} = \min\ \{95, 70 + 7\} = 77$
  and $P[1,3] := 4$
$D[2,1] := \min\{D[2,1], D[2,4] + D[4,1]\} = \min\ \{12, 9 + 14\} = 12$
$D[2,3] := \min\{D[2,3], D[2,4] + D[4,3]\} = \min\ \{5, 9 + 7\} = 5$
$D[3,1] := \min\{D[3,1], D[3,4] + D[4,1]\} = \min\ \{7, 4 + 14\} = 7$
$D[3,2] := \min\{D[3,2], D[3,4] + D[4,2]\} = \min\ \{97, 4 + 10\} = 14$
  and $P[3,2] := 4$

So we have finally

$$D = \begin{bmatrix} 0 & 80 & 77 & 70 \\ 12 & 0 & 5 & 9 \\ 7 & 14 & 0 & 4 \\ 14 & 10 & 7 & 0 \end{bmatrix} \text{ and } P = \begin{bmatrix} 0 & 4 & 4 & 0 \\ 3 & 0 & 0 & 3 \\ 0 & 4 & 0 & 0 \\ 3 & 0 & 0 & 0 \end{bmatrix}$$

The (i,j)-th entry of the matrix D is the length of the shortest path from vertex i to vertex j. To list the intermediate vertices we call the procedure path(i, j). Eventually we find

  Shortest path from 1 to 2 is 1, 4, 2 of length 80;
  Shortest path from 1 to 3 is 1, 4, 3 of length 77;
  Shortest path from 1 to 4 is 1, 4 of length 70;
  Shortest path from 2 to 1 is 2, 3, 1 of length 12;
  Shortest path from 2 to 3 is 2, 3 of length 5;
  Shortest path from 2 to 4 is 2, 3, 4 of length 9;
  Shortest path from 3 to 1 is 3, 1 of length 7;
  Shortest path from 3 to 2 is 3, 4, 2 of length 14;
  Shortest path from 3 to 4 is 3, 4 of length 4;
  Shortest path from 4 to 1 is 4, 3, 1 of length 14;
  Shortest path from 4 to 2 is 4, 2 of length 10;
  Shortest path from 4 to 3 is 4, 3 of length 7.

5. The execution of Floyd's algorithm clearly always requires n^3 comparisons; so the algorithm is $\Theta(n^3)$.

  This is the same order as an n-fold application of Dijkstra's algorithm, using each vertex in turn as initial vertex; but Floyd's algorithm requires space to store an $n \times n$ array.

6. Suppose we are looking for a shortest tour starting from and finishing at vertex 1.

For each vertex $i \neq 1$ we have $g(i, \emptyset) =$ cost of cheapest path from i to 1 with no intermediate vertex $= c_{i1}$. So

$$g(2, \emptyset) = c_{21} = 3$$
$$g(3, \emptyset) = c_{31} = 7$$
$$g(4, \emptyset) = c_{41} = 4$$
$$g(5, \emptyset) = c_{51} = 2$$

Next, for each $i \neq 1$ and each $k \neq 1, i$ we have

$$g(i, \{k\}) = \min_{j \in \{k\}}\{c_{ij} + g\{j, \emptyset\}\} = c_{ik} + g(k, \emptyset) = c_{ik} + c_{k1}.$$

So

$$g(2, \{3\}) = c_{23} + c_{31} = 3 + 7 = 10$$
$$g(2, \{4\}) = c_{24} + c_{41} = 4 + 4 = 8$$
$$g(2, \{5\}) = c_{25} + c_{51} = 6 + 2 = 8$$
$$g(3, \{2\}) = c_{32} + c_{21} = 3 + 3 = 6$$
$$g(3, \{4\}) = c_{34} + c_{41} = 8 + 4 = 12$$
$$g(3, \{5\}) = c_{35} + c_{51} = 6 + 2 = 8$$
$$g(4, \{2\}) = c_{42} + c_{21} = 4 + 3 = 7$$
$$g(4, \{3\}) = c_{43} + c_{31} = 8 + 7 = 15$$
$$g(4, \{5\}) = c_{45} + c_{51} = 5 + 2 = 7$$
$$g(5, \{2\}) = c_{52} + c_{21} = 6 + 3 = 9$$
$$g(5, \{3\}) = c_{53} + c_{31} = 6 + 7 = 13$$
$$g(5, \{4\}) = c_{54} + c_{41} = 5 + 4 = 9$$

Now for all appropriate i, j, k we have

$$g(i, \{j, k\}) = \min\{c_{ij} + g(j, \{k\}), c_{ik} + g(k, \{j\})\}.$$

So

$$g(2, \{3, 4\}) = \min \{c_{23} + g(3, \{4\}), c_{24} + g(4, \{3\})\}$$
$$= \min \{3 + 12, 4 + 15\} = 15, \text{ using } 2 \to 3$$
$$g(2, \{3, 5\}) = \min \{c_{23} + g(3, \{5\}), c_{25} + g(5, \{3\})\}$$
$$= \min \{3 + 8, 6 + 13\} = 11, \text{ using } 2 \to 3$$
$$g(2, \{4, 5\}) = \min \{c_{24} + g(4, \{5\}), c_{25} + g(5, \{4\})\}$$
$$= \min \{4 + 7, 6 + 9\} = 11, \text{ using } 2 \to 4$$

$$g(3, \{2,4\}) = \min \{c_{32} + g(2, \{4\}), c_{34} + g(4, \{2\})\}$$
$$= \min \{3 + 8, 8 + 7\} = 11, \text{ using } 3 \rightarrow 2$$
$$g(3, \{2,5\}) = \min \{c_{32} + g(2, \{5\}), c_{35} + g(5, \{2\})\}$$
$$= \min \{3 + 8, 6 + 9\} = 11, \text{ using } 3 \rightarrow 2$$
$$g(3, \{4,5\}) = \min \{c_{34} + g(4, \{5\}), c_{35} + g(5, \{4\})\}$$
$$= \min \{8 + 7, 6 + 9\} = 15,$$
$$\text{using either } 3 \rightarrow 4 \text{ or } 3 \rightarrow 5$$
$$g(4, \{2,3\}) = \min \{c_{42} + g(2, \{3\}), c_{43} + g(3, \{2\})\}$$
$$= \min \{4 + 10, 8 + 6\} = 14,$$
$$\text{using either } 4 \rightarrow 2 \text{ or } 4 \rightarrow 3$$
$$g(4, \{2,5\}) = \min \{c_{42} + g(2, \{5\}), c_{45} + g(5, \{2\})\}$$
$$= \min \{4 + 8, 5 + 9\} = 12, \text{ using } 4 \rightarrow 2$$
$$g(4, \{3,5\}) = \min \{c_{43} + g(3, \{5\}), c_{45} + g(5, \{3\})\}$$
$$= \min \{8 + 8, 5 + 13\} = 16, \text{ using } 4 \rightarrow 3$$
$$g(5, \{2,3\}) = \min \{c_{52} + g(2, \{3\}), c_{53} + g(3, \{2\})\}$$
$$= \min \{6 + 10, 6 + 6\} = 12, \text{ using } 5 \rightarrow 3$$
$$g(5, \{2,4\}) = \min \{c_{52} + g(2, \{4\}), c_{54} + g(4, \{2\})\}$$
$$= \min \{6 + 8, 5 + 7\} = 12, \text{ using } 5 \rightarrow 4$$
$$g(5, \{3,4\}) = \min \{c_{53} + g(3, \{4\}), c_{54} + g(4, \{3\})\}$$
$$= \min \{6 + 12, 5 + 15\} = 18, \text{ using } 5 \rightarrow 3$$

Next, for all appropriate i, j, k, l we have

$$g(i, \{j,k,l\}) = \min\{c_{ij} + g(j, \{k,l\}), c_{ik} + g(k, \{j,l\}), c_{il} + g(l, \{j,k\})\}.$$

So

$$g(2, \{3,4,5\}) = \min\{c_{23}+g(3, \{4,5\}), c_{24}+g(4, \{3,5\}), c_{25}+g(5, \{3,4\})\}$$
$$= \min\{3 + 15, 4 + 16, 6 + 18\} = 18, \text{ using } 2 \rightarrow 3$$
$$g(3, \{2,4,5\}) = \min\{c_{32}+g(2, \{4,5\}), c_{34}+g(4, \{2,5\}), c_{35}+g(5, \{2,4\})\}$$
$$= \min\{3 + 11, 8 + 12, 6 + 12\} = 14, \text{ using } 3 \rightarrow 2$$
$$g(4, \{2,3,5\}) = \min\{c_{42}+g(2, \{3,5\}), c_{43}+g(3, \{2,5\}), c_{45}+g(5, \{2,3\})\}$$
$$= \min\{4 + 11, 8 + 11, 5 + 12\} = 15, \text{ using } 4 \rightarrow 2$$
$$g(5, \{2,3,4\}) = \min\{c_{52}+g(2, \{3,4\}), c_{53}+g(3, \{2,4\}), c_{54}+g(4, \{2,3\})\}$$
$$= \min\{6 + 15, 6 + 11, 5 + 14\} = 17, \text{ using } 5 \rightarrow 3$$

Finally we have

$$g(1, \{2,3,4,5\}) = \min\{c_{12}+g(2,\{3,4,5\}), c_{13}+g(3,\{2,4,5\}),$$
$$c_{14}+g(4,\{2,3,5\}), c_{15}+g(5,\{2,3,4\}))\}$$
$$= \min\{3+18, 7+14, 4+15, 2+17\}$$
$$= 19, \text{ using either } 1 \to 4 \text{ or } 1 \to 5.$$

Thus the shortest tours are

1, 4, 2, 3, 5, 1 and 1, 5, 3, 2, 4, 1

7. (a) **Borůvka's algorithm.** $\mathbf{F}$ initially consists of 8 single-node trees, $(\{A\}, \emptyset), \ldots, (\{H\}, \emptyset)$.

Minimum weight edge from $(\{A\}, \emptyset)$ is AB of length 1;
Minimum weight edge from $(\{B\}, \emptyset)$ is BA of length 1;
Minimum weight edge from $(\{C\}, \emptyset)$ is CD of length 2;
Minimum weight edge from $(\{D\}, \emptyset)$ is DC of length 2;
Minimum weight edge from $(\{E\}, \emptyset)$ is EH of length 6;
Minimum weight edge from $(\{F\}, \emptyset)$ is FB of length 5;
Minimum weight edge from $(\{G\}, \emptyset)$ is GH of length 8;
Minimum weight edge from $(\{H\}, \emptyset)$ is HE of length 6.

Since $AB = BA$, $CD = DC$, $EH = HE$ each appear twice we take $\mathbf{F}_1$ to consist of the 5 single-node trees $(\{A\}, \emptyset)$, $(\{C\}, \emptyset)$, $(\{E\}, \emptyset)$, $(\{F\}, \emptyset)$, $(\{G\}, \emptyset)$ and apply the Blue Rule to their vertex sets, colouring AB, CD, EH, FB and GH blue.

$\dot{\mathbf{F}}$ now consists of the three blue trees

$T_1 = (\{A, B, F\}, \{AB, BF\});$
$T_2 = (\{C, D\}, \{CD\});$
$T_3 = (\{E, G, H\}, \{EH, GH\}).$

We now see that we have

Minimum weight edge from T_1 is BC of length 3;
Minimum weight edge from T_2 is CB of length 3;
Minimum weight edge from T_3 is DH of length 7.

Since $BC = CB$ occurs twice we take $\mathbf{F}_1$ to consist of T_1 and T_3 and apply the Blue Rule to their vertex sets, colouring BC and DH blue.

$\mathbf{F}$ now consists of a single blue tree, with edges AB, BC, CD, DH, EH, FB and GH; this is a minimum spanning tree, of total weight 32.

(b) **Kruskal's algorithm.** In increasing order of length we have

$$AB\ (1),\ CD\ (2),\ BC\ (3),\ AD\ (4),\ BF\ (5),\ EH\ (6),$$
$$DH\ (7),\ GH\ (8),\ AE\ (9),\ EF\ (10),\ FG\ (12),\ CG\ (14)$$

Originally there are 8 single-node blue trees

$$(\{A\}, \emptyset), (\{B\}, \emptyset), \ldots, (\{H\}, \emptyset).$$

AB has its endpoints in distinct blue trees; so we colour it blue. There are now 7 blue trees

$$(\{A, B\}, \{AB\}), (\{C\}, \emptyset), \ldots, (\{H\}, \emptyset).$$

CD has its endpoints in distinct blue trees; so we colour it blue. There are now 6 blue trees

$$(\{A, B\}, \{AB\}), (\{C, D\}, \{CD\}), (\{E\}, \emptyset), \ldots, (\{H\}, \emptyset).$$

BC has its endpoints in distinct blue trees; so we colour it blue. There are now 5 blue trees

$$(\{A, B, C, D\}, \{AB, BC, CD\}), (\{E\}, \emptyset), \ldots, (\{H\}, \emptyset).$$

AD has its endpoints in the same blue tree; so we colour it red. BF has its endpoints in distinct blue trees; so we colour it blue. There are now 4 blue trees

$$(\{A, B, C, D, F\}, \{AB, BC, CD, BF\}), (\{E\}, \emptyset), (\{G\}, \emptyset),$$
$$(\{H\}, \emptyset).$$

EH has its endpoints in distinct blue trees; so we colour it blue. There are now 3 blue trees

$$(\{A, B, C, D, F\}, \{AB, BC, CD, BF\}), (\{E, H\}, \{EH\}),$$
$$(\{G\}, \emptyset).$$

DH has its endpoints in distinct blue trees; so we colour it blue. There are now 2 blue trees

$$(\{A, B, C, D, E, F, H\}, \{AB, BC, CD, BF, EH, DH\}), (\{G\}, \emptyset).$$

GH has its endpoints in distinct blue trees; so we colour it blue. There is now just one blue tree with 7 edges,

$$(\{A, B, C, D, E, F, G, H\}, \{AB, BC, CD, BF, EH, DH, GH\}).$$

which is a minimum spanning tree.

(c) **Prim's algorithm.** 1. We begin with the 1-node tree $T = (\{A\}, \emptyset)$.

The edges protruding from T are AB (1), AD (4), AE (9) which are all uncoloured. We apply the Blue Rule to $\{A\}$ and colour AB blue.

2. T is now $(\{A, B\}, \{AB\})$.

The edges protruding from T are AD (4), AE (9), BF (5), BC (3) which are all uncoloured. Applying the Blue Rule to $\{A, B\}$ we colour BC blue.

3. T is now $(\{A, B, C\}, \{AB, BC\})$.

The edges protruding from T are AD (4), AE (9), BF (5), CG (14) and CD (2). These are all uncoloured; but AD and CD have the same endpoint D outside T—so we apply the Red Rule to the cycle A, B, C, D, A and colour AD red. The uncoloured edges protruding from T are now AE (9), BF (5), CG (14), CD (2). We apply the Blue Rule to $\{A, B, C\}$ and colour CD blue.

4. T now becomes $(\{A, B, C, D\}, \{AB, BC, CD\})$.

The protruding edges are AE (9), BF (5), CG (14), DH (7) which are all uncoloured and no two of which have the same endpoint outside T. Applying the Blue Rule to $\{A, B, C, D\}$ we colour BF blue.

5. T is now $(\{A, B, C, D, F\}, \{AB, BC, CD, BF\})$.

The edges protruding from T are AE (9), CG (14), DH (7), FE (10), FG (12) which are all uncoloured. AE and FE have the same endpoint E outside T; we apply the Red Rule to the cycle A, B, F, E, A and colour FE red. CG and FG have the same endpoint G outside T; we apply the Red Rule to the cycle C, B, F, G, C and colour CG red. The uncoloured edges protruding from T are now AE (9), DH (7), FG (12). Applying the Blue Rule to $\{A, B, C, D, F\}$ we colour DH blue.

6. T is now $(\{A, B, C, D, F, H\}, \{AB, BC, CD, BF, DH\})$.

The edges protruding from T are AE and CG, which are red and FE (10), FG (12), HE (6), HG (8). Now FE and HE have the same endpoint E outside T; we apply the Red Rule to the cycle F, B, C, D, H, E, F and colour FE red. FG and HG have the same endpoint G outside T; applying the Red Rule to the cycle F, B, C, D, H, G, F we colour FG red. The uncoloured edges protruding from T are now HE (6) and HG (8). We apply the Blue Rule to $\{A, B, C, D, F, H\}$ and colour HE blue.

7. T is now $(\{A, B, C, D, E, F, H\}, \{AB, BC, CD, BF, DH, HE\})$. The only edges protruding from T are FG, which is red, and HG (8), which is uncoloured. So we apply the Blue Rule to $\{A, B, C, D, E, F, H\}$ and colour HG blue.

As before we obtain a minimum spanning tree

$$(\{A, B, C, D, E, F, G, H\}, \{AB, BC, CD, BF, DH, HE, HG\}).$$

8. As in Floyd's algorithm we construct a sequence of arrays

$$P_0, P_1, \ldots, P_n$$

with **boolean** entries such that for $i, j, k = 1, \ldots, n$ we have $P[i,j] =$ **true** if and only if there is a path from vertex i to vertex j which has no intermediate vertex with number higher than k. Then clearly P_0 is the adjacency matrix and the (i, j)-th entry of P_n tells us whether or not there is a path in the graph from i to j.

We declare

$$\textbf{Var } P : \textbf{array } [1 .. n, 1 .. n] \textbf{ of boolean};$$

initialise P to be the adjacency matrix and then carry out the triple loop

```
for k:= 1 to n do
    for i:= 1 to n do
        for j:= 1 to n do
            P[i, j] := P[i, j] or (P[i, k] and P[k, j]);
```

Chapter 21

SOLUTIONS TO EXERCISES 9

1. (*a*) Old Russian multiplication.

10111001	10101110
101110010	1010111
1011100100	101011
10111001000	10101
101110010000	1010
1011100100000	101
10111001000000	10
101110010000000	1

So the product is the sum of

$$101110010$$
$$1011100100$$
$$10111001000$$
$$1011100100000$$
$$101110010000000$$

which is 0111110110111110.

(*b*) New Russian multiplication.

Let $x = 10111001$ and $y = 10101110$. Then

$$x_1 = 1011, \ x_0 = 1001, \ y_1 = 1010, \ y_0 = 1110,$$
$$x_1 - x_0 = 0010, \ y_0 - y_1 = 0100.$$

We now have to calculate the three products

$$p_2 = x_1 y_1, \ p_1 = (x_1 - x_0)(y_0 - y_1), \ p_0 = x_0 y_0.$$

For the calculation of p_2 we write $x = 1011$ and $y = 1010$. Then

$$x_1 = 10, \ x_0 = 11, \ y_1 = 10, \ y_0 = 10,$$
$$x_1 - x_0 = -01, \ y_0 - y_1 = 0.$$

Then we have

$$q_2 = x_1 y_1 = (10) \times (10) = 0100,$$
$$q_1 = (x_1 - x_0)(y_0 - y_1) = 0,$$
$$q_0 = x_0 y_0 = (11) \times (10) = 0110.$$

So the product p_2 is

$$0100 \times 2^4 + (0100 + 0 + 0110) \times 2^2 + 0110 =$$
$$01000000 + 101000 + 0110 = 01101110.$$

To calculate p_1 we write $x = 0010$ and $y = 0100$. Then

$$x_1 = 00, \ x_0 = 10, \ y_1 = 01, \ y_0 = 00,$$
$$x_1 - x_0 = -10, \ y_0 - y_1 = -01.$$

Then we have

$$q_2 = x_1 y_1 = (00) \times (01) = 0000,$$
$$q_1 = (x_1 - x_0)(y_0 - y_1) = (-10) \times (-01) = 0010,$$
$$q_0 = x_0 y_0 = (10) \times (00) = 0000.$$

So the product p_1 is

$$0000 \times 2^4 + 0010 \times 2^2 + 0000 = 00001000.$$

Finally we calculate p_0, starting by writing $x = 1001$ and $y = 1110$. Then

$$x_1 = 10,\ x_0 = 01,\ y_1 = 11,\ y_0 = 10,$$
$$x_1 - x_0 = 01,\ y_0 - y_1 = -01.$$

Then we have

$$q_2 = x_1 y_1 = (10) \times (11) = 0110,$$
$$q_1 = (x_1 - x_0)(y_0 - y_1) = (01) \times (-01) = -0001,$$
$$q_0 = x_0 y_0 = (01) \times (10) = 0010.$$

So the product p_0 is

$$0110 \times 2^4 + (0110 - 0001 + 0010) \times 2^2 + 0010 =$$
$$01100000 + 011100 + 0010 = 01111110.$$

The required product is now

$$01101110 \times 2^8 + (01111110 + 00001000 + 01101110) \times 2^4 + 01111110$$
$$= 0110111000000000 + 111101000000 + 01111110$$
$$= 0111110110111110.$$

2. Both methods must produce the same product 81468.

3. In the usual notation we have

$$m_{11} = m_{22} = m_{33} = m_{44} = 0,$$

$$m_{12} = 20 \times 10 \times 5 = 1000,$$
$$m_{23} = 10 \times 5 \times 100 = 5000,$$
$$m_{34} = 5 \times 100 \times 8 = 4000.$$

$$\begin{aligned}
m_{13} &= \min\{m_{11} + m_{23} + d_0 d_1 d_3,\ m_{12} + m_{33} + d_0 d_2 d_3\} \\
&= \min\ \{0 + 5000 + 20 \times 10 \times 100,\ 1000 + 0 + 20 \times 5 \times 100\} \\
&= 11000, \\
m_{24} &= \min\{m_{22} + m_{34} + d_1 d_2 d_4,\ m_{23} + m_{44} + d_1 d_3 d_4\} \\
&= \min\ \{0 + 4400 + 20 \times 10 \times 8,\ 5000 + 0 + 10 \times 100 \times 8\} \\
&= 4400.
\end{aligned}$$

Finally we have
$$\begin{aligned}
m_{14} &= \min\{m_{11} + m_{24} + d_0 d_1 d_4,\ m_{12} + m_{34} + d_0 d_2 d_4, \\
&\qquad\qquad m_{13} + m_{44} + d_0 d_3 d_4\} \\
&= \min\ \{0 + 4400 + 20 \times 10 \times 8,\ 1000 + 4000 + 20 \times 5 \times 8, \\
&\qquad\qquad 11000 + 0 + 20 \times 100 \times 8\ \} \\
&= 5800.
\end{aligned}$$

4. Suppose there are n matrices in the product. Then declare

Var m : **array** $[1 .. n]$ **of integer;**

and compute the entries $m[i,j]$ for $i \leq i \leq j \leq n$ using the definitions of the m_{ij} in the description of the algorithm. The required minimum number of multiplications is $m[1,n]$.

To produce the optimal bracketing we think of working with an array b of character strings (if our version of Pascal supports such a data type) with the idea that the array entry $b[i,j]$ should be the optimal bracketing of the partial product $A_i A_{i+1} \ldots A_j$. Clearly each $b[i,i]$ is the string consisting of the name of the ith factor of the product $(i = 1, \ldots, n)$ and for $i = 1, \ldots, n-1$ the entry $b[i,i+1]$ is the string consisting of a left parenthesis followed by the names of the ith and $(i+1)$st factors followed by a right parenthesis. When we are finding

$$m_{i,i+s} = \min_{i \leq k < i+s}\{m_{ik} + m_{k+1,i+s} + d_{i-1}d_k d_{i+s}\}$$

we can determine $b[i,i+s]$ by noting the index k which produces the minimum—call it k_0. Then $b[i,i+s]$ is the string consisting of a left parenthesis followed by $b[i,k_0]$ and then $b[k_0+1,i+s]$ followed by a right parenthesis.

The final optimal bracketing is the array entry $b[1,n]$.

5. (1) is unstable because α prefers C to his wife A and C prefers α to her husband γ. (There are two other unstable pairs: β prefers A to B and A prefers β to α; also β prefers C to B and C prefers β to γ.)
   (2) is stable.
   (3) is unstable because β prefers A to B and A prefers β to γ (and also because β prefers C to B and C prefers β to α).

6. The Gale-Shapley algorithm with the men doing the proposing proceeds as follows:

   (a) α asks C and they become engaged.

   (b) β asks B and they become engaged.

   (c) γ asks B, who prefers γ to her current fiancé β; so γ and B become engaged and β becomes free.

(d) β asks his second choice A who is free; so β and A become engaged.

(e) δ asks C who prefers him to her current partner α; so δ and C become engaged and α becomes free.

(f) α asks B who rejects his offer because she prefers her present partner γ.

(g) α asks D who is free and accepts him.

The resulting stable arrangement is

$$\alpha = D, \beta = A, \gamma = B, \delta = C.$$

7. (a) If A is paired with D (and hence B with C) the situation is unstable since A prefers C to D and C prefers A to B.

(b) If B is paired with D (so A with C) the situation is unstable since B prefers A to D and A prefers B to C.

(c) If C is paired with D (so A with B) then since C prefers B to D and B prefers C to A we again have an instability.

Chapter 22

SOLUTIONS TO
EXERCISES 10

1. (a) $(1 + 16)$ **div** $2 = 8$; $A[8] = 20$; $30 > 20$, so search in the subarray indexed by $9 \dots 16$.

   $(9 + 16)$ **div** $2 = 12$; $A[12] = 26$; $30 > 26$, so search in the subarray indexed by $13 \dots 16$.

   $(13 + 16)$ **div** $2 = 14$; $A[14] = 30$, so the required record in in $A[14]$.

   (b) $(1 + 16)$ **div** $2 = 8$; $A[8] = 20$; $14 < 20$, so search in the subarray indexed by $1 \dots 7$.

   $(1 + 7)$ **div** $2 = 4$; $A[4] = 10$; $14 > 10$, so search in the subarray indexed by $5 \dots 7$.

   $(5 + 7)$ **div** $2 = 6$; $A[6] = 15$; $14 < 15$, so search in the subarray indexed by $5 \dots 5$.

   $A[5] = 13 \neq 14$; so the required record is not present.

2. We should test that the program locates successfully the N entries we know to be present and that it reports failure for any chosen key less than $A[1].Key$, any chosen key between $A[i].Key$ and $A[i+1].Key$ $(i = 1, \ldots, N - 1)$ and any chosen key greater than $A[N].Key$.

3. The idea would be, given an array indexed by $lo \dots hi$, to choose two intermediate indices, say th and $twoth$, which subdivide the array into three roughly equal parts. Then, in searching for a record with Key field k, we would compare $A[th].Key$ with k—if they are equal then we have success at position th. If $k < A[th].Key$ then we would apply the ternary search procedure (recursively) to the subarray indexed

by $lo .. (th - 1)$. If $k > A[th].Key$ then we compare $A[twoth].Key$ with k—if they are equal then we have success at position $twoth$. If $k < A[twoth].Key$ then apply ternary search to the subarray indexed $(th + 1) .. (twoth - 1)$; otherwise, if $k > A[twoth].Key$ then apply ternary search to the subarray indexed by $(twoth) + 1 .. hi$.

4. We begin by evaluating the hash function for each of the keys:

k	534	702	105	523	959	699	821	883
$h(k)$	2	18	10	10	9	15	4	9

k	842	686	658	4	20	382	570	344
$h(k)$	6	2	12	4	1	2	0	2

(a) When we use linear probing to resolve collisions the entries in the hash table H are as follows, where, as usual, bracketed entries indicate unsuccessful attempts to find vacant positions for the records with these keys.

$H[0]$	570			
$H[1]$	20			
$H[2]$	534	(686)	(382)	(344)
$H[3]$	686	(382)	(344)	
$H[4]$	821	(4)	(382)	(344)
$H[5]$	4	(382)	(344)	
$H[6]$	842	(382)	(344)	
$H[7]$	382	(344)		
$H[8]$	344			
$H[9]$	959	(883)		

$H[10]$	105	(523)	(883)
$H[11]$	523	(883)	
$H[12]$	883	(658)	
$H[13]$	658		
$H[14]$			
$H[15]$	699		
$H[16]$			
$H[17]$			
$H[18]$	702		

9 of the entries are located in their home positions; 4 are one location removed from their home positions; one (the record with key 883) is 3 locations removed. For the record with key 382, whose home position is 2, we have to try positions 2, 3, 4, 5, 6, 7 (6 in all) before we find a vacant location. For the record with key 344, we have to try positions 2, 3, 4, 5, 6, 7, 8 (7 in all) . So the total number of comparisons required to search for all the entries is

$$(9 * 1) + (4 * 2) + (1 * 4) + (1 * 6) + (1 * 7) = 34.$$

So the average number of comparisons to locate a record which is present is 2.125.

(*b*) Using the first version of quadratic probing to handle collisions, we produce the hash table

$H[0]$	570	(344)			$H[10]$	105	(523)	(883)
$H[1]$	20				$H[11]$	523	(382)	(344)
$H[2]$	534	(686)	(382)	(344)	$H[12]$	658		
$H[3]$	686	(382)	(344)		$H[13]$	883	(344)	
$H[4]$	821	(4)			$H[14]$			
$H[5]$	4				$H[15]$	699		
$H[6]$	842	(382)	(344)		$H[16]$			
$H[7]$	344				$H[17]$			
$H[8]$	382	(344)			$H[18]$	702	(382)	(344)
$H[9]$	959	(883)						

In this case 10 of the entries are located in their home positions; 3 are one step along the probing sequence and one is 2 steps along the probing sequence. For the record with key 382, whose home position is 2, we have to try positions

$$2, 2 + 1, 2 + 4, 2 + 9, 2 + 16, 2 + 25 \equiv 8 \bmod 19 \ (6 \text{ in all})$$

before we find a vacant location. For the record with key 344, which also has home position 2, we must try positions

$$2, 2 + 1, 2 + 4, 2 + 9, 2 + 16, 2 + 25 \equiv 8 \bmod 19,$$
$$2 + 36 \equiv 0 \bmod 19, 2 + 49 \equiv 13 \bmod 19,$$
$$2 + 64 \equiv 9 \bmod 19, 2 + 81 \equiv 7 \bmod 19 \ (10 \text{ in all})$$

before we find a vacant location.

The total number of comparisons required to search for all the entries is thus

$$(10 * 1) + (3 * 2) + (1 * 3) + (1 * 6) + (1 * 10) = 35$$

and so the average number of comparisons is 2.1875

For the second version of quadratic probing we produce the hash table

$H[0]$	570	(344)			$H[10]$	105	(523)	(883)
$H[1]$	20	(382)	(344)		$H[11]$	523	(344)
$H[2]$	534	(686)	(382)	(344)	$H[12]$	658	(344)
$H[3]$	686	(382)	(344)		$H[13]$	344
$H[4]$	821	(4)	(344)		$H[14]$
$H[5]$	4	(344)			$H[15]$	699	(344)
$H[6]$	842	(382)	(344)		$H[16]$
$H[7]$					$H[17]$	382	(344)
$H[8]$	883	(344)			$H[18]$	702	(344)
$H[9]$	959	(883)

Here 10 of the records are located in their home positions; 3 have to move one step down the probing sequence and one has to move 2 steps down. To find a position for the record with key 382, for which the home position is 2, we must try positions

$$2, 2 + 1, 2 - 1, 2 + 4, 2 - 4 \equiv 17 \bmod 19 \text{ (5 in all)}$$

before we find a vacancy. For the last record, with key 344 and home position 2, we must try positions

$$2, 2 + 1, 2 - 1, 2 + 4, 2 - 4 \equiv 17 \bmod 19, 2 + 9,$$
$$2 - 9 \equiv 12 \bmod 19, 2 + 16, 2 - 16 \equiv 5 \bmod 19$$
$$2 + 25 \equiv 8 \bmod 19, 2 - 25 \equiv 15 \bmod 19, 2 + 36 \equiv 0 \bmod$$
$$19,$$
$$2 - 36 \equiv 4 \bmod 19, 2 + 49 \equiv 13 \bmod 19 \text{ (14 in all)}$$

before we find a vacant location.

The total number of comparisons is

$$(10 * 1) + (3 * 2) + (1 * 3) + (1 * 5) + (1 * 14) = 38$$

So the average number of comparisons is 2.375.

(c) We begin by evaluating the two hash functions for each of the keys:

k	534	702	105	523	959	699	821	883
$h(k)$	2	18	10	10	9	15	4	9
$h_1(k)$	8	6	4	14	8	3	6	17

k	842	686	658	4	20	382	570	344
$h(k)$	6	2	12	4	1	2	0	2
$h_1(k)$	10	7	13	5	4	9	10	5

Then we construct the hash table:

$H[0]$	570				$H[10]$	105	(523)	
$H[1]$	20				$H[11]$	382		
$H[2]$	534	(686)	(382)	(344)	$H[12]$	658	(344)	
$H[3]$					$H[13]$			
$H[4]$	821	(4)			$H[14]$	4		
$H[5]$	523				$H[15]$	699		
$H[6]$	842				$H[16]$	686		
$H[7]$	883	(334)			$H[17]$	344		
$H[8]$					$H[18]$	702		
$H[9]$	959	(883)	(686)	(4)				

Here 10 records are in their home position; for 3 records we had to try 2 positions; for 2 we had to try 3 positions; and for the record with key 344 we had to try 4 positions. Thus the total number of comparisons required to search for all the records in the table is

$$(10 * 1) + (3 * 2) + (2 * 3) + (1 * 4) = 26.$$

Thus the average number of comparisons is 1.625.

5. We calculate the values of the hash function h_1:

k	534	702	105	523	959	699	821	883
$h_1(k)$	1	0	1	3	10	10	2	12

k	842	686	658	4	20	382	570	344
$h_1(k)$	10	10	8	4	7	5	11	6

and obtain the following table of lists:

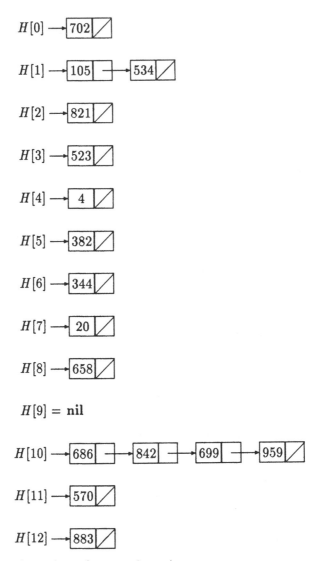

The total number of comparisons is

$$10 + (1 + 2) + (1 + 2 + 3 + 4)) = 23$$

So the average number of comparisons is 1.4375.

Chapter 23

SOLUTIONS TO EXERCISES 11

1. (a) Ordinary binary search tree insertion of 15 produces

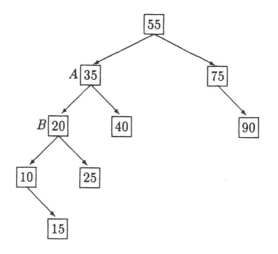

which is not an AVL-tree. The search path followed before this insertion was 55(1), 35(1), 20(0), 10(0), where the figures in parentheses are the *Balance* fields of the corresponding nodes. The pivot node *A* is the node containing 35. The insertion was made in the left subtree of *A*, with root the node *B* containing 20. Since the insertion was made to the left of *B* we are in the situation *LL*; following the *LL* instructions we restore the AVL property, obtaining

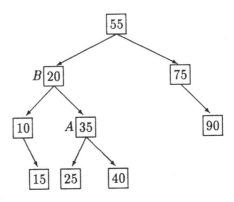

(b) When we insert 22 the ordinary insertion procedure produces

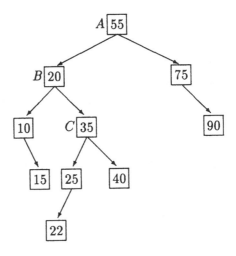

which is not an AVL-tree. The search path followed before the insertion of 22 was 55(1), 20(0), 35(0), 25(0); the pivot node *A* is the node containing 55. The insertion had to be made in the left subtree of *A*, with root *B*, the node containing 20. This time the insertion had to be made to the right of *B*, so we are in the situation *LR*, with the node containing 35 playing the rôle of *C*. Following the *LR* instructions we produce the AVL-tree

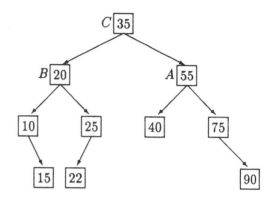

(c) When we insert 37, using ordinary binary search tree insertion, we obtain

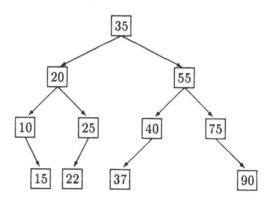

The search path for this insertion is $35(0)$, $55(-1)$, $40(0)$. The insertion is made to the left of 55; so the ordinary insertion procedure improves the balance of the node containing 55 and the tree produced is actually an AVL-tree.

(d) Inserting 39 by the ordinary binary search tree procedure gives the tree

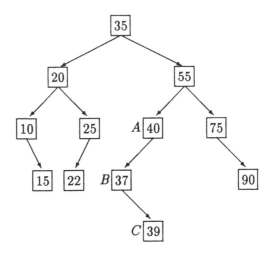

which is not an AVL-tree.

The search path before the insertion was 35(0), 55(0), 40(1), 37(0). The pivot node A is the node containing 40. The insertion is made to the left of A but to the right of its left child B (the node containing 37). So we are in the case LR with C the new node containing 39. Application of the LR rules produces the AVL-tree

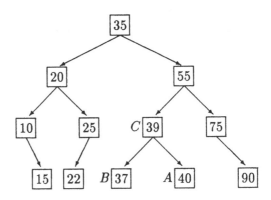

2. (a) When we insert hf in the tree

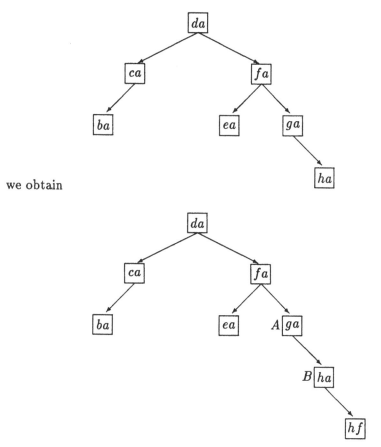

we obtain

which is unbalanced (Case *RR*: *A* is the node containing *ga*, *B* is the node containing *ha*). Rebalancing produces

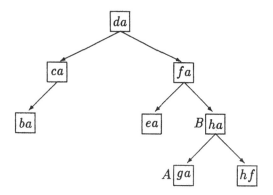

When we insert *ge* we obtain

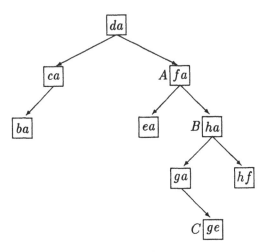

which has to be rebalanced (Case *RL*: *A*, *B*, *C* are the nodes containing *fa*, *ha*, *ge* respectively). Rebalancing produces

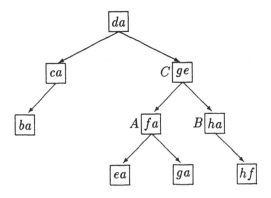

(b) We showed in (*a*) that the insertion of *hf* in the given AVL-tree produces, after rebalancing

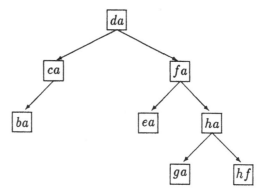

When we insert *df* in this tree we obtain

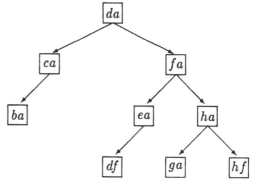

which satisfies the AVL conditions. Insertion of *bf* in this tree
leads to

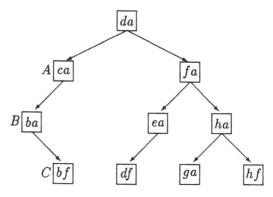

which has to be rebalanced (Case *LR*, with the nodes containing
ca, *ba*, *bf* playing the rôles of *A*, *B*, *C* respectively). Rebalancing

produces

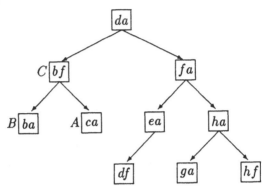

3. Ordinary binary search tree insertion of D, E, G produces

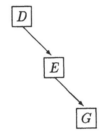

which is rebalanced (Case RR), producing

Inserting B produces the AVL-tree

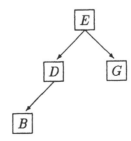

When we insert A we produce the tree

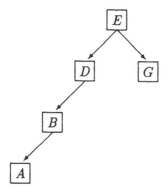

which has to be rebalanced (Case LL), producing

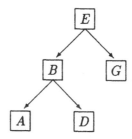

When we insert C using binary search tree insertion we have

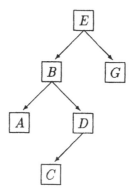

which is not an AVL-tree. It needs rebalancing (Case LR); this leads
to

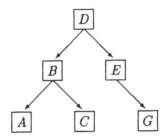

Finally, when we insert F we produce the tree

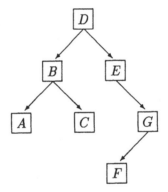

which has to be rebalanced (Case RL), giving eventually

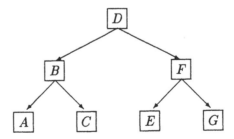

Chapter 24

SOLUTIONS TO EXERCISES 12

1.
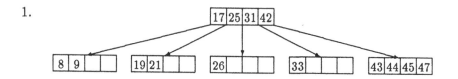

2.
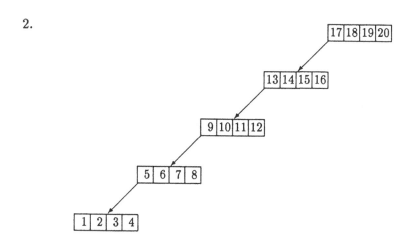

3. Inserting the first four elements produces the full root node

$$ba \mid ca \mid da \mid ea$$

To insert bf we must split the node, putting ba and bf to the left, da and ea to the right and ca up as single element of a new root node:

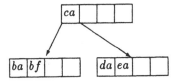

Insertion of df, ah, cg and bi produces eventually

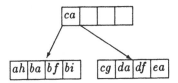

To insert cc we must split the second leaf node, sending cc and cg to the left, df and ea to the right and da up to the root node. This gives

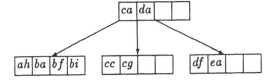

To insert af we must split the first leaf node, obtaining

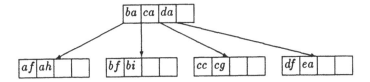

Insertion of *eg*, *bd*, *ec*, *ch*, *ai* produces

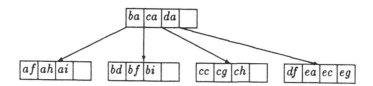

To insert *dc* we have to split the fourth leaf node; this yields

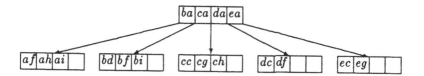

The next three insertions (of *di*, *ce* and *ef*) go into nodes which are not full, producing

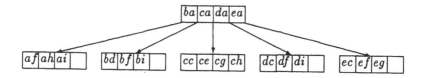

The final record, with *Key* field *cf* should go in the node

which is full. So we should split it into two nodes containing *cc*, *ce* and *cg*, *ch*, promoting *cf* to the root node

which is unfortunately full. So it must be split into two and a new

root node created with the middle element as its only entry. The final
B-tree is

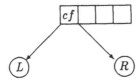

where the left subtree L of cf is

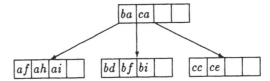

and its right subtree R is

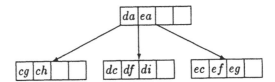

4. The record with key ff should be inserted in the node

$$\boxed{fa\,|\,fg\,|\,fh\,|\,fi}$$

But this node is full; so we must split it into two nodes containing fa,
ff and fh, fi, with fg promoted to the parent node

$$\boxed{df\,|\,ei\,|\,ga\,|\,gi}$$

But this is also full; so it is split with df, ei to the left, ga, gi to the
right and fg promoted to the root node

$$\boxed{af\,|\,ba\,|\,ca\,|\,da}$$

which is also full. So it is split—*af*, *ba* go to the left; *da*, *fg* go to the
right and *ca* is promoted to be the single entry of a new root node.
The resulting B-tree is

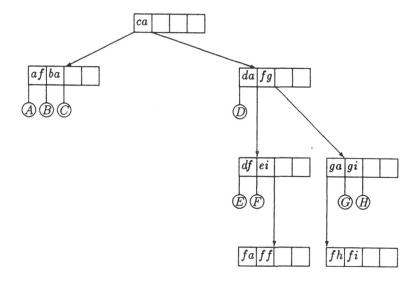

5. We shall distinguish between records and their keys by using the upper
case version of the key to represent the complete record (or key-and-
address pair)—thus, for example, *AB* will be used to denote the record
with key *ab*.

Insertion of the first four records (with keys *ca*, *ea*, *ba*, *da*) produces,
as in Exercise 1, the full node

$$\boxed{BA\,|\,CA\,|\,DA\,|\,EA}$$

To insert the record with key *bf* we have to consider the five elements

$$BA,\,BF,\,CA,\,DA,\,EA$$

and send the *key* of the middle record up to be the single element in a new root node. But all five records must appear in the leaves, so we have

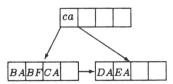

Insertion of the records with keys *df*, *ah*, *cg* produces eventually

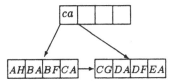

When we insert the record with key *bi* we have to split the first leaf, promoting the key of the middle element *BF*, and so obtaining

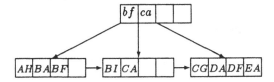

Similarly, when we insert the record with key *cc* we produce

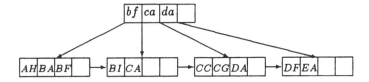

Inserting the records with keys *af* and *eg* does not require any node-splitting: we obtain

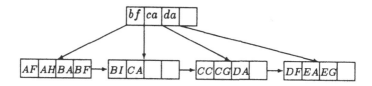

To insert the record with key *bd* we split the first node and get

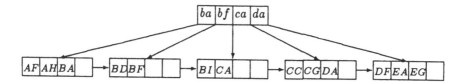

The next three records, with keys *ec*, *ch* and *ai*, can be inserted without any node splitting to obtain

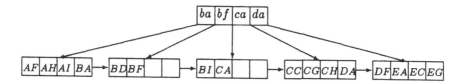

Finally, when we insert the record with key *dc* we have to split the last leaf, sending the middle key *ea* up to its parent, the root node, which must in turn be split, to produce finally the B$^+$-tree

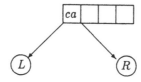

whose left subtree *L* is

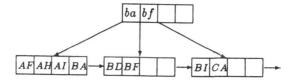

and whose right subtree R is

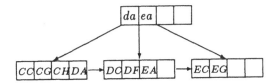

6. The root node of a B*-tree of order 7 may contain between 1 and 8 records. So the first 8 records in the input stream are stored in the root in increasing order of key:

ah	ba	bf	ca	cg	da	df	ea

For the insertion of *bi* we must split the root node—of the 9 records (8 in the root node and the new record) the one with the middle key remains as single entry in the root node, the first 4 in increasing order of key are put in the first leaf node and the last 4 in the second. So we have

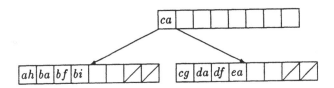

The non-root nodes of a B*-tree of order 7 must contain between 4 and 6 entries. So we may insert *cc*, *af*, *eg* and *bd* in the correct order of key in the appropriate leaf nodes, obtaining

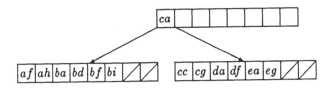

To insert *ec*, which should go in the second leaf node, where there is no room for it, we must consider the entries in the left sibling, the separating element in the parent, the entries in the node and the new entry, all arranged in increasing order of key:

af, ah, ba, bd, bf, bi, ca, cc, cg, da, df, ea, ec, eg.

We organise these into three nodes, with two separating elements, as shown:

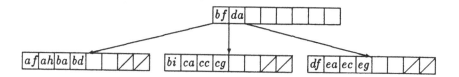

The next 5 records, with keys *ch, ai, dc, di, ce*, can be inserted (in proper order of key) in the appropriate leaves, producing

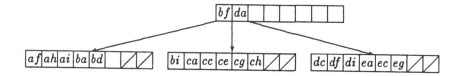

To insert *ef*, which should go in the already full third node, we examine the elements in the left sibling, the separating element in the parent, the elements of the third node and the new element, in increasing order of key—

bi, ca, cc, ce, cg, ch, da, dc, df, di, ea, ec, ef, eg

and organise them as three nodes with two separators. This produces the root node

```
bf cg di
```

and four leaf nodes

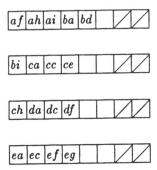

Finally the record with key cf goes into the second leaf node.

7. To remove cf from the B-tree

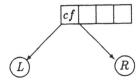

where the left subtree L of cf is

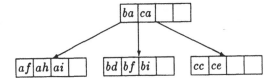

and the right subtree R is

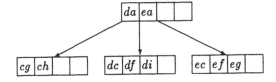

we replace cf by cg, the leftmost entry in the leftmost leaf of the right subtree of cf; when we remove cg from the node it no longer contains the minimum number of entries for a B-tree of order 5; its right sibling has one more than the minimum number, so we readjust the separating element in the parent node, obtaining

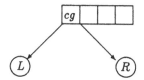

where the left subtree L of *cg* is

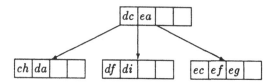

and its right subtree R is

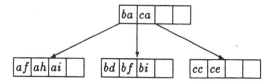

We may remove *ef* from its leaf node without further adjustment. But when we remove *ce* we have to readjust the separating element between its node and its left sibling. So when *ef* and *ce* are removed we have

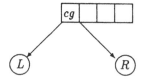

where the left subtree L of *cg* is

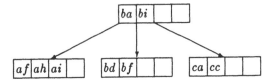

and its right subtree R is

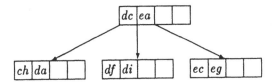

When we remove di from the node

its number of elements falls below the minimum allowed. Both siblings of this node have exactly the minimum number. So we amalgamate the node with its left sibling and the separating element, forming

$$\boxed{ch \mid da \mid dc \mid df}$$

But, by demoting dc to this new leaf node, we have reduced the number of elements in its node below the allowed minimum, so we amalgamate it with its left sibling and their separator to form a new root node, making the tree

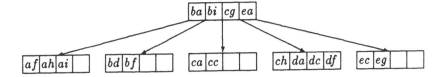

After dc and ch are removed we have

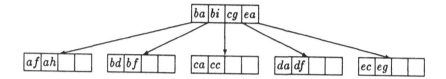

When we remove *eg* readjustment is required, resulting in

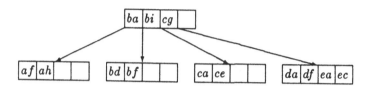

The removal of *bd* also requires readjustment, producing

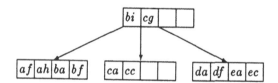

Removing *ec* and *af* produces

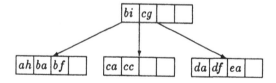

without any readjustment. But when we remove *cc* we must change the separator between the first and second leaves, obtaining

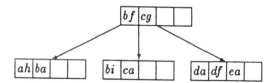

We now remove *bi* by changing the separator between the second and third leaves, whereupon we have

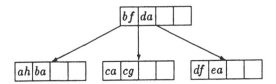

The remaining deletions, of *cg*, *ah*, *df* and *bf* produce in turn

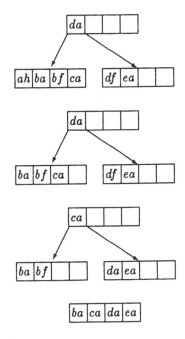

8. Starting with the B$^+$-tree

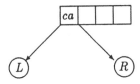

whose left subtree *L* is

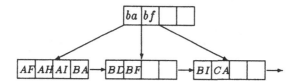

and whose right subtree R is

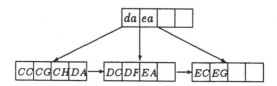

we may remove the records DC, AI, CH with keys dc, ai, ch from the leaf nodes containing them without further adjustment, since the nodes still have at least the minimum number of entries prescribed for non-root nodes of a B^+-tree of order 5. We obtain

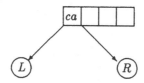

whose left subtree L is

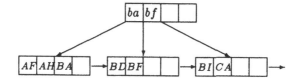

and whose right subtree R is

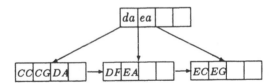

To remove the record EG with key eg we must amalgamate the fifth and sixth leaves, removing from their parent node the separating key ea (the record EA with key ea occurs in the amalgamated leaf node). But when we remove ea from the node containing it we reduce the number of entries below the minimum permissible. So we must amalgamate it with its left sibling and their separator, forming a new root node and making the tree

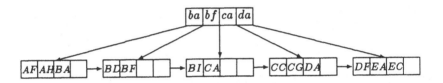

Removal of BD requires readjustment of the first two leaves; EC can be removed without further adjustment. After these two deletions we obtain

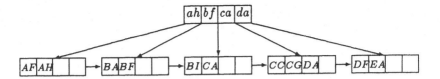

Removal of AF involves amalgamation of the first two leaves; CC can be removed without further adjustment. We obtain

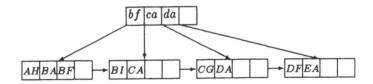

To remove BI we readjust the entries of the first two leaves and obtain

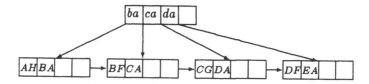

To delete CG we amalgamate the third and fourth leaves; this gives

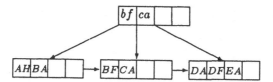

Deletion of AH requires amalgamation of the first and second leaves, producing

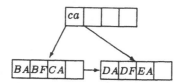

Removal of BF and DF proceeds without further adjustment, leading to

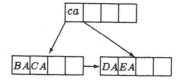

9. Using the conventions of the example in Section 12.3, with the four dots corresponding to a, r, t, s, we have the trie

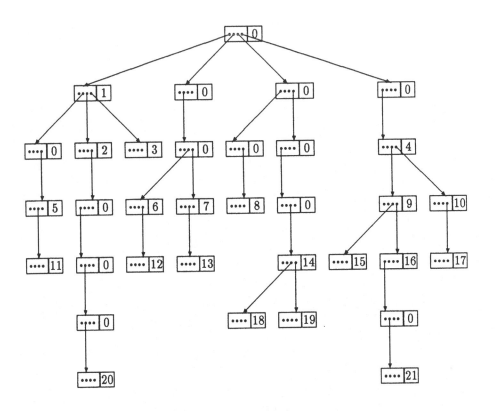

with the *Info* fields corresponding to the given words as follows:

1:	*a*	12:	*star*
2:	*art*	13:	*stars*
3:	*arts*	14:	*start*
4:	*as*	15:	*ta*
5:	*astart*	16:	*tar*
6:	*at*	17:	*tars*
7:	*ras*	18:	*tart*
8:	*rast*	19:	*tartar*
9:	*rat*	20:	*tat*
10:	*rats*	21:	*tatt*
11:	*sat*		

10. If we were to remove *hd* from the node

the node would be left with too few entries. Its left and right siblings each have only the minimum number of elements allowed in a non-root node of a B-tree of order 5. So we consider the elements *ga*, *gf* in its left sibling, the separating element *gi* and the remaining element *ha*; these form the node

$$\boxed{ga\;gf\;gi\;ha}$$

But when we demote *gi* to this new node we leave its previous node with only one entry, *hi*, which is too few for a non-root node. Again the left and right siblings have only the minimum permitted number of entries. So we consider the elements *bf*, *ca* from the left sibling, the separating element *cc* and the remaining element *hi*; these form the node

$$\boxed{bf\;ca\;cc\;hi}$$

Demotion of *cc* to this node leaves its previous node with only one element *ja*. This time the left sibling has one more than the minimum number of elements allowed, so we move *bb* up to the root in place of *be* and replace *cc* by *be*. Thus we obtain finally

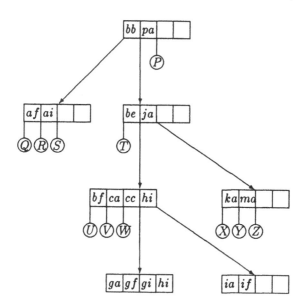

Index